Make Music
with Pro Tools

Avid Official Curriculum

For Pro Tools Artist 2023.3 Software

Make Music with Pro Tools

Avid Official Curriculum

Avid Technology, Inc.

ROWMAN & LITTLEFIELD
Lanham • Boulder • New York • London

Published by Rowman & Littlefield
An imprint of The Rowman & Littlefield Publishing Group, Inc.
4501 Forbes Boulevard, Suite 200, Lanham, Maryland 20706
www.rowman.com

86-90 Paul Street, London EC2A 4NE

British Library Cataloguing in Publication Information Available

Library of Congress Cataloging-in-Publication Data
ISBN 978-1-5381-7562-0 (paper : alk. paper)
ISBN 978-1-5381-7564-4 (electronic)

∞™ The paper used in this publication meets the minimum requirements of American National Standard for Information Sciences—Permanence of Paper for Printed Library Materials, ANSI/NISO Z39.48-1992.

The media provided with this book, and any accompanying course material, is to be used only to complete the exercises and projects contained herein. Rights are not granted to use the footage/sound materials in any commercial or non-commercial production or video. Product features, specifications, system requirements, and availability are subject to change without notice.

Trademarks

Avid, the Avid logo, Avid Everywhere, Media Composer, Pro Tools, Avid NEXIS, MediaCentral, iNEWS, AirSpeed®, Sibelius, Avid VENUE, FastServe, and Maestro, and all related product names and logos, are registered or unregistered trademarks of Avid Technology, Inc. in the United States and/or other countries. The Interplay name is used with the permission of the Interplay Entertainment Corp., which bears no responsibility for Avid products. All other trademarks are the property of their respective owners. For a full list of Avid trademarks, see: http://www.avid.com/US/about-avid/legal-notices/trademarks

PremiumBeat License Statement

The PremiumBeat music and sound effects included are licensed for use in the context of this Avid training only. If you wish to use the music or sound effects in other projects or applications, additional licensing must be purchased on PremiumBeat.com. Unlicensed use is unlawful and prohibited. The sale or distribution of this book without its cover is unauthorized. If you purchase this book without a cover, you should be aware that it was reported to the publisher as "unsold and destroyed." Neither the author nor the publisher has received payment for the sale of this "stripped" book.

About Avid

Avid delivers the most open and efficient media platform, connecting content creation with collaboration, asset protection, distribution, and consumption. Avid's preeminent customer community uses Avid's comprehensive tools and workflow solutions to create, distribute and monetize the most watched, loved and listened to media in the world—from prestigious and award-winning feature films to popular television shows, news programs and televised sporting events, and celebrated music recordings and live concerts. For more information about Avid solutions and services, visit www.avid.com.

Contents

Acknowledgments

This book is made possible through the involvement and input of numerous individuals at Avid Technology. Avid is the company behind Pro Tools software and hardware, along with many other products used in the digital media industry. The Avid Audio team is made up of dedicated professionals, all of them experts in their fields.

The material in this book is based primarily upon content written and provided by Andy Hagerman, Avid's Audio Curriculum Manager. Special thanks to Bryan Castle, Curtis Poole, and the entire worldwide training team at Avid for their input and support of this program.

About the Authors

Primary author **Andrew Hagerman** has been a professional musician and teacher for the majority of his 50+ years. Andy studied at the prestigious Northwestern University in Chicago, Illinois. During his time there, MIDI and computer music were in their infancy, and Andy recognized the usefulness of these technologies in aiding the creative process. His quest for the best in audio and music technology ultimately led him to use and teach Avid's Pro Tools.

Andy has experience as a performer, composer, arranger, and producer, including a stint as a musician for Walt Disney productions and composer and arranger on both music projects and post-production works. As an educator, he began teaching at Full Sail University in Winter Park, Florida, where he rose to the position of Associate Course Director of Advanced Audio Workstation Studies. In 2005, he joined the training team at Avid Technology as Training Services Manager for the Asia-Pacific region (with an office based in Tokyo Japan, where he resides today). He has authored numerous books on music and audio production and continues to create content to inspire the next generation of creative professionals.

Contributing author and editor **Frank D. Cook** is a musician, author, educator, and entrepreneur. He is the author of numerous books in pro audio, including multiple Pro Tools titles for the Avid Learning Series. He has worked closely with Avid for nearly 20 years in support of Avid's official training and certification programs.

Frank has taught digital audio at the college level since 2008. He currently runs the Multimedia Entrepreneurship program at Augustana University in Sioux Falls, South Dakota, where he helps prepare students for careers in digital media and technology. Frank is also an Avid Master Instructor, providing training and certification for educators. Through his company NextPoint Training, Inc., Frank develops tools and technology to empower students and educators, including the Elements|ED learning assessment platform (ElementsED.com).

Welcome to Pro Tools

First of all, congratulations on becoming a Pro Tools user. Pro Tools is the professional audio production standard, and your decision to learn it is a step in the right direction. Before jumping into details, here's an overview of the software and of our approach in this book.

What Is Pro Tools, Exactly?

In the world of modern audio production, several software products fall into the category of *Digital Audio Workstation* or DAW. The DAW's role in audio production is similar to that of a word processor in producing documents—you can create files, add and edit content, rearrange sections, and create impact using specialized tools. When you are finished recording and editing music in a DAW, you can export the song as an audio file that other people can listen to. Over the past 30 years, DAWs have become a key part of the professional production world.

When Avid says that their DAW, Pro Tools, is the industry standard, you can believe it. You'll find Pro Tools at all levels of audio production, from modest software-only systems that anyone can use, all the way up to high–end hardware and software systems (with advanced features and price tags to match) that produce Hollywood blockbuster films. As you go through this book, you'll see why pros have chosen Pro Tools, and how learning to use it puts you in very good company.

About This Book

In 2022, Avid introduced Pro Tools Artist, a version of their powerful Digital Audio Workstation aimed at music enthusiasts. This product provides a great introduction to the tools and workflows that people have used to create some of the world's most famous music. The goal of *Make Music with Pro Tools* (the first official Avid book focused on Pro Tools Artist software) is to give you a solid foundation in audio workflows that can take you anywhere you want to go in the world of audio production or music creation.

This book also serves as the official text for the Avid Learning Academy (ALA) program and the associated certification. The ALA program is designed for high schools and middle schools and provides curriculum for music creation, audio production, and video production. The program prepares students with the skills they need in their creative endeavors, on the job, or in continued study in their chosen field. Students who complete this program can become Avid Certified, thereby achieving a globally recognized industry credential.

Who This Book is Written For

Although this book is designed for use in the classroom, it also serves as a resource for anyone interested in using Pro Tools Artist, Pro Tools Studio, or Pro Tools Ultimate for music production. Users running the free Pro Tools Intro software can also use this text to master its features, although certain software limitations may apply.

This book is geared towards beginners with little or no experience working with a DAW. When it comes to audio production, the assumption will be that everything here is new, so basic key terms and concepts are described in plain English as we go along. That does not mean that the book is purely surface-level, however. Even experienced uses are sure to find information, details, and tips on features they did not know!

As you work your way through the text, you will find that it is quite thorough. Beginning users are encouraged to skip or gloss over the more advanced topics their first time through the curriculum. These topics can be explored in more depth on a second or even third pass through the course.

Don't worry if you're not a formally trained musician, or if you really haven't dealt with digital audio before. The beauty of Pro Tools—and computer music in general—is that even those without formal training can express their creativity! Of course, any general music or audio knowledge that you bring to the table is an added advantage, but it's certainly not a requirement for this book.

Pro Tools is a very deep program, and even the Artist tier has more features than we can cover in this book. As such, we've had to limit our scope. We assume that you've already mastered basic computer operation. However, you only need general computer knowledge for this course: how to download and locate files, install and launch applications, open and close documents, quit an application, and shut down or reboot your system.

To Learn More about the Avid Learning Academy

The Avid Learning Academy program, or ALA, is developed by Avid Technology and Rowman & Littlefield, with support from NextPoint Training, Inc. The ALA program provides schools and training organizations with high-quality, fully self-contained course offerings for students in the media arts.

Middle school and high school teachers who would like to join the Avid Learning Academy—and begin offering Avid Pro Tools certification for their students—can find additional information here:

- Avid Learning Academy on avid.com: https://www.avid.com/learning/avid-learning-academy
- Avid Learning Academy, Rowman & Littlefield: https://nxpt.us/RowmanALA

> **Not part of the Avid Learning Academy?** Learners who are studying this material independently can access additional resources to supplement this text from the *Make Music* Stage Pass module in ElementsED.com. For more information, visit nxpt.us/make-music.

Getting Started

Welcome to the world of Pro Tools! Throughout its decades-long history, Avid's Pro Tools has established itself as a leader in audio technology and the preeminent Digital Audio Workstation (DAW) worldwide. Pro Tools can be found in virtually every facet of the audio industry: from music production for streaming services to surround sound for movie soundtracks. The skills you will learn at the beginning of your journey can take you all the way to the top of the professional audio world.

This Lesson focuses on the basics: Sound—how does it exist in the physical world and the digital domain? How has digital audio technology evolved over the years, giving us the current powerful tools that we enjoy today? And why Pro Tools?

Learning Targets

- Learn how audio behaves in the real world

- Understand audio conversion to (and from) digital formats

- Learn about Digital Audio Workstations including Pro Tools

- Identify different components that make up a Pro Tools system

- Learn about the tools and processes involved in installing and supporting Pro Tools software

Media Files for this Course

To complete the Activities and Exercises in this course, you will need access to various media files and Pro Tools sessions. In an academic environment, your instructor can provide access to these files. Learners who are studying this material independently can access the associated media files using the *Make Music* Stage Pass module in ElementsED.com.

For more information, visit nxpt.us/make-music.

TOPIC 1.1:
CHARACTERISTICS OF SOUND

In this section, you will explore the fundamental characteristics of sound. What makes a piano sound *different* from a trumpet? Why does the D string on a guitar sound *higher* than the A string? Why is a shout *louder* than a whisper? Each sound that we hear has unique characteristics that allow our ears to interpret the sound, distinguish it from other sounds, and understand what the sound means to us.

Activity: Explore Basic Audio Characteristics

Open the Activity 1.1.ptx session file. Listen to the audio files on different tracks by soloing each track in turn. Take note of the different waveforms (sine, square, triangle, snare hit, trumpet, piano, voice), different frequencies, and different amplitudes on the tracks.

Discuss what you hear.

Discussion: Audio Basics

To understand audio production, we must first understand the nature of sound. The three most critical parts of the audio that you hear are **waveform**, **frequency**, and **amplitude**. Let's look at each of these aspects.

Waveform

Waveform is perhaps the most recognizable part of a sound. It refers to the shape of a sound. For example, here is an image of a sine wave with its distinctive smooth shape:

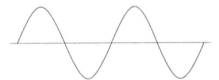

Figure 1.1 A sine wave

And here is an image of a square wave...

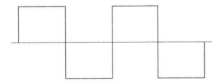

Figure 1.2 A square wave

And a triangle wave…

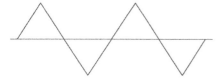

Figure 1.3 A triangle wave

You'll see here that even though the waveforms have different shapes, they share a few common features. For example, whenever we look at a waveform graph (which is what these images are), there is a horizontal line in the middle of the graph, which indicates zero energy.

A silent waveform would appear as a straight horizontal line following this zero line:

Figure 1.4 Silent audio

You'll also note that in each case (except for the silent audio), the waveform begins by ascending from the zero line. Since all sounds in the real world require energy, you'll see this same behavior in all naturally occurring audio waveforms.

This energy will reach its peak, and then return to the zero line. This part of the audio waveform—energy going up and then coming back down—is called the *compression* phase of an audio waveform. The term comes from the fact that air pressure increases in this part of an audio wave.

Sound has a natural back-and-forth motion (since its energy comes from something vibrating). So the energy will next drop below the zero line into negative territory. Here it will have a negative peak and return to the zero line. This is called the *rarefaction* phase of an audio waveform. This term is used to denote the fact that air pressure decreases in this part of the audio wave.

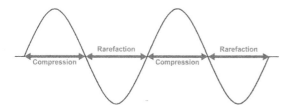

Figure 1.5 Compression and rarefaction phases of a sine wave

In the natural world, a sound never immediately stops. As the energy making the sound subsides, the waveform will settle down back to the zero line and silence. This is easy to see with a brief sound, like the snare drum hit shown below, as a brief burst of audio energy quickly settles back down to silence.

Figure 1.6 A snare drum hit

If that's what a waveform is, then how is it perceived? A sound's waveform is critically important—the shape of the audio waveform represents the tone or timbre of the sound. For example, a sine wave is a very simple and pure sound, quite different from a square wave of the same pitch and loudness. As sounds become more complex, their waveforms become more complex as well. You can see this in the waveform of a human voice:

Figure 1.7 The waveform of a human voice

Even though this waveform is highly detailed, it still follows the same general compression/rarefaction structure as every other sound. (Note that within each compression or rarefaction phase, there can be multiple peaks and dips.) In the real world, no two sounds are exactly alike (every sound-producing object vibrates differently), so every waveform has a distinctive shape.

Frequency

The frequency of a sound determines that sound's pitch. High-pitched sounds have a high frequency value, and low-pitched sounds have a low frequency value. On the surface, audio frequency is a very simple and straightforward matter, but let's dig a little deeper.

As you've already learned, waveforms have a compression phase followed by a rarefaction phase (followed by another compression phase, then another rarefaction phase, and so on until the sound ends). One period of compression followed by one period of rarefaction is called a cycle. (See Figure 1.8.)

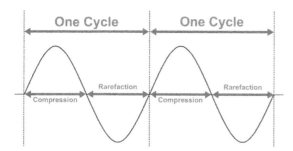

Figure 1.8 Two cycles of a sine wave

The illustrations above represent very short amounts of time: a single cycle translates to an imperceptibly brief sound. Any sound of significant duration has many cycles. Frequency is measured in cycles per second, in units called *Hertz* (Hz). A low-frequency sound has fewer cycles per second than a high-frequency sound.

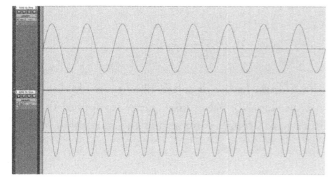

Figure 1.9 Two sine waves of different frequencies

Figure 1.9 shows how a low-frequency sound might appear, compared to a higher-frequency sound. In this case, both sounds are sine waves—they have similar waveforms; the only difference between them is the number of cycles that each has in a given amount of time.

Animals can hear different frequencies than humans. That's how a dog whistle works—it makes a loud sound at a frequency that dogs can hear, but humans cannot. The frequency range of human hearing is generally considered to be from 20 Hz to 20,000 Hz (or 20 *kilohertz*, abbreviated as kHz).

Although the range of 20 Hz to 20 kHz is used to estimate human hearing, it really doesn't apply to everyone. As we age, humans generally lose high-end frequency sensitivity. In general, our sensitivity to frequencies above 10 kHz begins to decrease significantly, beginning in our 30s.

 Frequent exposure to loud sounds can also affect hearing sensitivity. That is why it is so important to use hearing protection in loud environments; once you've suffered from lost or impaired hearing, you cannot repair the damage.

Amplitude

Amplitude, like frequency, is easy to recognize visually in a waveform. Amplitude refers to the energy level of a sound and is visually represented in a waveform by its height. Sound with greater amplitude will display a taller waveform, and sound with lower-amplitude will display a shorter (smaller) waveform.

Here you can see two sound waves that are identical in all aspects except one. They are both sine waves with the same frequency, but they represent sound at different amplitudes.

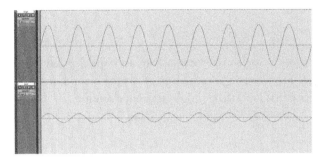

Figure 1.10 Two sine waves of different amplitudes

Amplitude can be affected in many ways—you can hit a drum harder or softer, blow more air through a tuba, or turn up the volume to send more voltage to a speaker. No matter how energy is supplied though, the result is the same: Waveforms with greater amplitude have stronger compression and rarefaction phases, move more air, and can be heard over greater distances.

The Decibel Scale

Just as the unit of measurement for frequency is Hertz, amplitude has its unit of measurement called the *Decibel* (dB). The range of Decibels in a recording is called the dynamic range. The maximum dynamic range that humans can perceive is from 0 dB (silence) up to around 120 to 130 dB, after which sound becomes painful. This range, often called the threshold of hearing to the threshold of pain, varies from person to person.

Decibel scales come in a few variations, depending upon the measurement being made. In the audio world, we use **dB SPL** (Sound Pressure Level) to measure the amplitude of sound traveling through the air, and **dB FS** (Full Scale) to measure the amplitude of digital audio signals in a DAW like Pro Tools.

Amplitude Versus Loudness

A few different terms could be used in place of amplitude, like volume, gain, or even voltage (when referring to an audio signal going to a speaker). Be careful, though, of using the word loudness if what you're really talking about is amplitude. Loudness deals with how sound is perceived, and the human ear is more sensitive to some frequencies than others. This means that two waveforms with identical shapes and amplitudes (for example, two sine waves at the same intensity), but with different frequencies, could be perceived by people as having different levels of loudness.

TOPIC 1.2:
CHARACTERISTICS OF DIGITAL AUDIO

In this section, you will begin exploring the nature of sound that is stored in a digital format. How do computers store and play sounds? How does the way a sound file is created affect how the file sounds when played back? How is digital audio different from the natural sound around us? How is it the same? When we record a sound, the way we capture and store the digital data impacts the sound's natural characteristics. This can then impact how we interpret, distinguish, and understand the sound.

Activity: Explore Characteristics of Digital Audio

- Open the Activity 1.2 folder and listen to examples of audio files created at different sample rates and bit depths.

- Listen to examples of 8-bit audio.

- Discuss what you hear. How would you describe these sounds? What is better with high sample rates/high bit depths? What is worse with low sample rates/low bit depths? How might these "degradations" be useful? What feelings to they convey/what do they make you think of?

Discussion: Audio in the Digital Domain

When audio is recorded (for example, from a microphone or guitar pickup), sonic energy is converted to electrical energy. This electrical signal can then be stored on a variety of media — from vinyl disks to magnetic tape, to a computer system's hard drive. From there, the signal can be edited, mixed, and played back, converting the stored data back to an electrical signal, and then to audible sound.

 When audio is recorded to a digital medium, the process is called analog-to-digital (A/D) conversion, and when it is played back, the process is known as digital-to-analog (D/A) conversion.

Samples and Sample Rates

The word sample is used in several ways in the audio world—from drum hits and short recordings, to the fundamental aspect of digital audio that we'll discuss here. For the purpose of this discussion, a *sample* can be defined as an instantaneous measurement of an audio signal. A sample measures one thing only, and that is the amplitude of an audio signal at a specific moment in time.

A single sample isn't nearly enough information to record or reproduce a sound. What's needed are many samples, spaced evenly in time, to properly map out a sound wave. Individually, a sample represents only a single amplitude value, but together they can represent a complete waveform!

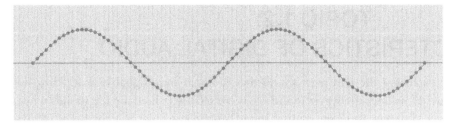

Figure 1.11 Sample points on a sine wave

The number of samples recorded per second is called the *sample rate*. Sample rates are measured in Hertz and Kilohertz, just like frequency. Here are some sample rates that are commonly used:

- 44.1 kHz (44,100 samples per second)

- 48 kHz (48,000 samples per second)

- 88.2 kHz (88,200 samples per second)

- 96 kHz (96,000 samples per second)

- 176.4 kHz (176,400 samples per second)

- 192 kHz (192,000 samples per second)

Sample rate theory gets its roots from a mathematician named Harry Nyquist, one of the fathers of digital audio and the co-creator of the *Nyquist-Shannon sampling theorem*. Put simply, the Nyquist-Shannon sampling theorem states that in order to accurately record or reproduce a sound, the sample rate must be at least twice the highest frequency of that sound. In other words, you need at least one sample in each compression phase, and one sample in each rarefaction phase.

A sine wave recorded with a sample rate that satisfies the Nyquist-Shannon sampling theorem can be accurately reproduced and played back.

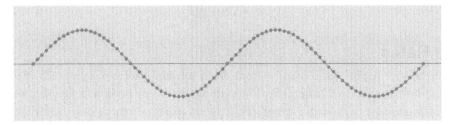

Figure 1.12 Plenty of samples for playback

Since the highest frequency that a human can hear is 20 kHz, a 44.1 kHz sample rate seems adequate (more than twice 20 kHz). However, when sound is recorded digitally, there is a small amount of distortion in the frequencies very near the Nyquist frequency (or one half of the sample rate). At 44.1 kHz, the Nyquist frequency is 22.05 kHz (44.1 divided by two). This high-frequency distortion can become audible—especially in sounds with a lot of high frequency content, like cymbals.

When recording at 96 kHz, however, the Nyquist frequency is 48 kHz, which is well above the audible range. And at 192 kHz, the Nyquist frequency is 96 kHz—even further beyond our ability to hear. In both cases, distortion near the Nyquist frequency is still there, but it's so far out of the human hearing range that it doesn't become a problem. While some professionals can hear a difference between 44.1 kHz audio and 48 kHz audio, few can distinguish between 48 kHz and 192 kHz.

Bit Depth

As you just learned, each sample is a digital measurement of the amplitude of a sound in an instant of time. As with all computer data, this measurement consists of ones and zeroes. The number of ones and zeros used to store each sample is what we call bit depth. In the audio production world, the most common bit depths are 16-bit and 24-bit.

Bit depth affects the accuracy of each measurement — the more bits in each sample, the more precise the measurement of amplitude can be. For example, 16-bit audio provides 65,536 discrete loudness levels (2^{16}). On the other hand, 24-bit audio (2^{24}) provides 16,777,216 loudness levels. This allows for more accurate measurements, and a more faithful recording of an audio signal.

Greater bit depths also result in a broader dynamic range. In fixed-point audio, each bit provides approximately 6 dB of dynamic range. Therefore, 16-bit audio has a maximum dynamic range of 96 dB (16x6) while 24-bit audio has a maximum dynamic range of 144 dB (24x6).

As you learned earlier, the theoretical dynamic range of human hearing is around 120 to 130 dB. A 16-bit audio file is limited to a 96 dB dynamic range, which is short of this dynamic range. On the other hand, 24-bit audio provides up to 144 dB of dynamic range—more than enough for human hearing. The trade off is that a 24-bit audio file will be 50% larger than a 16-bit file of the same sample rate and duration.

 16-bit and 24-bit audio use fixed point recording. Pro Tools also provides a 32-bit floating point option. Floating point is covered in other courses in the Avid Learning Series.

The Impact of Sample Rate and Bit Depth on File Size

The choices you make regarding sample rate and bit depth will affect the size of your recorded files. The more samples and bits you use, the more data must be stored on a hard drive and processed by the CPU. In practical terms, higher sample rates and bit-depths can translate into fewer tracks and plug-ins before your system reaches its storage and computing limits.

Here are a few standard figures to bear in mind when working with digital audio:

- One minute of 16-bit/44.1 kHz mono audio requires about 5 MB of storage space.

- One minute of 24-bit/44.1 kHz mono audio requires about 7.5 MB of storage space.

- One minute of 32-bit/44.1 kHz mono audio requires about 10 MB of storage.

From there, it's basic multiplication: if you double the sample rate, you'll double the file size. Stereo files (having two channels) will be twice the size of a mono file.

The chart below lists sample rates, bit-depths, and file sizes for a mono, one-minute audio file, rounded to the nearest tenth of a Megabyte.

Sample Rate, Bit-Depth, and Pro Tools File Sizes (Mono, 1 minute)			
	16-Bit	**24-Bit**	**32-Bit Float**
44.1kHz	5.3 MB	7.9 MB	10.6 MB
48kHz	5.8 MB	8.6 MB	11.5 MB
88.2kHz	10.6 MB	15.9 MB	21.1 MB
96kHz	11.5 MB	17.2 MB	23.0 MB
176.4kHz	21.1 MB	31.8 MB	42.3 MB
192kHz	23.0 MB	34.6 MB	46.0 MB

TOPIC 1.3:
AUDIO EDITING PRINCIPLES

Editing is a primary way to improve the digital audio we use to capture sound, communicate through sound, and create with sound. This unit introduces basic principles for working with audio files and file segments. Here you will explore the role of the digital audio workstation. You'll learn about tracks, audio files, and audio clips (or regions), and get an introduction to the nature of editing in a digital environment.

As you explore this topic, consider the following questions: How can editing be used to improve a recorded sound? How might editing change the meaning of a recording? Are such changes good or bad? What happens to audio you've removed or modified through editing? Are the changes you've made permanent?

When we edit a sound, the changes we make can impact the meaning, message, and emotion of the sound. When done skillfully, you can shape a listener's response to the sound to enhance your story or message.

Activity: Explore Audio Files and Clips

- Open the Activity 1.3.ptx session. This session has an audio recording on one track, followed by clips from the same audio file on another track.

- Solo each track and listen to them in turn. Describe the differences you hear.

- Use the Grabber tool (hand icon) to reposition the audio clips on the first track, removing the gaps. Solo and play back.

- Use the Grabber tool to rearrange the audio clips on the second track, changing their order. Solo and play back.

- Discuss the editing process. How might edits like these be beneficial? Can editing be dishonest or misleading?

Discussion: DAWs and Pro Tools – An Introduction

Before digital audio came on the scene, audio was recorded on magnetic tape, in expensive recording studios. In the mid-1980s, music technology took massive evolutionary leaps, introducing the MIDI protocol and digital audio that could be recorded to a hard drive as opposed to tape.

It was around this time that the company Digidesign introduced the digital audio recorder known as Sound Designer, which in turn evolved to the "tapeless studio system," Sound Tools. This then became the pioneering digital audio workstation (DAW) Pro Tools in 1991. In 1994, Digidesign merged with another company called Avid Technology (itself a leader in the video production world).

DAW Basics

Digital audio workstations combine comprehensive audio and MIDI recording, editing, and mixing tools, putting the power of a full audio production facility in a computer. Let's take a look at how DAWs work.

Sessions and Projects

DAWs generally have "master" files—files that bring together all the different media elements you need for your work. In Pro Tools, if you're working on media that resides in a local drive, that master file is called a *session* file. If your work resides in the cloud, the master file is called a *project*. Session files and project files are fairly small files themselves, but they are important because they are the master files for your work and enable you to interact with the media that you use.

Files and Clips

When you record audio into Pro Tools, an audio file is created. That file is not embedded in your session file; rather it is stored as a separate file on disk. Pro Tools enables users to access audio files through visual objects in the software called *clips*. A clip represents (or "points to") an audio file on your storage drive.

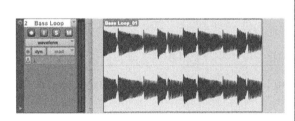 

Figure 1.13 An audio clip (left) and the corresponding audio file on disk (right)

Non-Linear, Non-Destructive

Working with clips has many advantages. For example, you can move clips earlier or later on the Pro Tools timeline and position them anywhere you want. An environment in which you can manipulate elements independently on the timeline is commonly described as being *non-linear*.

Another advantage of clip-based DAWs is that you can edit your audio *non-destructively*. This means that you can change the start and end times of clips (removing audio from your project's timeline) with no data loss. If you don't like an edit you've made, you can recover missing audio in the clip from the original file.

Real-Time Processing

In the early days of digital audio, computer power was relatively low. If we wanted effects on a track, we often needed to render out brand new files of processed audio. These days, most of the effects that we use in a session run in real time. This means that the effects are non-destructive; if you want to change a particular effect's settings in real time, you can do that easily.

Pro Tools—The Industry Standard

Despite the large number of DAWs on the market, the industry has picked Pro Tools to be their standard. Let's take a look at why so many pros choose Pro Tools.

Features and Workflows

Pro Tools is true to its digital audio roots, and throughout its evolution, audio quality has been a priority. Avid audio hardware captures and plays back audio with high fidelity, and audio processing (done within the Pro Tools software) preserves a clean signal, allowing professionals to get the best possible results.

But audio is not all that Pro Tools can do—Pro Tools has many powerful MIDI functions as well, which means that you can compose music, record live performances, and edit and mix MIDI and audio together, all in one software environment. And if you can read music notation, there's great news for you—you can view MIDI data as traditional notation, as well as in a "piano roll" view.

 You'll learn more about MIDI in Pro Tools in Lessons 9 and 10 of this course.

A word you'll commonly hear in discussions of audio production is *workflow*. This refers to a series of steps or features used to get a job done. Good software design provides the flexibility to work how you want in any situation. When it comes to recording, editing, and mixing, Pro Tools' workflow features are top-notch.

Pro Tools Versions

Today, four tiers of Pro Tools are available: Pro Tools Intro (free, feature-limited), Pro Tools Artist, Pro Tools Studio, and Pro Tools Ultimate. Though representing different levels of features, these tiers all share a common fundamental architecture. This means that the skills that you learn in Pro Tools Artist will also apply to the most advanced Pro Tools Ultimate systems.

Let's take a look at how the different commercial versions compare:

- **Inputs and outputs (I/O):** The more inputs and outputs you have, the more individual audio signals you can record and route to discrete outputs at once. Pro Tools Artist supports up to 16 channels of I/O, Pro Tools Studio supports up to 64, and Pro Tools Ultimate maxes out at a whopping 256 channels.

- **Tracks:** Pro Tools Artist supports up to 32 simultaneous Audio tracks, plus MIDI tracks, Instrument tracks, and more. Track counts progressively increase as you upgrade to Pro Tools Studio and Pro Tools Ultimate. You'll learn about specific track types and track counts later in this course.

- **Mixing:** You can create *stereo* mixes in Pro Tools Artist, with full access to standard automation features. For *Surround* mixing and advanced automation, Pro Tools Studio or Pro Tools Ultimate is required.

TOPIC 1.4:
COMPONENTS OF A DIGITAL AUDIO WORKSTATION

To get started making music or other audio creations, you will need a computer capable of running your digital audio application. Typically called a DAW, this application is really only one component of a digital audio system. In this section, you will explore the hardware and software components that make up a typical audio production system.

Activity: Design a Pro Tools System

Do some research to determine what kinds of devices can run Pro Tools Artist: Phone? Tablet? Chromebook? Laptop? Desktop? Mac? Windows?

- Check Avid's compatibility documents for system requirements:
  https://avid.secure.force.com/pkb/articles/compatibility/Pro-Tools-System-Requirements

- What else might you need in order to record and produce music, besides a computer and Pro Tools? What other devices would you consider buying?

Discussion: What Makes Up a Pro Tools System?

Pro Tools software is a key part of your audio production system, but it's not the only part. Many different components work together to make a complete audio production system.

The Heart of Your DAW: The Computer

Your computer is the cornerstone of your Pro Tools system. Pro Tools software can run on both Windows and Mac-based desktop computers and laptops. However, it's important to have the right kind of power to make the most out of Pro Tools.

Mac or Windows?

When building a Pro Tools system, the computer's operating system is often one of the first considerations. Mac or Windows? The biggest difference between the two platforms—beyond the operating system itself— relates to the modifier keys and shortcuts that Pro Tools will use.

Even if you're more comfortable on one platform than the other, you can still easily switch between them by bearing in mind the keyboard shortcut equivalents shown in the table below.

Mac	Windows
Command	Ctrl
Option	Alt
Control	Start
Shift	Shift
Return	Enter

CPU

Pro Tools systems can operate in one of two ways: *Native*, where the host computer is responsible for all processing tasks, or *DSP*, where specific hardware has been added to offload some of these tasks, increasing capacity and improving performance.

Pro Tools Artist and Pro Tools Studio systems operate natively, meaning that the computer's *Central Processing Unit* (or CPU) will do everything from mixing to real-time effects processing and more. The faster your computer's CPU is, the more powerful your Pro Tools software can be.

Pro Tools Ultimate can operate as either a native or DSP system, depending upon the system setup. Advanced DSP system configurations are discussed in advanced courses in the Avid Learning Series.

RAM/Unified Memory

In addition to CPU power, your computer's *Random-Access Memory* (RAM) or *Unified Memory* (UM) plays an important role in how your Pro Tools system will perform. RAM/UM serves as a short-term memory for your CPU, and here again, more is generally better. Pro Tools Artist requires a minimum of 8 GB of RAM to run, but Avid recommends 32 GB or more (especially for higher tiers of Pro Tools).

Storage Drives

DAWs rely on storage drives to store their audio. Two key factors for Pro Tools drives are *size* and *speed*. A larger-capacity drive enables you to store more audio data, higher-resolution data, or both. Most recording studios require multiple terabytes of drive space. It's also important that the data can be retrieved quickly, so the speed of the drive is very important. Avid recommends drives that have a minimum rotational speed of 7200 RPM (for traditional hard drives), or the use of solid state drives (SSDs).

Beginners might be tempted to use their computer's internal system drive for all their audio tasks. While this can work for small jobs, at a certain point your system drive won't be adequate. For that reason, it's highly recommended to use a separate drive dedicated to audio data storage when using Pro Tools.

Not to be Overlooked — Mice, Trackballs, Keyboards

Technical specifications aside, it's important to have a comfortable work setup, as Pro Tools users tend to spend long hours at their computers. Make sure that your keyboard is comfortable to type on, to avoid wrist fatigue. Also, spend the extra money to invest in an extended keyboard for your Pro Tools system; many Pro Tools keyboard shortcuts and operations utilize the numeric keypad on an extended keyboard.

Choosing a mouse, trackball, or trackpad is a matter of personal preference. Trackballs and trackpads generally take up less space, and so are commonly seen on professional recording studio desks.

There's no single right answer for what to use. Choose what is comfortable and what will stand up to many hours of use—you'll be glad you did in the long run.

 This course covers several functions and workflows that require the use of the numeric keypad. A full-sized, extended keyboard is highly recommended.

Getting Audio In, Getting Audio Out: Audio Interfaces

Your computer probably has a built-in microphone and speakers, but these won't be good enough for any kind of serious work. To get high-quality audio in and out of your computer, you need to use an *audio interface*. The good news is that there are a lot of choices, and you won't need to break the bank.

Computer Connections

Audio interfaces can connect to your computer using USB, Thunderbolt, or other connections. As a general rule, the faster the connection between the interface and the computer, the more channels of input and output or the higher quality audio you will be able to play and record.

Analog Audio Connections

The number and types of inputs that an interface has is important. Your needs will determine what you should purchase. If you're working by yourself and only recording one instrument at a time, an audio interface with just one or two inputs might be just fine. If you want to record multiple musicians at the same time, however, you'll need more channels of input.

You'll want to make sure that the gear you purchase can accommodate devices you want to attach to it:

- **Line level** inputs are generally used for connecting synthesizers, drum machines, and audio and video media players. Line inputs usually use a quarter-inch phone connector.

- **Microphone** inputs are used to connect microphones to your interface. These generally use 3-pin XLR-type connectors.

 Some microphones require extra voltage to operate, called phantom power. This is sometimes labeled as "48v" on an interface. If your microphone requires phantom power, make sure that your interface can supply it.

■   **Instrument** inputs are typically used to connect an electric guitar or bass directly into Pro Tools. This type of input, sometimes referred to as a **DI** (for *Direct Inject* or *Direct Input*), is where you will plug in your instrument. Instrument/DI inputs also use a quarter-inch phone connection.

The types of outputs on your interface are also crucial. Monitor speakers (discussed later in this lesson) commonly use quarter-inch or XLR connectors. Make sure that your audio interface supports the same connection as your speakers. A headphone output is also convenient to have.

Digital Audio Connections

Many audio interfaces, including some entry-level products, have digital audio inputs and outputs of some extent. Digital inputs are commonly used to receive signals from other digital devices, and digital outputs will often go to speakers that have digital inputs.

Digital audio formats include coaxial S/PDIF, optical S/PDIF, ADAT optical, or AES/EBU. Here again, make sure you have the kinds of connections that your digital peripheral gear requires (if you have any).

    The topic of digital audio connections is beyond the scope of this book but is covered in detail in other courses of the Avid Learning Series.

Hearing the Real Mix: Monitor Speakers

In order to hear Pro Tools, you'll need speakers—specifically, studio monitor speakers. Monitor speakers are different than normal consumer-level speakers.

What to Look for in Monitor Speakers

When it comes to studio speakers, you may be tempted to choose speakers that make music sound fantastic, boosting frequencies like ground-shaking lows or accentuated highs. While that might be great for end-user listening systems, that's not really the job of monitor speakers.

The goal of good monitor speakers is to give you an honest reproduction of your recordings and mixes, without any sonic enhancements. It's only when you can hear your mix with all its imperfections that you can fix problems, so that your work will sound great on a wide range of playback systems in the real world.

Case in point: For decades, Yamaha NS-10M speakers were many professionals' choice. Even though they've been out of production for years, they can be found in many studios today. They were never particularly expensive and were originally designed to be home bookshelf speakers. Did they sound especially great? No—their value as studio monitor speakers was that they were so average that they effectively represented a typical playback system. If your audio work sounded good through those speakers, they'd sound pretty good anywhere.

Figure 1.14 A pair of Yamaha NS-10M speakers

Here are a few things to look for in monitor speakers:

■   **Frequency response:** As a general rule, you want an even frequency response over the audible frequency range: the speaker shouldn't artificially boost or cut any frequencies. Most speaker manufacturers publish frequency response charts for their products. The flatter the shape between 20 Hz and 20 kHz, the better.

■   **Size:** If you're working in a small room, you don't need huge monitor speakers. However, if you've got a large studio, small speakers will not provide the power that you need. Shop around for speakers designed to match the size of your production room.

■   **Ports:** Some speakers have a hole in the cabinet, called a *port*, to enhance low frequencies. Rear-ported speakers need some space. The back of the speaker should be at least 1 meter (or 3 feet) away from the wall behind it. If you have a small production studio and cannot position your speakers that far from the wall, it might be better to choose front-ported speakers.

Speakers versus Headphones

Headphones can be useful, but they can't completely replace your monitor speakers. With monitor speakers, some of the sound coming from the left speaker will be heard by your right ear and vice versa, which can't happen with headphones. What you hear can also change when sounds from the left speaker and the right speaker interact with each other in the air, and this can significantly affect your mix. With headphones, the left and right channels are completely isolated and separated by your head, so this interaction won't occur.

However, headphones can be an important tool for audio production. Just as with studio monitor speakers, there are headphones that are specifically suited for mixing, with an even frequency response.

The construction of headphones is also important:

■   Most headphones on the market are called *closed-back*. This means that the outer cover of the headphone is solid and does not allow sound to pass through. This is useful when you're recording a vocal performance and you don't want the microphone to pick up what's being played through the headphones. Closed-back headphones are a good choice for recording.

- Open-back headphones on the other hand, have an outer case that allows sound from the speaker to pass through. Due to their more accurate sound reproduction, most professional mixing headphones (as opposed to recording headphones) have an open-back design.

Figure 1.15 An example of open-backed headphones: Sennheiser's HD650

Great Resources

Here are a few places to get up-to-date answers as you put together your system.

COMPATIBILITY DOCUMENTS—Avid maintains a list of Pro Tools system requirements, which it updates as new versions are released. To check on requirements for your computer and find out what you need to run Pro Tools, go here:

- https://avid.secure.force.com/pkb/articles/compatibility/Pro-Tools-System-Requirements.

KNOWLEDGE BASE—Avid also has a database called the *Knowledge Base*, where you can search for information on a variety of technical topics. To access the Knowledge Base, go here:

- https://www.avid.com/search#t=KB&sort=relevancy.

IN-APPLICATION HELP—Once you've installed Pro Tools (discussed below), you can use the **HELP** menu to search topics based on keywords, or to access Pro Tools online help and support.

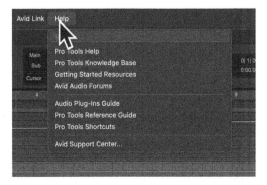

Figure 1.16 The Pro Tools Help menu

TOPIC 1.5:
SOFTWARE INSTALLATION AND CONFIGURATION

This section explores the process of installing Pro Tools software, associated plug-ins, and other software components that come with a subscription. It also discusses PACE iLok authorization, which is required to run all Pro Tools software tiers.

Discussion: Installing Pro Tools

To install Pro Tools, you will need to create an Avid account and authorize the software using an iLok USB key or an iLok Cloud session. You can download installers from your Avid account, or you can use the Avid Link application.

Creating an Avid Account

Your Avid account will be your portal to download any software you have purchased and to access a variety of Avid services. To get started, do the following:

1. Go to avid.com and click the **SIGN-IN** link in the top right-hand corner of the window.

Figure 1.17 Clicking the Sign In link on the Avid website

2. To create a new account, enter your details in the right-hand side of the resulting screen.

WELCOME TO YOUR AVID ACCOUNT

SIGN IN

CREATE A NEW ACCOUNT

Email *

Password *

First Name *

Last Name *

Country *   United States

User Name

This is business account
This is personal account

Email *

Figure 1.18 The my.avid.com web page

3.   Click the **CREATE AN ACCOUNT** button at the bottom of the page to complete the process.

Using iLok Protection

Pro Tools and the plug-ins that come with it require licenses. Avid uses PACE anti-piracy software to manage those licenses. PACE can authorize your licenses using an iLok Cloud session (requires an internet connection) or an iLok USB key.

Figure 1.19 A PACE iLok USB key

Many industry manufacturers also use the PACE iLok system. iLok keys are a common fixture in many studios. An iLok key can hold hundreds of authorizations for all your iLok-enabled software. After a software license is placed on an iLok key, you can use it to authorize the software on any computer.

When you purchase Pro Tools and register the software to your Avid account, you will be prompted to create an iLok account, if you don't have one already. (The onscreen instructions will walk you through this process.) In most cases, it is simplest to use the same username and password for your iLok account that you use for your Avid account. However, it is important to recognize that these are two separate accounts.

 To learn more about PACE and iLok, including the activation of your iLok Cloud- or iLok USB-based licenses, go to www.ilok.com.

Installing Pro Tools

Once you have purchased Pro Tools, you will be able to access the installers you need through your Avid Account:

1.   Log in to your Avid account on avid.com.

2.   Navigate to the **My Products** section.

3.   Click the **VIEW MY PRODUCTS** link. (See Figure 1.20.)

 You can also install Pro Tools using the Avid Link application. See the discussion later in this Lesson and the process described in Exercise 1.

Figure 1.20 Viewing your purchased products in your Avid account

4.   In the **My Products** page, you'll see each purchased product represented as a horizontal black row. Click on the Pro Tools listing to expand it and drill down.

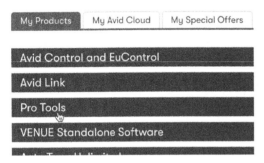

Figure 1.21 Accessing Pro Tools installers

5.   Click the **VIEW SOFTWARE DOWNLOAD LINKS & PRODUCT DETAILS** link.

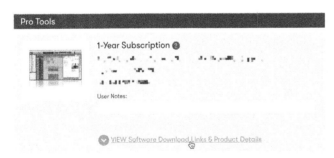

Figure 1.22 Showing Pro Tools installers in your Avid account

6.   From the list that appears, click on the desired version of the software. The installer will begin downloading.

7.   Once downloaded, launch the installation program. Installation from this point on is straightforward and follows normal installation processes based on your computer's operating system.

Installing Plug-Ins

In the world of Pro Tools, plug-ins provide software processing equivalent to traditional hardware effects and synthesizers. These include everything from EQ to compression, reverb, delay, and virtual instruments.

A number of plug-ins are automatically installed with Pro Tools. You will find other plug-in installers in your Avid account. These will appear in the **Software Download Links & Product Details** section, under your Pro Tools product listing.

Some plug-ins and bundles you will want to install for this course include the following:

- AIR Effects Bundle

- AIR Instruments Bundle

- Pro Tools | GrooveCell

- Pro Tools | SynthCell

- Pro Tools | PlayCell

- XPand!2

Avid Link

When you install Pro Tools, another application called Avid Link is also installed. Avid Link is a useful utility that can help you manage your software licenses, keep up to date with the latest versions, and more.

If you have an Avid account, but have not yet installed Pro Tools, you can install Avid Link individually. Just log into your Avid account and click the Avid Link item in your My Products page.

You can learn more about Avid link from the Avid Link product page. Visit https://www.avid.com/products/avid-link. From here, you can download Avid Link by clicking the Download Now button in the top right corner of the page.

Opening Avid Link

If you're working on a Mac computer, you can open Avid Link from the menu bar icon. On a Windows machine, you can open it from the taskbar icon or from the Start menu. Note that the Avid Link app is NOT the same as the Avid Link in-application browser that is available from within Pro Tools.

Avid Link and Software Updates

One of the central functions of Avid Link is to manage your licenses and update them easily:

1. After launching the Avid Link application, click the **PROFILE** icon at the top left corner to get to the Sign-In page.

2. Enter the email address and password that you have set up for your Avid account.

3. Click the **SIGN IN** button.

Figure 1.23 Signing into your Avid account via Avid Link

Click the **PRODUCTS** icon (left-hand side of the window) to see a list of all your Avid licenses. (This list may take a while to populate, as Avid Link synchronizes with your Avid account.) Next to each item in the list, you'll see a button that allows you to open the application, install a product, or update a product that is out of date.

LESSON 1 CONCLUSION

This Lesson provided an overview of the characteristics of analog and digital audio and introduced the concept of a digital audio workstation for editing and manipulating audio.

Discussion: Summary of Key Concepts

In this Lesson, you learned:

- How audio behaves in the real world, in terms of waveform, frequency, and amplitude

- How audio is converted to (and from) a digital format

- The importance of sample rate and bit depth

- What DAWs are, how they work, and why Pro Tools is the industry standard

- The different components that make up a Pro Tools system, from computers to interfaces to monitor speakers

- The process of installing Pro Tools, including creating an Avid Account, using an iLok account, and keeping up to date with Avid Link

Activity: Lesson 1 Knowledge Check

This quiz will check your knowledge of material covered in the Getting Started lesson.

1. Match the audio term to the characteristic it represents.

   Waveform   Pitch

   Amplitude   Intensity

   Frequency   Shape

2. Frequency is measured in cycles per second, commonly expressed as:

   Sine

   Hertz

   Decibels

   Ohms

3. The amplitude of a sound is commonly measured in:

   Beats

   Hertz

   Decibels

   Ohms

4. The highest frequency that can generally be heard by a human being is:

   20 Hz

   120 Hz

   10 kHz

   20 kHz

   32 kHz

5. The Nyquist-Shannon sampling theorem states that in order to accurately reproduce a signal, the sound wave should be sampled at a rate that is _____ times the highest frequency you wish to record.

6. What is the maximum dynamic range of 24-bit audio?

7. What is a clip in Pro Tools? How is it different from a file on disk?

8. Of the three commercial tiers of Pro Tools software, which support surround mixing?

    Pro Tools Artist

    Pro Tools Studio

    Pro Tools Ultimate

9. Avid uses which anti-piracy software to manage Pro Tools licenses?

    Red Points

    3DS

    NAGRA

    PACE/iLok

    Hudson Analytix

10. True or False? When you install Pro Tools, another application called Avid Link is also installed.

Installing Pro Tools

This exercise covers basic installation of Pro Tools software. If you plan to use Pro Tools on your personal computer, this exercise will help you get started.

 This exercise may be considered optional in an academic setting, where students are using preconfigured Pro Tools systems in a school lab or studio. Your course instructor will provide further guidance.

Exercise Details

■ **Required Media:** None

■ **Exercise Duration**: Around 30 Minutes

Qualify Your System

Before installing any software, you'll need to verify that your computer system meets all of the software requirements. If your computer does not meet the requirements for Pro Tools Artist, the software may either fail to install or fail to launch. In some cases, the software may launch, but it will not run properly.

Verify your system compatibility, as follows:

■ Go to https://avid.secure.force.com/pkb/articles/compatibility/Pro-Tools-System-Requirements.

■ Review the computer hardware specifications: minimum available storage/drive space, minimum RAM requirements, and qualified processors/CPUs.

■ Review compatible operating systems.

If your system isn't qualified for the latest version of Pro Tools, you've got two options: install an older version of Pro Tools for which the system is qualified, or upgrade to a qualified system.

Get Your Pro Tools License

If you've already purchased a Pro Tools license (perpetual or subscription), you've likely completed some of the following steps. In that case, simply skip ahead to the parts you have not done yet.

For most new Pro Tools users, the simplest way to get started is to install Avid's free 30-day trial. At any point during or after the trial, you can purchase a license to extend your access.

Sign up for the free trial:

1. Go to https://my.avid.com/get/pro-tools-trial.

2. Enter your email address.

3. Follow the onscreen instructions. For new users, this process will include:

   - Creating a new Avid account. (Be sure to use a valid email address that you have access to.)

   - Creating an iLok account, with the same email address and password as your Avid account.

   - Installing the Avid Link application.

Install Pro Tools and Related Software

The easiest way to install Pro Tools software, associated plug-ins, and sound libraries is to use the Avid Link application. After completing the above process for the free trial, Avid Link will be installed on your system. Avid Link will run in the background during normal operation.

Install Pro Tools software:

1. Click the Avid Link icon in the top menu bar area of the screen (Mac) or the bottom tray area (Windows) and select **SHOW** from the popup menu.

Figure 1.24 Clicking on the Avid Link icon

   The Avid Link user interface will display.

2. Click on the **PROFILE** button in the top left corner of Avid Link and enter your credentials to log into your Avid account.

3. Click on the **PRODUCTS** button on the left to access your products page.

Figure 1.25 The Products page of Avid Link

4. Click the **INSTALL** button next to the Pro Tools listing.

Install plug-ins and sound libraries:

1. Click on the Included Apps & Plugins link under the Pro Tools listing to drill down.

2. On the resulting page, click the **INSTALL** buttons for each of the following primary components:

   - AIR Effects Bundle
   - AIR Instruments Bundle
   - Avid Loopmasters Sample Pack

Figure 1.26 Plug-ins and sound library to install for this course

3. Scroll down to locate and install each of the following for use in this course:

- GrooveCell plug-in

- PlayCell plug-in

- SynthCell plug-in

- Xpand!2 plug-in

4. Optionally install other components as desired.

Authorize Pro Tools with iLok License Manager

Your Pro Tools license can be activated using either an iLok Cloud-based authorization or an iLok USB key. For most beginning Pro Tools users, authorizing through iLok Cloud is the easiest way to get started.

Activate your license with iLok Cloud:

1. Launch the iLok License Manager (installed with Pro Tools) using the conventions for your operating system.

2. Click the **SIGN IN** button at the top left and log in with your account credentials.

3. From the **FILE** menu, select **OPEN YOUR CLOUD SESSION**.

4. Select all of the products listed in the right pane. (Click the first one; then shift-click the last one.)

Figure 1.27 Products selected in iLok License Manager

5. From the **LICENSES** menu, select **ACTIVATE**.

6. In the resulting dialog box, select your iLok Cloud session as the destination, if not already selected, and click the **ACTIVATE** button. (See Figure 1.28.)

Figure 1.28 Selecting the iLok Cloud session as the destination for Pro Tools licenses

7. If prompted to set iLok Cloud to Managed Mode, click **AGREE**.

8. Quit iLok License Manager when finished.

Verify Installation

To verify proper installation and authorization, you can simply launch Pro Tools. If it starts up ok, then you have completed the above steps without issue.

Test Pro Tools:

1. Launch Pro Tools according to the conventions for your operating system. Once startup completes, you should see the Pro Tools Dashboard. This is enough to verify the installation.

2. (Optional) Close Pro Tools when finished:

   - Click the **CANCEL** button at the bottom of the Dashboard.

   - Quit the Pro Tools application according to the conventions for your operating system.

That completes this exercise.

Getting Inside Pro Tools

Now that you've gotten to know a bit about sound, digital audio, and Pro Tools systems, it's time to start exploring the basic functionality of Pro Tools Artist software.

 This course focuses on the entry-level Pro Tools Artist software. Unless otherwise indicated, everything you learn here will apply equally to Pro Tools Studio and Pro Tools Ultimate software, as well.

This Lesson covers a lot of ground—from opening a session and playing it back, to creating a new session from scratch. You will also learn to recognize the session components and the role they each play in the session hierarchy. Understanding these fundamentals is an important step on the road to Pro Tools mastery.

Learning Targets

- Power up and launch Pro Tools

- Open and play back a Pro Tools session

- Create a new session

- Understand the file hierarchy of a Pro Tools session

TOPIC 2.1:
POWERING UP PRO TOOLS

In this section, you will learn about turning on an audio system that includes a computer, an audio interface, and monitor speakers. As you explore, consider why it might be important to start up the equipment in a certain order. What might happen if the equipment is started in the wrong order? Have you ever before experienced issues using a computer system and connecting or disconnecting devices? What kinds of problems have you run into? Electronic equipment can be sensitive, so it's important to understand the proper startup procedure... and what to do when things stop working!

Discussion: Launching Pro Tools

When computers and audio interfaces are turned on or off, they can send a spike of voltage from their outputs. If your speakers are on, that voltage spike will sound like a loud pop or thump. Over time, these pops and thumps will wear out your speakers. So, here is a cardinal rule among audio professionals:

Your monitor speakers should be the last thing you turn on when starting up a Pro Tools system, and the first thing that you turn off when shutting it down.

If you have spent significant money and time on your setup, you'll want to make sure your gear is taken care of properly. Ensuring that speakers aren't accidentally damaged when powering on or off is not just professional etiquette. It is a good habit to get into from the start to protect your gear.

Start-Up Sequence

Beyond your monitor speakers, here's the recommended order for powering up a Pro Tools system:

1.   Start with all devices powered down.

2.   Turn on any devices (other than the computer) that use external power. This can include external drives, audio or MIDI interfaces, and so on. Wait for each device to initialize, as needed.

3.   Power up your computer. If some devices are USB-powered, wait for them to initialize as well.

4.   Launch Pro Tools.

5.   Turn on your monitor speakers.

(i)   More complex systems often require special power-up processes. Refer to your equipment's documentation for specific details.

Many audio interfaces are muted upon startup, as an extra precaution to protect the attached speakers. For these devices, remember to unmute the interface after your system is completely powered up.

Troubleshooting

If your equipment is not functioning properly after startup, or if it stops functioning at some point while you're working, here are some simple steps you can take.

If Pro Tools is behaving strangely:

■ For playback issues, choose **SETUP > PLAYBACK ENGINE** and check the following:

- If you are not hearing playback, verify that your audio interface is displayed in the Playback Engine pop-up menu. If not, select the audio interface and click **OK** to enable it. The session will save and close. Reopen the session once the process completes.

- If your audio interface is not available in the Playback Engine dialog box, first close the session. Then unplug and reconnect your audio interface, and check the Playback Engine dialog box again. If the audio interface displays in the pop-up menu, select it and reopen the session.

  Otherwise, quit Pro Tools and visit the audio interface manufacturer's website to locate the appropriate driver. After downloading and installing the driver, restart Pro Tools and verify that the audio interface is selected in the Playback Engine dialog box. Then reopen the session.

- If you are hearing distorted playback, change the **H/W BUFFER SIZE** setting to a different value and click **OK** to close the dialog box. This will clear the buffer and reset it. Often this step alone will fix the problem. Afterward, you can reset the H/W Buffer Size to its original setting.

 For more information about the Playback Engine dialog box, see Topic 2.2 later in this Lesson.

■ For other issues, or if the above steps don't help, take the followings steps, in order, until the problem is resolved:

- Close and reopen the session. This can often clear minor issues with Pro Tools behavior.

- Quit and relaunch the Pro Tools software. This process can clear problems at the application level.

- Power down and restart your system, including peripheral devices that use external power. This can clear problems with the computer at the operating system level as well as any problems you might be having with external devices.

TOPIC 2.2:
OPENING AND PLAYING A PRO TOOLS SESSION

In this section, you will learn how to open a Pro Tools session and configure Pro Tools' basic settings. You will also learn how to control playback and how to use various transport controls. As you complete this unit, consider what operations in Pro Tools may be familiar to you based on other software or devices you've used. What operations or behaviors are unfamiliar? Does anything seem strange, redundant, or pointless about the controls? What aspects of this unit do you think may not apply to you or the work you hope to do in Pro Tools?

Activity: Exploring Transport Controls

- Open the Activity 2.2.ptx session.

- Press spacebar to start playback. Let the session play for several seconds. Press spacebar again to stop.

- Repeat the above. What observations can you make about playback in Pro Tools?

- Try using the various transport controls. What do they each do? How might you use these functions?

- Discuss the transport controls. Do the buttons make sense to you?

Discussion: Working with a Session

When Pro Tools users create a session, they're creating a master file that can refer to other media, such as audio files, on any connected storage drive. The amount of audio that a session can use is limited only by the amount of available storage. Pro Tools is very flexible about where files and folders can be located.

Let's go through the basic steps of opening and playing a session.

To open an existing session:

1. Launch Pro Tools software, according to the conventions of your computer's operating system.

    Once launched, Pro Tools will display the Dashboard. (See Figure 2.1.)

Figure 2.1 The Pro Tools Dashboard

On the left-hand side of the Dashboard, you'll find four tabs: **CREATE**, **RECENT**, **PROJECTS**, and **GETTING STARTED**. The Recent tab will display a list of your 10 most recently created and opened sessions or projects for easy access. If you're just getting started with Pro Tools, this list will be empty.

2. In the lower right-hand portion of the Dashboard, click the **OPEN FROM DISK** button.

Figure 2.2 Opening a session from disk

3. In the browser window that appears, navigate to the folder that contains the desired session file.

(i)   Pro Tools session files have a .PTX file extension.

Figure 2.3 Locating a Pro Tools session file

4. Click on the session file to select it and then click the **OPEN** button, or simply double-click the session file to open it.

Playback Engine and Hardware Setup

With a session open and ready to play, you'll want to verify that it will play through the correct device. Pro Tools can be configured to use an audio interface connected to your computer, your computer's built-in speakers, or some other device. A quick look at the **PLAYBACK ENGINE** and **HARDWARE SETUP** dialog boxes will make sure that things are set up correctly.

The Playback Engine Dialog Box

When you launch Pro Tools, the software will typically default to your audio interface or the built-in inputs and outputs (speakers) on your computer. If you need to change the device that Pro Tools is using, you can do so from the Playback Engine dialog box:

1. From the **SETUP** menu, choose **PLAYBACK ENGINE**. The Playback Engine dialog box will appear.

Figure 2.4 Opening the Playback Engine dialog box

2. In the **DEVICE** field, choose the hardware that is attached to your speakers or headphones.

Figure 2.5 Choosing a device in the Playback Engine dialog box

ⓘ If your audio interface does not show up on the Device list, you might be missing the driver. Make sure that your hardware drivers are installed and up to date.

ⓘ Mac computers use the "Pro Tools Aggregate I/O" setting to access the computer's built-in inputs and outputs for recording and playback.

ⓘ If a session is open when you change the Playback Engine device, a message will display letting you know that Pro Tools will save and close your session. You will need to reopen the session to use the new Playback Engine settings.

3. Click the **OK** button in the lower right of the Playback Engine dialog box to apply your changes.

The Hardware Setup Dialog Box

After choosing an audio interface in the Playback Engine dialog box, you can configure it from the Hardware Setup dialog box. (Note, this step may not be necessary when using your computer's built-in audio.)

1. From the **SETUP** menu, choose **HARDWARE**. The Hardware Setup dialog box will appear.

Figure 2.6 Opening the Hardware Setup dialog box

2. The Hardware Setup dialog box will vary depending on the interface connected to your computer. The device selected in the Playback Engine dialog box will display in the upper left-hand corner of the dialog box. For some devices, hardware setup options can be configured directly in this window. Others will use a dedicated control app that can be launched from this dialog box.

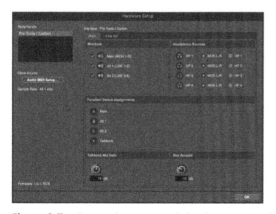 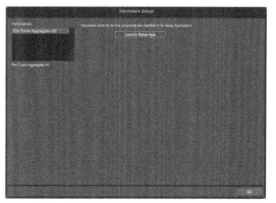

Figure 2.7 The Hardware Setup dialog box: Pro Tools | Carbon (left) and Pro Tools Aggregate I/O (right)

(i)   The Pro Tools Aggregate I/O option is available on Mac-based computers only.

3.   Once you've configured your settings, click the **OK** button to close the Hardware Setup dialog box.

Starting and Stopping Playback

To begin experimenting with session playback, you'll want to work in the Edit window (**WINDOW > EDIT**). The colored blocks in this window are audio and MIDI clips. For each session, the details of those clips will be different, but the overall look of the window will be similar.

Figure 2.8 The Pro Tools Edit window

    MIDI clips are explored in detail in Lesson 9 in this course.

    If you're not seeing the Edit window, you can show it by going to the Window menu and choosing Edit.

Later in this Lesson, you'll learn the Pro Tools user interface in detail. For now, let's go through some of the basic ways to play and hear your session.

One way of controlling playback is from the Pro Tools Transport window:

1.   From the **WINDOW** menu, choose **TRANSPORT**. (See Figure 2.9.) The Transport window will open.

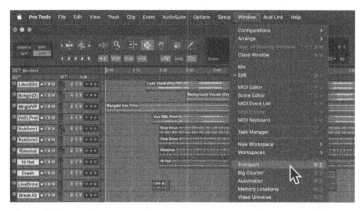

Figure 2.9 Opening the Transport window from the Window menu

 The shortcut for opening (and closing) the Transport window is Command+[1] (on the numeric keypad) on a Mac, or Ctrl+[1] (on the numeric keypad) on Windows.

2. Click the green triangular button to begin playback.

Figure 2.10 Starting playback from the Transport window

As your session plays, you will see a vertical line moving from left to right. This is commonly called the *playback cursor*. This line indicates where the playback point is in the session's timeline.

You will also see large green numbers at the top of the Edit window. These show the playback cursor location numerically, in minutes and seconds, bars and beats, or other measurement units.

Figure 2.11 The playback cursor moving across the Edit window during session playback

On the left-hand side of the Edit window, you'll see level meters showing the volume level of each individual row (or *track*).

Figure 2.12 Track level meters in the Edit window

3. To stop playback, click the square **STOP** button (left of the Play button) in the Transport window.

Figure 2.13 Stopping playback from the Transport window

> You can also press the Spacebar on your computer keyboard to start and stop playback.

The Transport window includes a few other useful navigational buttons:

■ Clicking the **RETURN TO ZERO** button will place the cursor at the beginning of the session's timeline.

Figure 2.14 The Return to Zero button

■ Clicking and holding the **REWIND** button will move the playback cursor backwards on the timeline; clicking and holding the **FAST FORWARD** button will move the cursor forward on the timeline.

Figure 2.15 The Rewind button (left) and the Fast Forward button (right)

■ Clicking the **GO TO END** button will take your cursor to the end of your session's timeline.

Figure 2.16 The Go to End button

> ## Navigation Shortcuts
>
> Here are two shortcuts that you will find useful when navigating your session's timeline:
>
> • To get back to the beginning of the timeline, press **RETURN** (Mac) or **ENTER** (Windows).
>
> • To go to the end of your timeline, press **OPTION+RETURN** (Mac) or **ALT+ENTER** (Windows).

Closing a Session and Quitting Pro Tools

When you're done with your work, you will want to save what you've done and safely quit the Pro Tools software. The process follows the typical rules of your computer's operating system:

1. Navigate to the **FILE** menu and do one of the following:

    • Select **SAVE** to overwrite the session file with any changes you've made.

    • Select **SAVE AS** to save a new session with your changes, leaving the original session unchanged.

 Press Command+S (Mac) or Ctrl+S (Windows) at anytime to save your session.

 Press Command+Control+S (Mac) or Ctrl+Start+S (Windows) at anytime to activate the Save As command.

2. Select **CLOSE SESSION** to close the session when finished.

 Closing the Pro Tools windows will NOT close your session; the session will still be open with its windows closed. If you save it in this state, it will save (and later reopen) with the windows closed.

Quitting the Pro Tools application follows the convention of your computer's operating system.

On a Mac computer, do the following:

1. Navigate to the **PRO TOOLS** menu.

2. Select **QUIT PRO TOOLS**.

On a Windows computer, do the following:

1. Navigate to the **FILE** menu.

2. Select **EXIT**.

TOPIC 2.3:
CREATING A PRO TOOLS SESSION

In this section, you will create a new session from scratch. As with many things in Pro Tools, there are a few different ways that you can approach this. You will explore the processes of creating a new blank session, creating a new session from a template, and selecting session parameters.

As you prepare to create a session, you'll want to think about the kind of work you are setting out to do: What is the purpose of your session? Will you be composing music? Creating sound effects? Recording narration? Who will be listening to your production? What will be the delivery medium? How might your work be used in the future? The answers to these questions will help you determine the choices you need to make when you are first getting started.

Activity: Explore Uses of Audio

■   Consider common audio activities as a class:

- Music production

- Podcast production

- Radio/broadcast advertisements

- Sound effects for film, TV, games, theater, and broadcast

- Audio books

- Game audio

- Foley sound

- Recording / broadcasting live events

- Audio restoration

- Music remixing

- Post production

■   Discuss how the requirements might be different for the audio you create for each of these activities.

- Which activities can you complete using lower quality recordings and equipment? Which might require a higher-end production value?

- Which do you think can be done using a limited dynamic range and a limited frequency spectrum? Which do you think will require a broad dynamic range or wide frequency spectrum?

- What other considerations might apply?

Discussion: Creating a Session

To get started working on a new production in Pro Tools, you will need to create a session. The session consists of a collection of files and folders that work together. This collection will grow in size as you work.

Creating a Blank Session

Let's start off by creating a blank session—in other words, a session that has no tracks in it.

To create a blank session:

1. Launch Pro Tools.

2. Click the **CREATE** tab in the Dashboard, if it isn't already selected.

 If the Dashboard is not visible, click on the FILE menu and choose CREATE NEW. The Dashboard window will appear with the CREATE tab selected.

 You can also use the shortcut Command+N (Mac) or Ctrl+N (Windows) to create a new session.

3. Name your session descriptively—the default name ("Untitled") doesn't provide any information about the session!

Illegal Characters

Certain characters are "illegal" in both Windows and Mac computer systems, and should be avoided when naming a session:

* | " : < > ? / \

It's worth noting that you *can* use these characters when working within Pro Tools (for things like naming tracks), but not for naming a session file.

---

4. Choose the **LOCAL STORAGE (SESSION)** radio button in the Dashboard.

5. Make sure the **CREATE FROM TEMPLATE** checkbox is unchecked. (See Figure 2.17.)

Figure 2.17 Creating a blank session (not from a template)

6.   Choose the **FILE TYPE** that your session will use. This will determine file format that will be used for audio files that you record in the session. You have two choices:

   •   **BWF (.WAV):** This option will create *.wav* files (short for Waveform Audio File) when recording in Pro Tools. Pro Tools uses the Broadcast Wave Format (BWF) as its default audio file format.

   •   **AIFF:** This option will create *.aiff* files (Audio Interchange File Format). Originally a Mac-only format, Pro Tools provides this option on both Mac and Windows-based systems. AIFF can be used in circumstances where you might share files with applications that don't support *.wav* files.

7.   Choose a **SAMPLE RATE** for your session. Available options will vary depending upon the audio interface (or other device) that you've chosen in the Playback Engine dialog box.

8.   Choose a **BIT DEPTH** for your session. Your choices are 16-bit, 24-bit, and 32-bit float.

9.   Select **I/O SETTINGS** to determine the number, naming, and organization of your audio inputs and outputs. You'll find more detail on this later in this course; for now, consider these two settings:

   •   **Last Used:** This is the default setting. This option reuses the I/O settings from the most recent session opened on that system.

   •   **Stereo Mix:** This option will load default input and output settings for the audio device currently selected in the Playback Engine dialog box. This is often a good starting point, especially if you are creating a Pro Tools session on an unfamiliar system.

10.   (Optional) Enable the **INTERLEAVED** checkbox. This determines how stereo recordings are treated:

   •   **Unchecked:** Audio recorded on a stereo track will be stored as two mono audio files (one for the left channel and one for the right channel). This is also known as split-stereo or multi-mono.

   •   **Checked:** Audio recorded on a stereo track will be stored as a single stereo audio file, comprising both left and right channels.

(i)   The choice to use interleaved files or not has no impact on how Pro Tools functions or on the quality of the recorded files. This setting affects only the type and quantity of audio files created on disk (in the Audio Files folder).

Figure 2.18 Choosing audio parameter settings for your session

11. Near the bottom of the Dashboard, you'll find two radio buttons. These enable you to control where your session will be created:

    • If you select the **PROMPT FOR LOCATION** radio button, Pro Tools will present a dialog box allowing you to choose a location for your session from among your local drives.

    • If you select the fixed location radio button, Pro Tools will automatically create your session in the indicated folder. (The default location is your Documents folder.) You can change this location by clicking the **LOCATION** button and navigating to the desired destination.

Figure 2.19 Location options for your new session

(i) Most professionals choose to store their sessions using a dedicated audio storage drive or location rather than in the default Documents folder.

12. To complete the process, click the **CREATE** button in the lower right-hand corner of the window. If you chose the **PROMPT FOR LOCATION** option, you will be prompted to choose a location for your session. Otherwise, your session will be created in the folder selected for the fixed location.

(i) Pro Tools allows only a single session to be open at a time. If you already have a session open when you create a new one, you'll be given the option to save and close the session before the new session opens.

After creating a new session, you'll see the Pro Tools Mix and/or Edit window with no tracks displayed.

Creating a Session from a Template

You can also create a new session from a template. When you create a session from a template, you'll be starting from a preconfigured set of tracks rather than an empty Mix and Edit window.

To create a session from a template:

1. Access the Dashboard and click the **CREATE** tab.

2. Select the **LOCAL STORAGE (SESSION)** option as before.

3. In this case, make sure the **CREATE FROM TEMPLATE** checkbox is enabled. You will see a list of templates that you can choose from.

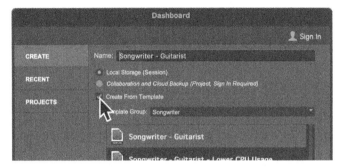

Figure 2.20 Creating a session from a template

4. Click the **TEMPLATE GROUP** pop-up menu and choose a template category. The list of templates will update to display all templates in that category.

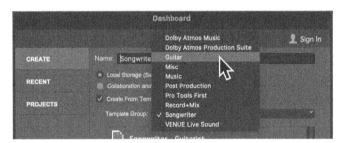

Figure 2.21 Changing template categories

5. Choose the template that you wish to use for your new session.

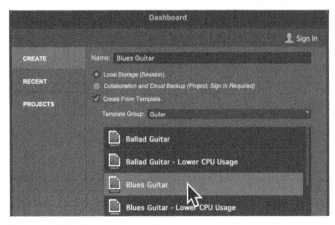

Figure 2.22 Choosing a template

6. Specify a name for the new session in the Name field at the top of the Dashboard. (Pro Tools auto-populates the name field with the template name; however, you should get into the habit of naming your sessions descriptively.)

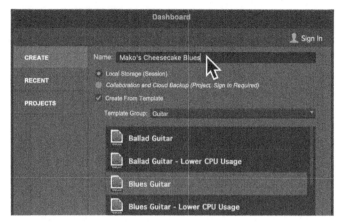

Figure 2.23 Naming your new session

After this, the process is identical to the steps used to create a blank session.

7. Choose your session settings:

    • File Type

    • Sample Rate

    • Bit Depth

    • I/O Settings

    • Interleaved option

8. Choose a save location for your new session.

9. Click the **CREATE** button. A new session will be created with the contents from the selected template.

When you create a session from a template, your session will come preloaded with tracks. You'll see these in both the Edit window and the Mix window.

Session Audio Settings

In the first Lesson, you learned about sample rate and bit-depth, and how those parameters relate to the frequencies and amplitude levels that can be recorded and played back. Choosing the right audio specs for your session is important; this is something that is best decided early in the production process.

Sample Rate and Bit-Depth Considerations

As a rule, larger files will use more CPU and consume more drive space. That translates to fewer minutes of audio, and fewer possible tracks and effects. Higher sample rate and bit-depth settings will result in larger files. Consider the following points:

■ Higher sample rates are not always better. A recording at a sample rate of 176.4 kHz includes <u>four times</u> as many samples as the same recording at a sample rate of 44.1 kHz. This means the file will be four times as large. Although a higher sample rate allows for more accurate high frequencies, for many home- and semi-professional recordings, the difference will be inaudible.

■ At any given sample rate, a 24-bit file will be 50% larger then a 16-bit file. That additional file size can give you significant benefits when recording material with a broad dynamic range, such as orchestral music. In these cases, 16-bit audio may fall short of the dynamic range you need, while 24-bit audio provides more than enough to cover the entire usable range of audible sound.

The session sample rate and bit-depth don't need to match the settings used for the final output. Professionals often record, edit, and mix at higher settings than they use in their stereo file. Higher specs can provide better results, even if you reduce sample rate and bit-depth for the final export.

Audio File Formats

All versions of Pro Tools support WAV or AIFF files as native formats. WAV files are the popular choice, for a number of reasons. First, WAV files are more broadly compatible than AIFF files. Secondly, Pro Tools uses Broadcast Wave Format (BWF) files, which can include additional information (metadata) that is useful in professional post-production workflows (production for a video medium).

WAV and AIFF files are both uncompressed Pulse Code Modulation (PCM) files. As such, there is no difference in sound quality between the two formats.

Split Stereo versus Interleaved

The decision to use interleaved files or not won't affect sound quality, drive usage, CPU load, or Pro Tools workflow. The only significant difference is the format and number of files that you will have in your session's Audio Files folder. Choosing interleaved files means that you will have fewer files to keep track of (each stereo recording will result in one file rather than two). It also means that you can more easily use or play the stereo recordings from your Audio Files folder outside of Pro Tools.

TOPIC 2.4:
COMPONENTS OF A PRO TOOLS SESSION

After creating a new Pro Tools document, you might reasonably assume that you've created a session file, and you'd be right—but that's not the only thing that you've created! A Pro Tools session consists of an ecosystem of different elements that work together to get the job done.

This section takes a look at the different files and folders that make up the Pro Tools session hierarchy. This discussion addresses questions like, "Why does a session require so many files? Why doesn't Pro Tools use a single, self-contained document for each session?" As you progress through this unit, also consider why some session content is saved within the session file and other content is saved externally.

Activity: Explore a Pro Tools Session Folder

- Open the session folder for **Activity 2.4**. What files and folders are included inside?

- Open each subfolder. What kinds of content do you find in each?

- Open the session by double-clicking the **Activity 2.4.ptx** file. Do you recognize anything from the session folder?

- Return to the open session folder. What has changed? Why do you think the content is different?

- Optional: Return to Pro Tools and record something to a track and bounce the session.

- Return again to the session folder and explore. What new files do you find?

- Close the Pro Tools session. What effect does that have on the session folder?

- Discuss what you've observed and try to draw some conclusions about the files Pro Tools creates.

Discussion: Pro Tools File Hierarchy

When you create a Pro Tools session, the software creates a top-level session folder. Insider of this folder is a hierarchy of additional files and folders that work together to allow the session to function.

Session Folder

When you create a session, Pro Tools will automatically create a folder to put it and the other elements of the session into for easy organization. In the case of a session called **My Next Big Hit**, you can see some of the typical elements of a Pro Tools session. Note that the folder is named for the session that you've created.

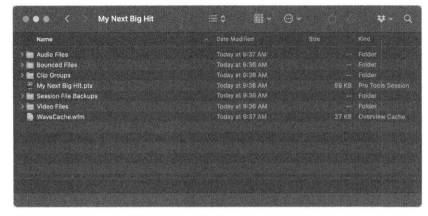

Figure 2.24 Contents of a typical Pro Tools session folder

Session Components

Within the session folder, you'll find different files and folders that contribute to how a Pro Tools session operates. Let's take a look at each element individually and the role that it plays.

 Certain folders are created automatically when you create a session, others may be created later as needed. If you don't see all of the folders discussed below in one of your sessions, it's likely because the session doesn't need them.

Session File

Your Pro Tools session file is the nexus of your Pro Tools work. This is where you'll be doing all of your recording, editing, mixing, and more.

My Next Big Hit.ptx

Figure 2.25 A Pro Tools session file

You can perform a number of production tasks using the Pro Tools session file only—working with MIDI and balancing levels of different tracks to name a few—but for other jobs, a Pro Tools session acts as a map, pointing to media files on your system and controlling when they will play back on your session's timeline.

When you create a Pro Tools session, a Pro Tools session file is created within the session folder. Both the session folder and session file will have the same name, with the session file having a .ptx file extension.

WaveCache File

When you view audio clips in Pro Tools, you'll see a visual representation of each audio file's waveform. These visual representations of your session's audio are stored in a file named WaveCache.wfm.

The WaveCache file is automatically created by Pro Tools within the session folder.

Figure 2.26 A Pro Tools WaveCache file

Deleting or losing the WaveCache file will not harm a session. When the session file is next opened, Pro Tools will simply reconstruct the WaveCache file in the session folder, without data loss.

 If your session doesn't include any audio clips, you won't see a WaveCache.wfm file in your session folder.

Subfolders

Pro Tools also creates a variety of subfolders to handle the needs of the session. These subfolders can include:

- **Audio Files:** This is the default location for any audio files that are created as a result of recording to Audio tracks in Pro Tools. Each recording is typically stored as a separate file within this folder.

 Within the Audio Files folder, WAV files will have the .wav file extension, and AIFF files will have the .aif file extension.

- **Video Files:** In certain workflows, video files used in Pro Tools will be placed in the Video Files subfolder. This applies only in situations where the video is copied into the session.

 Pro Tools Artist does not support video files, so no Video Files folder is created.

- **Rendered Files:** A number of features within Pro Tools will temporarily render an audio file. The Rendered Files subfolder is created to store these files. Rendered files will be in either .wav or .aif format and are dynamically managed by Pro Tools (being created and deleted as needed).

- **Bounced Files:** When you finish your mixing work, you can export a mixdown, or *bounce*, of the file. This process creates a single stereo audio file that can be listened to outside of the Pro Tools environment. The default location for the resulting audio file is the Bounced Files folder.

- **Clip Groups:** Clip groups combine multiple clips into a single editable object on the Pro Tools timeline. Clip groups are normally included within the session file, but they can be exported for use in other sessions. The default location for exported clip groups is the Clip Groups folder.

 The topic of Clip Groups is covered in the Pro Tools 110 course.

- **Session File Backups:** Pro Tools periodically creates auto backups of your session file to protect you from losing all your work if something goes wrong. In the Pro Tools Preferences dialog box, you can choose how many backups to keep, and how frequently new backup files are created. The files used for auto backups are saved in the Session File Backups folder.

ⓘ To set your Auto Backup preferences, choose Setup > Preferences and select the Operation tab.

ⓘ Auto Backup files are named after the Session, with file suffixes that aid in organization. Naming is structured as [Session Name].bak.[backup number].ptx.

LESSON 2 CONCLUSION

In this Lesson, you explored processes for launching and troubleshooting Pro Tools. You learned about opening existing sessions and creating new sessions of your own, and you saw how to control the Pro Tools transport. Along the way, you also learned about audio file formats and the hierarchy of files used in a Pro Tools session.

Discussion: Summary of Key Concepts

In this Lesson, you learned:

- The proper order in which to power up and shut down your system, and why it's important

- How to launch Pro Tools and open a session

- How to change the playback device in the Playback Engine and Hardware Setup dialog boxes

- How to control basic playback and positioning in a Pro Tools session

- Steps required to create a new blank session

- The file hierarchy of a Pro Tools session, and the function of the various files and folders it includes

Essential Keyboard Commands and Shortcuts

Below is a summary of modifier behaviors and shortcut operations that you should know from this Lesson:

- Press Spacebar to start and stop playback.

- Press the **RETURN** key (Mac) or the **ENTER** key (Windows) to move the Edit cursor to the beginning of the session's timeline.

- Press **OPTION+RETURN** (Mac) or **ALT+ENTER** (Windows) to move the Edit cursor to the end of the session's timeline.

- Press **COMMAND+S** (Mac) or **CTRL+S** (Windows) to save an open session.

- Press **COMMAND+N** (Mac) or **CTRL+N** (Windows) to create a new session.

Activity: Lesson 2 Knowledge Check

This quiz will check your knowledge of material covered in this Lesson.

1.   When powering up your Pro Tools system, which device should be turned on last?

   Computer

   Audio interface

   MIDI Interface

   External Hard Drives

   Monitor Speakers

2.   Which of the following steps are recommended if Pro Tools is not playing audio properly?

   Toggle between the Mix and Edit windows

   Verify that your audio interface is selected in the Playback Engine dialog box

   Change the H/W Buffer Size setting in the Playback Engine dialog box

   Open a session template and save it as a new session

3.   What dialog box lets you change the device or audio interface that Pro Tools uses for audio playback?

4.   A quick way to start or stop playback is to press the _____ key.

5.   What is the name of the small floating window that provides access play, stop, fast-forward, and rewind buttons?

6.   Rather than creating a session from scratch, you can choose to create a session from a _____ to start from a preconfigured set of tracks.

7.   When creating a new session, which two audio file types are available to choose from for the session?

8.   What is the difference between interleaved stereo and split-stereo files? Does it matter which option you use in Pro Tools?

9.   Match the file or folder to its description.

Session File	Database for graphic representation of audio files in your session
WaveCache.wfm	A "pointer" to other media files on your system
Session File Backups folder	Default location for recorded audio
Audio Files folder	Temporary storage for audio files, dynamically managed by Pro Tools
Rendered Files folder	Storage for safety copies of Pro Tools sessions

10.   True or False? When you create a session, Pro Tools will automatically create a session folder to contain all the elements of the session for easy organization.

Creating a Session

In this exercise, you will create a Pro Tools session, configuring the session parameters as needed for a simple radio advertisement. Once you've created the session, you will display the Edit window and the Transport window. You will then use the Save As command to save the session with a different name for use in subsequent exercises.

Exercise Details

- **Required Media:** None

- **Exercise Duration:** 10 to 15 Minutes

Getting Started

To get started, you will need to create a new 44.1 kHz, 24-bit session. You can do this by launching your Pro Tools software and configuring the **CREATE** tab in the Dashboard.

Launch Pro Tools and create a session:

1. Power up your computer and any connected hardware, as described in Lesson 2.

2. Do one of the following to launch Pro Tools:

   - Double-click on the **PRO TOOLS** shortcut icon on the desktop.

   - Click the **PRO TOOLS** icon in the Dock (Mac).

   - Click **START > PRO TOOLS** (Windows).

3. In the Dashboard, select the **CREATE** tab at the top left, and enable **LOCAL STORAGE (SESSION)**.

4. Make sure the **CREATE FROM TEMPLATE** checkbox is NOT selected (unchecked).

5. At the top of the Dashboard, name your session **Exercises-XXX**, where **XXX** is your initials.

Specify the session parameters:

1. At the bottom of the Dashboard, set the audio parameters as follows:

    •   File Type: BWF (.WAV)

    •   Bit Depth: 24 Bit

    •   Sample Rate: 44.1 kHz

    •   I/O Settings: Stereo Mix

    •   Interleaved: Checked

    •   Prompt for Location: Selected

Figure 2.27 Session Parameters configured in the Dashboard

2. Next, click the **CREATE** button.

3. Navigate to an appropriate location to save your session, as directed by your instructor.

4. Click **SAVE** to save the session in the selected location.

Displaying Pro Tools Windows

In the next few exercises, you will be working primarily in the Edit window. This window will let you work with media on your tracks, change your playback location, and more.

Configure the Edit window, as follows:

1. Make sure the Edit window is displayed by choosing **WINDOW > EDIT**.

2. Then maximize or resize the window as needed to utilize the available space on your desktop. This is an important step to be able to work efficiently.

    • On macOS systems, hold the **OPTION** key while clicking the green Maximize button at the top left of the Edit window. This will make the window full-size without obscuring the main menus.

    • On Windows systems, click the square Maximize button at the top right of the Edit window.

As you work, you may also need to access the Transport controls from time to time. These are available in the Transport window and may also be available in the Edit window toolbar.

For now, open the Transport window so that its controls will be readily available:

■   Choose **WINDOW > TRANSPORT**.

With the window open, you can position it anywhere on screen that feels comfortable. When finished, your session should look something like this.

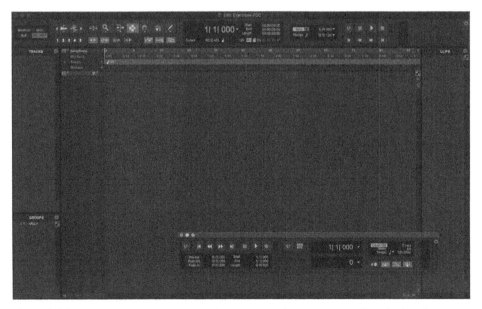

Figure 2.28 Exercise 2 session with the Edit window and Transport window displayed

Finishing Up

To complete this exercise, you will need to save your work under a new name and close the session. Note that you will be reusing this session in subsequent exercises, so it is important to save the work you've done.

Finish your work:

1. Choose **FILE > SAVE AS** to create a copy of the session.

2. In the **SAVE SESSION AS** dialog box, rename the session as Exercise02-XXX (where XXX is your initials), and click **SAVE**.

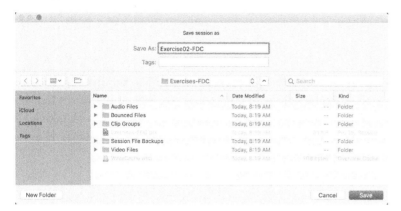

Figure 2.29 The Save As dialog box on a macOS system

 Do not move the renamed session to a different location. The exercise revisions you create in this book should all remain within the original Exercises folder.

3. Choose **FILE > CLOSE SESSION** to close the session when finished.

 You cannot close a Pro Tools session by closing the Mix and Edit windows. This common mistake leaves the session open with no active windows. Instead, you must choose CLOSE SESSION from the FILE menu.

That completes this exercise.

Getting to Know Pro Tools

This Lesson explores the Pro Tools user interface and its primary windows. First, we dive into the Pro Tools Edit window and examine its layout, tools, and component parts. Next, we look at the Mix window and its component parts. Then we move on to the Transport window. We wrap up this Lesson by taking a look at ways to customize the appearance of the Pro Tools windows through themes and views. Here we also provide an overview of the main Pro Tools menus.

Learning Targets

- Learn the layout and function of the Pro Tools Edit window

- Learn the layout and function of the Pro Tools Mix window

- Learn the layout and function of the Pro Tools Transport window

- Learn how to customize the Pro Tools display

- Learn how to work with various views and menus available in Pro Tools

TOPIC 3.1:
THE EDIT WINDOW

The first step to using any software is to get familiar with the user interface. The Pro Tools user interface is comprised of its main windows. The Edit window is generally where you will start work on a session. In this unit, you'll learn how to customize the Edit window to suit your personal style.

Activity: Explore the Edit Window Interface

- Open the Activity 3.1.ptx session. This session will open with the Edit window displayed.

- Maximize the Edit window as needed by double-clicking on title bar at the top of the window.

- Click on each of the four Edit mode buttons on the far left side of the Edit window toolbar: SHUFFLE, SLIP, SPOT, and GRID. Notice the colors associated with each mode. What do you think each color represents?

- Position your mouse over each of the Edit tool buttons in the Edit window toolbar, starting with the magnifying glass icon and working your way to the right.

  Hover over each button long enough for the Tool Tip text to appear, showing the name of the tool. What do you think each tool is used for?

- Spend some time experimenting with the Edit tools and Edit modes. What conclusions can you draw from your observations?

Discussion: Working in the Edit Window

The Edit window is where many professionals do most of their work. It's where you will import your media, arrange your clips, and (as the name suggests) do your editing. It may look complex at first, but if you break it down to its component parts, it's pretty easy to get around. (See Figure 3.1.)

 To show the Edit window in Pro Tools, go to the Window menu and choose Edit. Displayed windows are indicated by check marks in this menu.

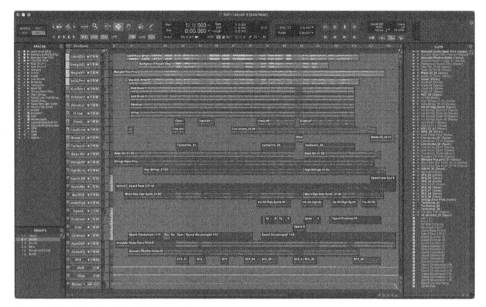

Figure 3.1 The Pro Tools Edit window

Edit Window Toolbar

At the top of the Edit window, you'll see a row of buttons and icons, collectively known as the Edit window toolbar. Here, tools are arranged in clusters according to their function.

Figure 3.2 The Edit window toolbar

In this Lesson, we will discuss the Edit window toolbar by naming its clusters and describing them in general terms. Throughout the course, you'll learn how to use each of these tools in detail.

Edit Mode Buttons

The cluster of buttons at the far left of the toolbar shows the Edit modes. You'll learn more about these modes later in this course, but for now, just know that you have four of them: Shuffle, Slip, Spot, and Grid.

Figure 3.3 Edit Mode buttons, with Grid mode active

Edit Tools

The Edit tools are grouped together in the cluster shown in Figure 3.4. From left to right, these are as follows:

- Zoomer tool (magnifying glass icon)

- Trim tool

- Selector tool

- Grabber tool (hand icon)

- Scrubber tool (speaker icon)

- Pencil tool

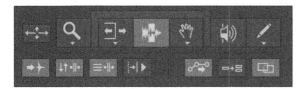

Figure 3.4 Edit Tools (top) and option buttons (bottom)

At the left and across the bottom, from left to right, are the following option buttons:

- Zoom Toggle button (arrows pointing each direction, left of the Zoomer tool)

- Tab to Transient button (bottom left)

- Link Timeline and Edit Selection button

- Link Track and Edit Selection button

- Insertion Follows Playback button

- Automation Follows Edit button

- Mirrored MIDI Editing button

- Layered Editing button

Counter and Edit Selection Area

The Counter and Edit Selection area will give you very important information. On the top left, you'll see the Main Counter, which tells you exactly where your timeline insertion is on your session's timeline. This counter can show position in a number of time scales (Minutes and Seconds, Bars and Beats, Timecode, and so on) and can even show two scales simultaneously. (Figure 3.5 shows Bars and Beats in the Main Counter on the top, and Minutes and Seconds in the Sub Counter below).

To the right of the Main Counter, you'll see Edit Selection indicators, which will tell you the start, end, and duration (length) of any selection you might have made on the timeline. The bottom row of the Counter and Edit Selection area has a collection of indicators as well, including the position of your cursor and various status indicators.

Figure 3.5 Counter and Edit Selection area of the Edit window toolbar

Grid and Nudge Values

The Grid and Nudge functions are based on user-adjustable increments. You can easily choose the scale and increment for either of these by clicking the appropriate selector (triangle button) to the right of the value.

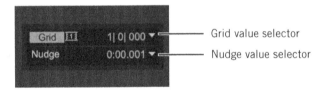

Figure 3.6 Grid and Nudge values

Additional tool clusters can be shown or hidden in the toolbar as needed. These include Zoom controls, Transport controls, MIDI controls, and Output Meters.

Zoom Controls

Zoom controls allow you to quickly zoom in or out horizontally on the timeline, or vertically for audio or MIDI clips in the session. Zoom levels can also be saved as one of five Zoom Presets, accessible from the bottom row of buttons.

Figure 3.7 Zoom controls

Transport/Expanded Transport

You may have already worked with Transport controls in the Transport window. You can also show these controls in the Edit window toolbar, in two ways:

- **Transport:** This includes basic transport controls only.

- **Expanded Transport:** This includes extra controls, including Pre-roll, Post-roll, Fade-in, and timeline selection Start, End, and Length.

Figure 3.8 Transport controls (Left) and Expanded Transport controls (right)

MIDI Controls

When you're working with MIDI information (short for Musical Instrument Digital Interface), you'll want to be able control aspects of your session like Tempo, Meter, and Count Off. The MIDI Controls cluster enables you to do that, and more.

Figure 3.9 MIDI controls

Output Meters

The session's Output Meters will show the total signal level coming out of your designated outputs. It is commonly used to show the level of signals that are routed to your speakers or headphones.

Figure 3.10 Output Meters

Rulers Area

Just below the Edit window toolbar, you'll find another horizontal strip subdivided into segments. These are your session's rulers, which measure and mark the passage of time in different ways. The rulers display your current position within the session. They also enable you to set start and end points for playback and recording.

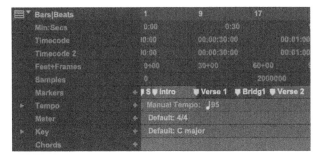

Figure 3.11 Rulers in the Pro Tools Edit window (Pro Tools Studio shown)

You can show or hide any of the following rulers in the Edit window. These rulers are divided into two categories: Timebase rulers, which indicate the progress of time, and Conductor rulers, which display other important events that can occur as your session plays.

The Timebase rulers in Pro Tools Artist include:

- Bars|Beats (Bars and Beats)

- Min:Secs (Minutes and Seconds)

- Timecode (SMPTE timecode)

- Samples

And the Conductor rulers include:

- Markers

- Tempo

- Meter

- Key

- Chords

 As you work in Pro Tools, you may notice a thin vertical red line in your ruler area. This indicator displays whenever your cursor is positioned in the Tracks area of the Edit window. If you can't find your cursor, look for the red line in the rulers!

Tracks List and Groups List

The column on the left-hand side of the Edit window is comprised of two sections: From top to bottom they are the Tracks List and the Groups List.

The Tracks List shows a list of all tracks in your session, in the order that they appear in the main area of the Edit window. Here, you can select, show, hide, or reorder your tracks.

Figure 3.12 The Tracks List

The Groups List in the Edit window is directly below the Tracks List. Here, you can view and work with various Edit Groups that you create in a session.

 Edit Groups allow the user to make changes on multiple grouped tracks simultaneously.

 Edit Groups are beyond the scope of this course. They are discussed in detail in the Pro Tools 110 course of the Avid Learning Series.

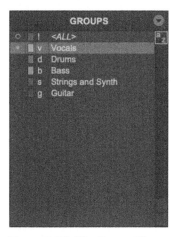

Figure 3.13 The Groups List

Clips List

On the right side of the Edit window, you'll see the Clips List. Just as the Tracks List shows all tracks in your session, the Clips List displays clips of various types that are in your session (whether they are actively used in tracks or not). Your Clips List is a comprehensive list of the media in your session.

Figure 3.14 The Clips List

 In Pro Tools Artist or Pro Tools Studio, only audio, MIDI, and clip group clips are shown. In a Pro Tools Ultimate, video clips are also shown in the Clips List.

Tracks Area

In the main part of the Edit window is the tracks area. This is where you'll see horizontal strips with descriptive names like Vocals, SFX, Strings, and so on displayed to the left of each row. Each one of these rows is a track, and the colored blocks on the strips are called clips. The number of tracks in your session, and the number of clips on each track will vary, depending on the work that you're doing. (If you haven't created any tracks in your session, this area will be blank.)

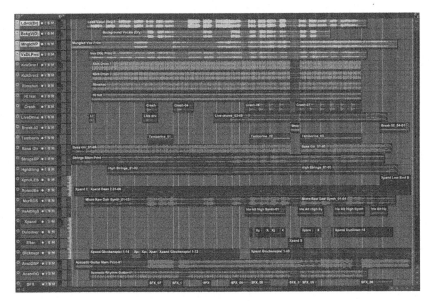

Figure 3.15 The Edit window tracks area

There's a term that you'll learn more about in later courses—playlists. Simply put, an edit playlist is a sequence of clips on a track, including the order and position of the clips. For that reason, the tracks area of the Edit window is also referred to as the playlist area.

Customizing the Edit Window

Different workflows will require different window layouts—here are a few ways that you can make the most of the Edit window.

In the upper right-hand corner of the Edit window, you will see a small circular icon with a downward-facing triangle, called the Edit window pop-up menu. This menu lets you select items to show or hide. The top section of the menu includes Edit window toolbar controls, with a check mark indicating which controls are shown. Clicking outside of the menu will close the pop-up menu.

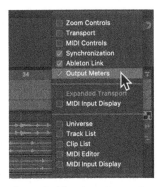

Figure 3.16 The Edit window pop-up menu

You can move different control clusters laterally along the Edit window toolbar to suit your preference. While holding the **COMMAND** key (Mac) or **CTRL** key (Windows), move your cursor to the control cluster that you want to move. When the icon is displayed as a hand, click and drag the cluster to your desired location. As you move along the Edit window toolbar, you'll see a yellow bar indicating where the tool cluster will be positioned when your mouse is released.

In the Grid and Nudge controls, the word Grid isn't just a label—it's also the Show Grid Lines button. When the word Grid is displayed in black text against a green background, grid lines will be visible in the tracks area. When the word is in green text against a black background, the grid lines are hidden.

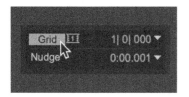

Figure 3.17 The Show Grid Lines button

You can show or hide either the left or right columns (the Tracks/Groups Lists or the Clips List) by clicking the small side-facing arrow buttons in the lower corners of the track's area.

You can also customize your Edit window by changing the width of your side columns. Just move your cursor to the border between the column and the tracks area—your cursor will then change to a double arrow. Resize the column by dragging left or right to suit your needs.

> (i) Professionals keep track names as short as possible. This serves two purposes: First, names can be displayed without being abbreviated. Second, the Tracks List can be narrower, leaving more room in the Edit window for other things.

> (i) Double-clicking with the cursor positioned at the column border (where the cursor changes to a double arrow) will hide the column.

TOPIC 3.2:
THE MIX WINDOW

In this unit, you will learn about the Pro Tools Mix window. You'll learn different ways to access the window and what the primary components of the window are. You will also learn about different ways to customize the Mix window.

Activity: Mix Window Controls

- Open the Activity 3.2.ptx session. This session will open with the Mix window displayed.

- Press the spacebar to begin playback and observe what happens. What do you see and hear?

- Drag a fader up and down. What effect does this have?

- Click and drag up/down on a pan knob. What effect does this have?

- Close the Mix window by clicking the Close button in the upper left or right corner. What happens to playback? What can you infer about the session based on this observation?

- Go to the **WINDOW** menu and choose **MIX**. What happens?

- Stop playback and choose **FILE > CLOSE SESSION**.

Discussion: Working in the Mix Window

The process of combining multiple individual tracks into a final cohesive product is called mixing. Though it's certainly common to do some mixing in the Edit window, Pro Tools has a window dedicated to this process, appropriately called the Mix window.

Pro Tools provides two easy ways to get to the Mix window:

- From the **WINDOW** menu, select **MIX**.

- From the computer keyboard, press **COMMAND+=** (Mac) or **CTRL+=** (Windows). This shortcut will toggle from the Edit window to the Mix window and vice versa.

The Mix window is a bit simpler than the Edit window and will look familiar to anyone who's ever sat behind a mixer.

Figure 3.18 The Pro Tools Mix window

Tracks Area

Like the Edit window, the Mix window has a large tracks area. Each of the vertical strips in the Mix window represents a track, in the same order as they appear in the Edit window. (Tracks are listed from top to bottom in the Edit window and from left to right in the Mix window). Just as with the Edit window, if your session doesn't have any tracks, this area will be blank.

Figure 3.19 The Mix window Tracks area

Tracks List and Groups List

The Mix window's tracks area doesn't show clips, so there is no purpose for a Clips List on the right side of the window. However, there is a left-hand column that comprises the Tracks List and the Groups List, similar to the left column of the Edit window.

Just as in the Edit window, the Tracks List will show you a list of all tracks in your session, in the order that they appear in the Tracks area of the Mix window. Here you can select, show, hide, or reorder your tracks.

Figure 3.20 The Tracks List in the Mix window

Note that the Tracks List in the Edit window and the Tracks List in the Mix window are linked, meaning that the changes that you make in one will also apply to the other. The tracks shown and selected in the Tracks area of the Mix and Edit windows are identical.

Mix Groups are helpful when mixing a large session, enabling you to make changes to multiple grouped tracks at once. The Groups List in the Mix window is directly below the Tracks List.

Figure 3.21 The Groups List in the Mix window

 The use of Mix Groups is beyond the scope of this course. Mix and Edit Groups are discussed in detail in the Pro Tools 110 course of the Avid Learning Series.

Customizing the Mix Window

Though critical to audio production, the Mix window is simple to navigate. Pro Tools provides a few easy ways to customize your mixing space.

You can show or hide the Mix window side column by clicking the small side-facing arrow button in the lower corner of the track's area.

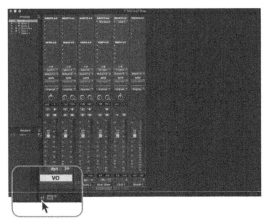

Figure 3.22 Button for showing and hiding the Mix window side column

You can also change the width of the Mix window side column. Just move your cursor to the border between the column and the tracks area—the cursor will change appearance to a double arrow. Resize the column by dragging left or right to suit your needs.

Figure 3.23 Resizing the Mix window column

In sessions that have many tracks, it can be useful to fit more tracks on screen at once. This is where choosing Narrow Mix view can help—from the **VIEW** menu, choose **NARROW MIX**. The width of each track's strip will decrease, showing more tracks in the window.

The keyboard shortcut to change between Narrow Mix view and normal view is Command+Option+M (Mac) or Ctrl+Alt+M (Windows).

TOPIC 3.3:
THE TRANSPORT WINDOW

In this section, you will learn about the Pro Tools Transport window. You'll learn different ways to access the window and get an overview of the primary components of the window and when you might need them. You will also learn how to customize the Transport window so that it shows the controls you need.

Activity: Transport Window Controls

■ Open the Activity 3.3.ptx session. This session will open with the Transport window displayed.

■ Click the **PLAY** button; after a few seconds, click the **STOP** button.

■ Click **PLAY** again. Observe the result. Where does playback begin?

■ Click the on the **FFW** button one time and release it. Click it a second time and note the cursor location. What effect did that have?

■ Click and hold the **FFW** button for a few seconds. What effect does this have?

■ Click the **RETURN TO ZERO** button. Then click the **GO TO END** button. What do these buttons do?

■ Experiment with other transport functions. What other observations are you able to make?

Discussion: Working with the Transport Window

While the Edit window and the Mix window are the most important environments in which you'll work, another main window you'll often use in Pro Tools is the Transport window.

Figure 3.24 The Transport window

Here are two easy ways to show or hide the Transport window:

■ From the **WINDOW** menu, choose **TRANSPORT**.

■ Press **COMMAND+[1]** (on the numeric keypad) from a Mac computer or **CTRL+[1]** (on the numeric keypad) from a Windows computer.

You must use the numeric keypad for this shortcut. Using the number keys at the top of your keyboard won't work.

 The numeric keypad has many uses in Pro Tools, so you'll usually see keyboards with numeric keypads in professional studios.

You've seen most of the Transport window's controls before in the Edit window.

The Primary Transport Window Controls

The Transport window includes controls similar to those seen in the Edit window toolbar.

Playback Controls

On the top from, left to right, are the Online, Return to Zero, Rewind, Fast Forward, Go to End, Stop, Play, and Record Enable buttons. Below these buttons, on the left-hand side, you'll see Pre-roll and Post-roll (important in the recording process), and below them is a Fade-in option. To the right of these, you'll see Start, End, and Length fields for the current Timeline selection.

Figure 3.25 Transport Controls

Counter Controls

To the right of this area, you will see the Counter controls, showing the Main Counter and Sub-Counter.

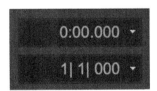

Figure 3.26 Counter Controls

These fields enable you to see the passage of time in two scales. In the example above, the Main Counter's time scale is set to Minutes and Seconds, and the Sub-Counter is set to Bars and Beats.

MIDI Controls

The Transport window's MIDI Controls mirror the MIDI Controls in the Edit window.

Figure 3.27 MIDI Controls

Output Meters

The session's Output Meters will show the total level coming out of any outputs that you choose. This display is commonly used to show the output level going to your speakers or headphones.

Figure 3.28 Output Meters

 The Transport window also includes controls for Synchronization and Ableton Link. These topics are beyond the scope of this course.

Customizing the Transport Window

In the upper right-hand corner of the Transport window, you'll see the Transport window pop-up menu button. Clicking it will display a menu that will let you show or hide sections of the Transport window.

Figure 3.29 The Transport window pop-up menu (right)

You can show or hide the displays for Counters, MIDI Controls, Synchronization, Ableton Link, and Output Meters by selecting them in the menu. Displayed controls will be indicated by a check mark.

Toggling the Expanded Transport menu option will show or hide the bottom row of the Transport window.

TOPIC 3.4:
THEMES, VIEWS, AND MENUS

In this unit, you will learn how to customize the Pro Tools display. You will also learn rules about each of the main Pro Tools menus so you know where to look for the various commands, windows, and operations you will use in Pro Tools.

Discussion: Customizing the Display and Using Menus

Three more aspects to working with Pro Tools bear mentioning before we close this Lesson: color themes, window views, and the Pro Tools menus.

Color Themes

Pro Tools Artist provides two preset color themes to choose from—Dark and Classic. The theme you choose is a matter of personal taste and preference for your working conditions.

To choose your preferred theme:

1. From the **SETUP** menu, choose **PREFERENCES**. The Preferences dialog box will appear.

2. Click the **DISPLAY** tab at the top of the Preferences dialog box.

3. In the Basics section, click the **UI THEME** menu. A choice of Classic or Dark will appear.

4. Select the theme that you prefer. The Pro Tools display will instantly change to match.

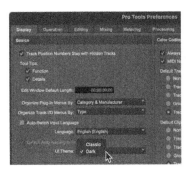

Figure 3.30 Choosing a color theme

5. Click **OK** in the Preferences dialog box to confirm your choice.

 The majority of images presented in this course use the Dark UI theme. The layout of controls and operation of Pro Tools is identical with either theme.

Views

When we refer to views in Pro Tools, we're talking about the display areas *within* a window—or what we might call the *parts* of a window. The following view options are available in the different windows.

Ruler Views

Various different rulers can be shown or hidden in the Edit window, based upon your needs. Here are two ways to show or hide rulers:

- Choose the **VIEW** menu, select **RULERS**, and enable/disable an individual ruler from the submenu.

Figure 3.31 Working with rulers from the View menu

- Click on the small rectangular icon in the upper right-hand corner of the rulers area (called the **RULER VIEW SELECTOR**) and enable/disable each of the rulers you wish to show or hide.

Figure 3.32 The Edit window's Ruler View selector

Edit Window Views

Additional elements of the Edit window can be shown, hidden, or adjusted to suit your workflow. These are known as the Edit window views. The Edit window views in Pro Tools Artist include:

- Comments

- Instrument

- Inserts A-E

- Inserts F-J

- Sends A-E

- Sends F-J

- I/O

- Real-Time Properties

- Track Color

As with rulers, there are two ways to show or hide individual Edit window views:

- Choose the **VIEW** menu, select **EDIT WINDOW VIEWS**, and enable/disable an individual view from the submenu.

Figure 3.33 Working with Edit window views from the View menu

- Click the small rectangular icon in the upper right-hand corner of the Tracks area (called the **EDIT WINDOW VIEW SELECTOR**) and enable/disable each of the views you wish to show and hide. (See Figure 3.34.)

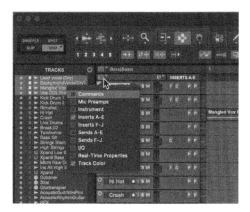

Figure 3.34 The Edit Window View selector

 You can also access the Edit Window View menu by right-clicking on the heading of any displayed Edit window column.

 To hide any Edit window view, Option-click (Mac) or Alt-click (Windows) on the heading of the Edit window column.

Mix Window Views

Like the Edit window, the Mix window has its own views that can be shown or hidden. The Mix window views in Pro Tools Artist include:

- Instrument

- Inserts A-E

- Inserts F-J

- Sends A-E

- Sends F-J

- EQ Curve

- Meters and Faders

- I/O

- Delay Compensation

- Track Color

- Comments

As in the Edit window, there are two ways to show or hide the Mix window views:

■   From the **VIEW** menu, select **MIX WINDOW VIEWS** and enable/disable a view from the submenu.

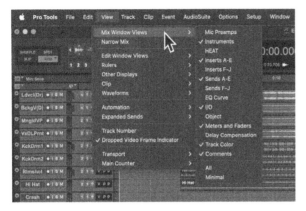

Figure 3.35 Working with Mix window views from the View menu

■   Click the small rectangular icon in the bottom left corner of the Mix window (called the **MIX WINDOW VIEW SELECTOR**) and enable/disable each of the views you wish to show and hide.

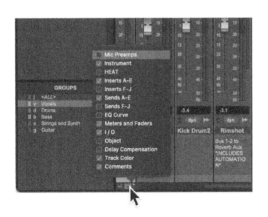

Figure 3.36 The Mix Window View selector (left); views displayed in the Mix window (right)

Whereas Edit window views appear as columns to the left side of each track, Mix window views appear as rows across the mixer. The views shown in the image above include Inserts A-E, Sends A-E, EQ Curve, I/O, and Meters and Faders.

You can also reveal the Mix Window View menu by right-clicking on the heading of any Mix window view on any track's channel strip.

 To hide any Mix window view, Option-click (Mac) or Alt-click (Windows) on the heading of the Mix window view on any track's channel strip.

Menu Structure

Above the Pro Tools windows, you'll find a number of menus. While it's not important to memorize everything in these menus at this point, it is important to get a sense of what each menu covers. Each menu has unique characteristics, so knowing what the menus are designed for will help you locate a specific command or feature that you need.

Figure 3.37 The Pro Tools Menus at the top of the screen

- FILE—This menu provides *file-based* commands, allowing you to open and close a Pro Tools document (session file), save the document, and so on. Here, you can also import audio and MIDI files and export your final mix as a file.

- EDIT—Here you'll find *edit* commands, such as cutting, copying, and pasting selections and more. This menu provides access to all of the selection-based editing commands discussed in this and other Avid Learning Series courses.

- VIEW—As you've already seen, the View menu lets you show or hide Rulers, Edit window views, and Mix window views. To show or hide any display *within* a window, you'll go to the View menu.

- TRACK—This menu is for *track-based* commands that affect one or more selected tracks. Commands related to the creation, duplication, deletion, or modification of tracks, you'll find in the Track menu.

- CLIP—The Clip menu can be thought of as a sibling of the Edit menu, but focused specifically on clips. This is where you can perform *clip-based* commands that affect one or more selected clips.

Clips are pieces of media within a Pro Tools session or project.

- **EVENT**—Here's a simple rule: to make adjustments to time or MIDI, look first in the Event menu. This menu affects how and when events occur in time.

- **AUDIOSUITE**—Plug-in effects come in two types: real-time processors and file-based (non-real-time) processors. In the AudioSuite menu, you will find all of the *file-based* plug-ins.

- **OPTIONS**—Individual functions can toggle *on* or *off* (either *enabled* or *disabled*) can be found in the Options menu (think "O" for On or Off, and "O" for Options). Items in this menu are either active or inactive; either checked or unchecked.

 In the Options menu, enabled features display a check mark; disabled features do not. You can enable or disable any feature by clicking on it in this menu to toggle its state.

- **SETUP**—The Setup menu lets you configure multiple behaviors within a *dialog box*. Examples include the Playback Engine and Preferences. The selections under this menu all lead to dialog boxes.

- **WINDOW**—the Window menu is easy to understand: it's used to show, hide, or arrange Pro Tools windows. All of Pro Tools' main windows are found under the Window menu.

- **AVID LINK**—This menu allows you to access various functions included in the Avid Link application without leaving Pro Tools.

⚠ The Avid Link menu opens an in-application browser in Pro Tools that lets you access certain Avid Link functionality. This menu does NOT launch the Avid Link application. For full functionality, launch Avid Link outside of Pro Tools.

- **HELP**—The Help menu lets you search for commands, find information on a topic by keyword, or access Pro Tools online help and support pages. It also provides important documentation, such as the Pro Tools Reference Guide and a comprehensive list of shortcuts.

LESSON 3 CONCLUSION

This Lesson provided an overview of the Pro Tools Edit, Mix, and Transport windows. It also discussed how to customize the Pro Tools appearance using color themes and optional views. Lastly, it introduced the Pro Tools menu system and provided rules for understanding what you will find under each main menu.

Discussion: Summary of Key Concepts

In this Lesson, you learned:

- The layout and function of the Pro Tools Edit window

- The layout and function of the Pro Tools Mix window

- The layout and function of the Pro Tools Transport window

- How to set the color theme for the Pro Tools user interface

- How to configure available views in the Edit and Mix windows

- The basic functions of each of the Pro Tools main menus

Essential Keyboard Commands and Shortcuts

Below is a summary of modifier behaviors and shortcut operations that you should know from this Lesson:

- Press **COMMAND+=** (Mac) or **CTRL+=** (Windows) to toggle from the Edit window to the Mix window and vice versa.

- Press **COMMAND+OPTION+M** (Mac) or **CTRL+ALT+M** (Windows) to change between Narrow Mix view and normal view in the Mix window.

- Press **COMMAND+[1]** (Mac) or **CTRL+[1]** (Windows) using the numeric keypad to show or hide the Transport window.

- To hide any Edit window view, **OPTION-CLICK** (Mac) or **ALT-CLICK** (Windows) on the heading at the top of the column for that view.

- To hide any Mix window view, **OPTION-CLICK** (Mac) or **ALT-CLICK** (Windows) on the heading above the view on any track's channel strip.

Activity: Lesson 3 Knowledge Check

This quiz will check your knowledge of material covered in this Lesson.

1. Refer to the Image: The Pro Tools window shown below is called the _____ window.

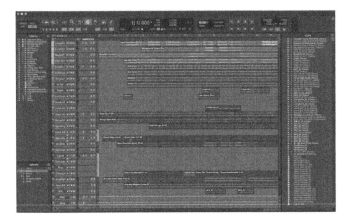

2. Refer to the Image: The Pro Tools window shown below is called the _____ window.

3. Refer to the Image: The Pro Tools window shown below is called the _____ window.

4.   Which *two* of the following can you use to show or hide the I/O view in the Edit window?

A. The Ruler View selector

B. The Track View selector

C. The File menu

D. The Edit Window View selector

E. The View menu

5.   Which *two* of the following can you use to show or hide the **Tempo** ruler in the Edit window?

A. The Ruler View selector

B. The Track View selector

C. The File menu

D. The Edit Window View selector

E. The View menu

6. What keyboard shortcut can you use to toggle between the Mix and Edit windows in Pro Tools?

    A. SHIFT+W

    B. COMMAND+= (Mac) or CTRL+= (Windows)

    C. COMMAND+T (Mac) or CTRL+T (Windows)

    D. The [5] key on the numeric keypad

7. True or False. The Track List is available in both the Edit window and the Mix window.

8. The Group List is displayed directly beneath the _____ List in the Mix window.

9. True or False. The Clip List is available in both the Edit window and the Mix window.

10. Match the Pro Tools menu name to its description.

View menu	Used for file-based commands, such as opening, closing, and saving sessions
File menu	Used to show or hide parts of a window
Options menu	Used to configure the behavior of a Pro Tools system through dialog boxes
Window menu	Used for toggling features on or off
Setup menu	Used to access (show, hide) and arrange whole windows in Pro Tools

Configuring a Session

In this exercise, you will open the Pro Tools session you created in Exercise 2 and continue work. You will configure the Main Time Scale, rulers, color theme, and other display options for the session. You will then save the session for use in subsequent exercises.

Exercise Details

- **Required Media:** None

- **Exercise Duration:** 10 to 15 Minutes

Media Files

To complete the exercises in this book, you will be using various files included in the **PT Academy Media Files** folder. You can download the media files from your course learning module in ElementsED.com. Consult your instructor or visit nxpt.us/make-music for more details.

Getting Started

You will start by opening the Pro Tools session you saved at the end of Exercise 2. If that session is not available, you can use the provided Exercise03-Starter file in the 01. Starter Sessions folder.

Open the session and save it as Exercise 3:

1. Open the session file that you created in Exercise 2: Storage Drive/Folder > Exercises-XXX > Exercise02-XXX.ptx.

   Alternatively, you can use the Exercise03 Starter file: PT Academy Media Files > 01. Starter Sessions > Exercise03-Starter.ptx.

2. Choose FILE > SAVE AS and name the session Exercise03-XXX. Keep the session inside the original Exercises-XXX folder (or move it into Exercises-XXX if working from the starter file).

The session will open with the Edit and Transport windows displayed, as they were when you saved it.

Setting Display Options

In this section, you will set the Main Time Scale, Sub Time Scale, and other display options for the session.

Set the Main Time Scale and Sub Time Scale:

1. Choose **VIEW > MAIN COUNTER > BARS|BEATS** to set the Main Time Scale to Bars|Beats.

    The Bars|Beats Ruler will display highlighted above the tracks in the Edit window, and the Main Counter will display its location information in Bars|Beats.

2. If the Sub Counter is not already displayed, click the down arrow next to the Main Counter and select **SHOW SUB COUNTER** from the pop-up menu. The Sub Counter will display under the Main Counter.

Figure 3.38 Selecting the option to show the Sub Counter

3. Next, click on the down arrow next to the Sub Counter and select **MIN:SECS** for the Sub Time Scale.

4. Verify that the Min:Secs ruler is displayed (**VIEW > RULERS > MIN:SECS**).

Display the side columns (Tracks List and Clips List):

■   If needed, click the arrow icons in the bottom left and right corners of the Edit window to display the Edit window side columns. (See Figure 3.39.)

    The Tracks List will display in the left side column of the Edit window, and the Clips List will display in the right side column.

Figure 3.39 Clicking the arrow icon in the bottom left corner of the Edit window to display the left side column

Set the color theme:

1. Choose **SETUP > PREFERENCES** to open the Preferences dialog box.

2. Click the **DISPLAY** tab at the top of the dialog box.

3. In the Basics section, click the **UI THEME** menu.

4. Toggle between the Classic and Dark theme to select the color theme of your choice. The Pro Tools display will update instantly as you change themes.

Figure 3.40　Choosing a color theme

5. Once you've selected your preferred option, click **OK** to close the Preferences dialog box.

Finishing Up

To complete this exercise, you will need to verify your settings and save your work. Note that you will be reusing this session in Exercise 4, so it is important to save the work you've done.

Save your work:

1. Verify that your Edit window has been configured properly. Check the Counters area (top center), the side columns (left and right), and the color theme.

    Your Edit window should look similar to Figure 3.41 below.

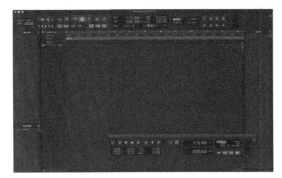 

Figure 3.41 The Edit window: dark theme (left) and classic theme (right)

2. Make adjustments as needed.

> (i) We will use the Classic theme for screenshots in the remaining exercises in this book. You may wish to set your Preferences to match; however, either option will work. The choice is yours.

3. Choose **FILE > SAVE** to save the changes you've made.

4. Choose **FILE > CLOSE SESSION** to close the session.

> (i) You cannot close a Pro Tools session by closing the Mix and Edit windows. This common mistake leaves the session open with no active windows. Instead, you must choose CLOSE SESSION from the FILE menu.

That completes this exercise.

Basic Track Techniques

In Lesson 2, you learned how to create a blank session. While a blank session is a great starting-off point, you'll also want to create some tracks and begin getting some media onto them!

In this Lesson, you will learn about different track types available in Pro Tools and what each track type is designed to do. You'll learn how to create tracks and how to configure track routing. You'll also learn how to manage the tracks that you create in your session and adjust their visual display.

Learning Targets

- Recognize the different track types available in Pro Tools Artist

- Create new tracks in a session

- Set track inputs and outputs

- Work with the display and playback characteristics of different tracks

TOPIC 4.1:
TRACK TYPES

In this unit, you will explore the different types of tracks available in Pro Tools. What is the difference between an Audio track and an Aux Input track? When would you want to use an Instrument track? Should your tracks be mono or stereo?

Before you can start creating tracks, it's important to understand the types of tracks available to you, and how each type of track functions within a session.

Activity: Explore Track Types

This activity can be completed individually or as an instructor-guided exploration. If working individually, consult your instructor for assistance, as needed.

- Open the Activity 4.1.ptx session. This session has various types of media in the Clips List.

- Using the **NEW** command under the **TRACK** menu, create tracks of different types.

- Drag the clips of different media onto the different track types and observe what happens.

- Play the session and observe what happens.

Discuss what you learn. What types of tracks can you put audio clips on? What types of tracks can you put MIDI clips on? What restrictions apply? What do different tracks look like and sound like?

Discussion: Track Types in Pro Tools Artist

To make the most of your work in Pro Tools, you first need to understand what types of tracks are available and what each track type is used for.

Audio Tracks

Audio tracks are the foundation upon which Pro Tools stands. Audio tracks are used any time you want to record an audio signal, regardless of its sound source. When you record audio, the sound that you capture will appear on an Audio track as a waveform.

Audio Track Type Icon

In the Mix window and the Tracks List, each track type is associated with a different track type icon. Audio tracks are represented by a waveform icon. You'll see this icon next to the track name in the Tracks List, and just above the track name in the Mix window. (See Figure 4.1.)

Figure 4.1 An Audio track in the Mix window (left) and a close-up view of the Audio track type icon (waveform icon: right)

Audio Track Counts

Each Pro Tools tier supports different track counts. In Pro Tools Artist, you can add a maximum of 32 mono or stereo Audio tracks to a session.

Aux Input Tracks

Aux Input tracks (often called Aux tracks for short) are like Audio tracks, with one important difference: An Aux Input track cannot hold audio clips. Aux Input tracks route audio through the mixer, but they cannot record audio.

In the Mix window or Tracks List, Aux Input tracks are indicated by a down-pointing arrow icon. Pro Tools Artist supports up to 32 mono or stereo Aux Input tracks.

Figure 4.2 The Aux Input track type icon (down arrow)

MIDI Tracks

MIDI tracks are one of two track types that support MIDI recording and MIDI clips. A MIDI track cannot be heard on its own; however, it can be used in combination with a virtual instrument on an Aux Input track.

MIDI tracks are indicated by a circular MIDI 5-pin connector icon in the Mix window and Tracks List. (See Figure 4.3.) Pro Tools Artist supports up to 64 MIDI tracks.

Figure 4.3 The MIDI track type icon (5-pin connector)

Instrument Tracks

Instrument tracks are the other kind of track that supports MIDI recording and MIDI clips. This track type can be thought of as the combination of a MIDI track *and* an Aux Input track, allowing the MIDI data to generate sound from the track, through the use of a virtual instrument placed directly on the track.

 Details on working with MIDI and virtual instruments are provided in Lessons 9 and 10.

In the Mix window or Tracks List, Instrument tracks are indicated by a keyboard icon. Pro Tools Artist supports up to 32 mono or stereo Instrument tracks.

Figure 4.4 The Instrument track type icon (keyboard)

Master Fader Tracks

Master Fader tracks are important when you're mixing. These tracks cannot hold clips; instead they are used to control the output level for a session. Master Faders are often misused, so we'll pay special attention to this track type—and how to use it—when we discuss the mixing process.

In the Mix window and the Tracks List, Master Fader tracks can be distinguished by the Greek letter, Sigma (Σ). This symbol represents a sum in mathematical terms, just as a Master Fader represents a sum of the audio in a session. Pro Tools Artist supports a single mono or stereo Master Fader track.

Figure 4.5 The Master Fader track type icon

Folder Tracks

Folder tracks are tracks that you use to contain other tracks, simplifying sessions that have a high number of tracks. Folder tracks are available in two types: Basic Folders and Routing Folders.

Basic Folders are used simply for organizing tracks. Although a Basic Folder has some control over the tracks it contains, it lacks the more sophisticated functionality of a Routing Folder track.

Routing Folders combine the organizational convenience of a Basic Folder with the signal flow of an Aux Input track. These tracks help simplify larger sessions, and they play an important role in the mixing process.

In the Mix window's tracks area, Folder tracks can be identified by a folder icon just above the track name. In the Tracks List, Folder tracks are indicated by a triangle icon next to the track name.

Figure 4.6 The Folder track type icon: Basic Folder (left) and Routing Folder (right)

Pro Tools Artist supports both Basic Folder tracks (up to 2000) and Routing Folder tracks (up to 32).

 The topic of Folder tracks is covered in the Pro Tools 110 course.

Mono Tracks versus Stereo Tracks

In Pro Tools Artist, tracks that route audio can be either mono (meaning that they only have one input channel) or stereo (meaning they have two input channels—left and right). Mono audio clips can only be placed on a mono Audio track. Stereo clips (with both left and a right channels) need to be placed on a stereo Audio track.

The track format (mono or stereo) relates to the *input* of the track, not the output. Both mono and stereo Audio tracks are typically routed to the session's stereo outputs.

 Since MIDI on its own makes no sound, a MIDI track is neither mono nor stereo.

TOPIC 4.2:
CREATING TRACKS

In this unit, you will begin exploring how to add tracks to your session. Start by considering what types of tracks you want and how many of each you will need. What do you plan to record? How many different sound sources do you need to capture? Will you be using a MIDI keyboard? Will you use virtual instruments?

You may not know all of the answers to these questions up front, but the more complete your plan is at the beginning, the better you will be able to anticipate your track needs for the session.

 Before proceeding, double-check your Preferences (Setup > Preferences) for compatibility. Uncheck the New Tracks Default to Tick Timebase and Enable Elastic Audio on New Tracks options under the EDITING and PROCESSING tabs, respectively.

Activity: Evaluate the Tracks in a Session

■ Open the Activity 4.2.ptx session. This session includes tracks of different types and formats.

■ Examine the tracks in the Edit window. Can you tell which track is which type? Which are Audio tracks? Which are MIDI tracks? Which are Instrument tracks? Which are Aux Inputs?

■ Can you tell which tracks are mono and which are stereo?

■ Switch to the Mix window and examine the tracks there. Is it easier or harder to identify track types and formats in this window? What other observations can you make about the tracks by looking at them in the Mix and Edit windows?

Discussion: Creating Tracks for Your Session

Making new tracks is pretty straightforward. To get started, you can open the New Tracks dialog box.

■ From the TRACK menu, choose NEW.

■ Press the keyboard shortcut COMMAND+SHIFT+N (Mac) or CTRL+SHIFT+N (Windows).

The New Tracks dialog box will appear.

Figure 4.7 The New Tracks dialog box (Dark color theme shown)

To select track parameters, work from left to right in the New Tracks dialog box:

1. Enter the number of tracks you want of a given type in the **CREATE** field at the left.

2. Choose the channel width of your track(s) (mono or stereo) under the **TRACK FORMAT** menu.

3. Select the kind of track you want to create from the **TRACK TYPE** menu.

4. For this course, leave the track timebase set to its default.

(i) **The track timebase determines whether the track is affected by tempo changes made to the session.**

5. Provide a descriptive name for the track(s) in the field at the right.

6. Optionally click the **+** symbol at the end of the row to add another row and repeat the process.

(i) **Adding multiple rows to the New Tracks dialog box allows you to simultaneously add tracks of different types or different channel widths.**

(i) **To rearrange rows, click and hold on the Move Row icon at the far right of a row. A blue outline will appear around the row. Drag the row up or down, as needed.**

When finished, click the **CREATE** button to add the track(s) to your session. The tracks will be added in the order that they were listed in the New Tracks dialog box.

Track Names and Multiples

When you create multiple tracks in a single row of the New Tracks dialog box, Pro Tools will add a number to the end of the track name to distinguish between the tracks. For example, if you create 3 mono audio tracks with the name "Vocal" in the name field...

Figure 4.8 Creating three mono audio tracks named Vocal

...the result will be three tracks in your session, named Vocal 1, Vocal 2, and Vocal 3.

TOPIC 4.3:
ROUTING YOUR TRACKS

Once tracks have been created, your next job is to make sure that you can hear them. If you're recording, you also need to make sure the input signal is routed properly. That's where a track's input and output selectors come into play.

In this section, you'll learn how to display inputs and outputs in your Pro Tools session. You will also learn how to route signals into your tracks for recording and how to route signals out of your tracks for playback. Things you'll want to consider include: What do you want to record? How can the sound or signal be connected to your computer? How will Pro Tools know which connected signals to record on each track? What will you use to listen to playback from your tracks? How will Pro Tools know where to send the signal from each track so you can hear it?

Activity: Explore Track Routing

■   Open the Activity 4.3.ptx session. This session has a variety of track types included and is showing the I/O view at the head of each track in the Edit window.

■   Observe the differences in the I/O sections of different tracks. Why might this section look different for some tracks than others? Does this tell us anything about the individual tracks?

■   Try selecting Bus 1 as the input for each track. What tracks does this work for? What tracks does it not work for? What options are available on different tracks? What conclusions can you make based on these observations?

Discussion: Routing Inputs and Outputs

You can set a track's input and output (or I/O) from the I/O view in the Edit or Mix windows. The I/O view is available as a column in the Edit window.

Figure 4.9 The I/O view in the Edit window

This view is also available above a track's pan and automation controls in the Mix window. (See Figure 4.10.)

Figure 4.10 The I/O view in the Mix window

The I/O view in each window shares a similar design. Any changes you make to a track's input or output in one window will be reflected in the other window.

 In the Edit window, the I/O view changes at different track heights. For example, when a track is small, the Input and Output Path selectors will be side-by-side rather than top and bottom.

The images in the following sections show the process of setting inputs and outputs in the Mix window. The process is identical in the Edit window.

Setting Track Inputs

At the top of the I/O view is the Input Path selector. Clicking on this will allow you to choose where the input signal is coming from for a given track.

To set a track's input:

1.   Click the track's Input Path selector. A menu will appear. (See Figure 4.11.) This menu will vary based on your audio interface and I/O setup.

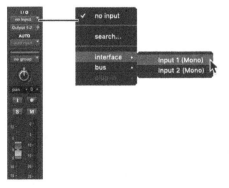

Figure 4.11 Clicking an Audio track's Input Path selector and selecting an interface input

2.   From the menu, select the desired input. The menu will close, and the selection will be applied.

Figure 4.12 Input 1 displayed on the track

 Throughout this course, you'll need to route inputs in a variety of different situations. However, an Audio track that's simply playing back an audio clip will not use its input path; it can be set to anything, including No Input.

Setting Track Outputs

Directly below the Input Path selector is the Output Path selector. This selector allows you to choose where a given track's signal is going for playback. For example, if a track's Output Path selector reads **No Output**, you won't hear that track. Selecting an output that is connected to your speakers fixes the problem.

To set a track's output:

1.   Click the desired track's Output Path selector. A menu will appear. (See Figure 4.13.) As with the inputs, this menu will be based on your audio interface and I/O setup.

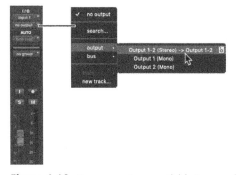

Figure 4.13 Output options available in a track's Output Path selector

2.   From the menu, select on the desired output. The menu will close, and the selection will be applied.

Figure 4.14 Output 1-2 displayed on the track

Setting Default Inputs and Outputs

If you've set your Playback Engine properly but aren't seeing the inputs or outputs that you expect, the problem might lie in the I/O Setup dialog box. This dialog box can get quite involved, but here are some basics to get the default inputs and outputs you need:

1. Go to the **SETUP** menu and choose **I/O**. The I/O Setup dialog box will appear.

2. In the **INPUT** tab, click the **DEFAULT** button.

3. In the **OUTPUT** tab, click the **DEFAULT** button.

4. In the **BUS** tab, click the **DEFAULT** button.

5. Click the **OK** button. The I/O Setup dialog box will close, and your inputs and outputs will be set to the default settings for your audio device.

TOPIC 4.4:
WORKING WITH TRACKS

Once you have tracks in your session, you may at times need to make some changes to the tracks. In this unit, we explore various ways to modify your tracks and change how your tracks appear on screen.

Activity: Modify Track Displays

■ Open the Activity 4.4.ptx session. This is an example of a session that contains multiple tracks.

■ Place your mouse pointer at the head of the tracks area and position it along the border between the Shaker and Drums tracks. A double-headed arrow will appear (see red outline below).

Figure 4.15 Positioning the mouse between tracks

■ Click and drag up or down with the double-headed arrow. What happens?

■ Now position your mouse over the track nameplate for the Drums track.

■ Click on the nameplate and drag up or down. What happens?

■ Based on your observations, how can you change a track's height? How can you rearrange the order of the tracks in a session?

Discussion: Working with Tracks in a Session

Pro Tools provides a great deal of flexibility when it comes to working with tracks. You can select tracks to target them for track-based operations. You can temporarily hide tracks to focus on other tracks. You can also change the order of tracks, and more.

Selecting and Deselecting Tracks

You can select and deselect tracks from the Tracks List in either the Edit or Mix windows. You can also select and deselect tracks from the Tracks area.

Selecting a Track

Here are three ways to select a track:

- In the Tracks List (in either the Mix or Edit window), click the name of a track to select it.

Figure 4.16 Selecting a track in the Tracks List

- In the Edit window, click on a track name at the head of the track. This area is known as the track nameplate.

Figure 4.17 Selecting a track in the Edit window

- In the Mix window, click on a track nameplate at the bottom of the track.

Figure 4.18 Selecting a track in the Mix window

No matter how you do it, the result will be the same: the name of any clicked track will become highlighted in the Tracks List, the Edit window, and the Mix window.

Deselecting a Track

Deselecting a selected track is not as simple as just clicking on the track name. Here are a couple ways to deselect a track:

- Hold the **COMMAND** key (Mac) or the **CTRL** key (Windows) while clicking on a track nameplate in the Tracks area (or while clicking a track name in the Tracks List). This modifier is used to add or remove individual tracks from the selection.

- Hold the **OPTION** key (Mac) or the **ALT** key (Windows) while clicking on a track nameplate. This modifier is used to add or remove *all* tracks from the selection.

(i) When you click a track to select it, any other selected track(s) will be deselected. By holding Command (Mac) or Ctrl (Windows) while you select a track, the new track will be selected without deselecting any already-selected tracks.

(i) You can select a range of tracks by clicking on the first track in the range and then holding the Shift key while clicking on the last track in the range.

Showing and Hiding Tracks

By default, you'll see all the tracks that have been added to your session. But at times, you'll want to show certain tracks and hide others. It's easy to do this in Pro Tools.

In the Tracks List, you'll find a circular dot to the left of each track name, called the Track Show/Hide icon. A dim-colored dot indicates that the track is hidden, while a solid-colored dot indicates that the track is visible. In the image below, three tracks are visible while the rest are hidden.

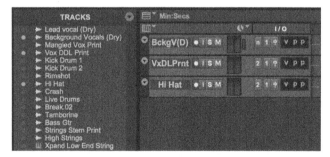

Figure 4.19 Shown and hidden tracks in the Tracks List

 Hidden tracks are still audible. When you hide a track, you simply remove it from view, not from your mix.

To show or hide a track, just click on the track's corresponding Track Show/Hide icon, changing the track's view state. This will affect the tracks shown in both the Edit window and the Mix window.

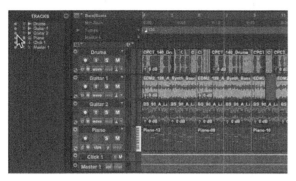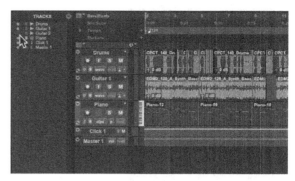

Figure 4.20 Hiding the Guitar 2 track: before (left) and after (right)

To show or hide multiple successive tracks, you can click and drag across a range of Track Show/Hide icons.

 You can show (or hide) all tracks in your session by clicking any track's Show/Hide icon while holding the Option key (Mac) or Alt key (Windows).

 You can also hide a track by right-clicking on the track name and selecting Hide from the pop-up menu.

Naming and Renaming Tracks

Track names are very important. You can name your tracks when you create them, and you can rename them later at any time.

To rename a track after it has been created:

1. Do one of the following:

    *   In the Edit or Mix window, double-click the nameplate of the track you want to change.

    *   Right-click the name of the track to be changed and select **RENAME** from the pop-up menu. (See Figure 4.21.)

Figure 4.21 Changing a track's name by right-clicking the nameplate

2. In the dialog box that appears, type a new name for the track. When using the double-click method, you can navigate through your tracks using the **PREVIOUS** and **NEXT** buttons at the bottom of the dialog box.

3. When finished, click the **OK** button.

Figure 4.22 Renaming a track

 In the Track Rename dialog box, hold Command (Mac) or Ctrl (Windows) while pressing the Right or Left Arrow keys to advance to the next track or return to the previous track, respectively.

Changing Track Order

At some point, you may want to re-order your tracks after you've created them. Here are three ways:

- In the Tracks List, click and drag the track name for the desired track up or down.

- In the Edit window tracks area, click the track nameplate and drag the track up or down.

- In the Mix window tracks area, click the track nameplate and drag the track left or right.

In all three instances, a yellow line will indicate where the track will be placed once you release the mouse.

Changing Track Height

In the Edit window, you can also change individual track heights as well. For example, if you have a large number of tracks and you want to see more of them in your Edit window, you can make them smaller. On the other hand, if you want to get a closer look at a track's waveform, you can make the track bigger.

Tracks can be resized individually to any of the following preset heights:

- Micro

- Mini

- Small

- Medium

- Large

- Jumbo

- Extreme

- Fit to window

Here is one way to change your track height:

1. Click in the area immediately to the left of the track's clip area. (See Figure 4.23.) This area is called the Vertical Zoom Scale.

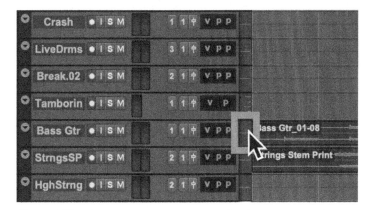

Figure 4.23 The Vertical Zoom Scale area for the Bass Gtr track

2. A menu will appear, giving you a choice of different heights for the track. Choose the desired option, and the track height will change accordingly.

You can also click on the Track Options menu button (the small circular icon to the left of each track name). Depending on the current track height, different menus may appear, one of which will be Track Height. From here, you can choose the desired height option.

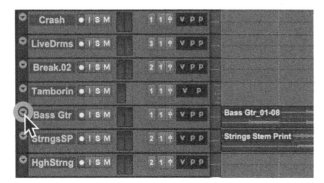

Figure 4.24 Clicking the Track Options menu for the Bass Gtr track

 At smaller track heights, some controls are resized, rearranged, or hidden. Click the Track Options menu to access the hidden controls.

As a third and potentially easier option, just move your cursor to the bottom boundary of the track that you want to resize. A double arrow icon will appear—then, click and drag up or down to set your desired height.

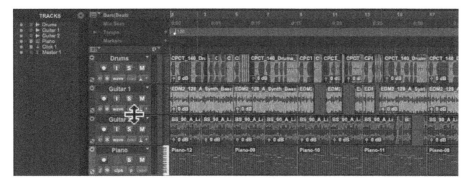

Figure 4.25 Clicking and dragging to resize the Guitar 1 track

 Hold the Control key (Mac) or Start key (Windows) and press the Up or Down Arrow keys to change the height of any track containing the Edit cursor.

 Change the height of all tracks simultaneously by holding the Option key (Mac) or Alt key (Windows) while changing the height of any one track.

Muting and Soloing

Sometimes, you don't want to hear a given track in your mix, or you want to hear it in isolation, without other distractions. That's where the Mute and Solo buttons come into play.

When a track is soloed, that track will be the only one heard—all non-soloed tracks will be silent (or implicitly muted). To solo a track, click the Solo button (marked with an **S**) in the Edit or Mix window. The adjacent Mute button (marked with an **M**) on any non-soloed tracks will be a dark orange color, indicating that they have been muted as a result of another track being soloed.

Figure 4.26 A soloed track as it appears in the Edit and Mix windows

A track that is muted will not be heard. To mute a track, just click the track's Mute (**M**) button in the Mix or Edit window.

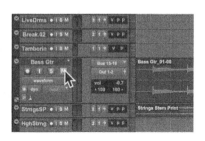

Figure 4.27 A muted track as it appears in the Edit and Mix windows

You can toggle solos or mutes for all tracks in a session by holding Option (Mac) or Alt (Windows) while clicking the solo or mute button on any one track.

Modifier Behaviors

In Pro Tools, a frequently used key is the **OPTION** key (Mac) or the **ALT** key (Windows). Among other useful functions, this modifier key enables you to make changes on one track and apply them across all of the tracks in your session.

This modifier behavior is referred to as **DO TO ALL**, and the **OPTION/ALT** key is likewise commonly called the Do To All modifier.

Multiple modifier keys can work in combination, and that is the case here as well.

The **SHIFT** key often relates to working with selections (think **S** for Shift, **S** for Selection). When you add this key to the Option/Alt key, you can apply changes to all selected tracks: **OPTION+SHIFT** (Mac) or **ALT+SHIFT** (Windows). This modifier key combination is often referred to as the **DO TO SELECTED** modifier set.

Deleting Tracks

Deleting tracks is easy to do — perhaps too easy. Beware: deleting tracks in Pro Tools is irreversible (not undoable). When you delete a track, it's gone forever, so make doubly sure that you don't need that track before deleting it!

 Deleting a track will also clear your session's Undo History. This means you cannot undo deleting the track, and you also cannot undo any action completed before deleting the track.

With that warning in mind, here are two ways you can delete a track.

- From the **TRACK** menu, choose **DELETE**.

- Right-click on the track name of a track and choose **DELETE** from the menu that appears.

With either method, all selected tracks will be deleted.

 Deleting a track will not remove its clips from the Clips List.

LESSON 4 CONCLUSION

This Lesson gave you an overview of track types and track operations in Pro Tools. You learned how to create tracks, how to assign inputs and outputs to tracks, and how to change the appearance and order of your tracks.

Discussion: Summary of Key Concepts

In this Lesson, you learned:

- The different track types and their unique functions within Pro Tools

- How to create new tracks—individually or by creating multiple tracks at once

- How to set a track's inputs and outputs

- How to manage your tracks, including selecting, showing, naming, and reordering tracks

- How to mute and solo your tracks

Essential Keyboard Commands and Shortcuts

Below is a summary of modifier behaviors and shortcut operations that you should know from this Lesson:

- To open the New Tracks dialog box, press **COMMAND+SHIFT+N** (Mac) or **CTRL+SHIFT+N** (Windows).

- To select or deselect all tracks in the Mix or Edit window, **OPTION-CLICK** (Mac) or **ALT-CLICK** (Windows) on any track's nameplate.

- To add or remove an individual track from the track selection in the Mix or Edit window, hold **COMMAND** (Mac) or **CTRL** (Windows) and click on the track nameplate.

- To select a range of tracks, select the first track by clicking its nameplate; then hold **SHIFT** while selecting the last track in the range by clicking its nameplate.

- To show or hide all tracks in a session, **OPTION-CLICK** (Mac) or **ALT-CLICK** (Windows) on any track's Show/Hide icon in the Tracks List.

- To change the height of all tracks in a session, hold **OPTION** (Mac) or **ALT** (Windows) while changing the height of any track.

- To toggle solos or mutes for all tracks in a session, hold **OPTION** (Mac) or **ALT** (Windows) while clicking a solo or mute button for any track.

Activity: Lesson 4 Knowledge Check

This quiz will check your knowledge of material covered in the Basic Track Techniques lesson.

1. Match the track type with its description.

Instrument	Audio is recorded to this kind of track.
Master Fader	Track is identified in the Tracks List and Mix window by a down-facing arrow icon
Aux Input	Commonly used in conjunction with an Aux Input track
MIDI	MIDI can be recorded to this track type and heard audibly
Audio	Controls the level of an output

2. Which are types of Folder tracks? (Choose Two)

   Simple Folder

   Basic Folder

   Sub Folder

   Root Folder

   Routing Folder

3. The track type icon for an Aux Input track is:

   An audio waveform

   A down arrow

   A keyboard

   A triangle

4. Which Pro Tools menu can you use to create a track?

5. What is the keyboard shortcut to open the New Tracks dialog box?

6.   Which Edit or Mix window view can you use to set a track's Input?

Inserts A-E

Inserts F-J

Sends A-E

Sends F-J

Instrument

I/O

7.   True or False? In the image shown, the **Kick Drum 1** track is currently shown (visible) in the tracks area of the Edit window.

8.   What track control can you use to hear an individual track in isolation, silencing all other tracks? What control can you use to silence an individual track while allowing all other tracks to continue to play back?

9.   True or False? Deleting a track can be undone.

10. What will be the result if you hold the **OPTION** key (Mac) or **ALT** key (Windows) while you change the height of a track in your session?

Only that track will resize.

Only selected tracks will resize.

All tracks in the session will resize.

Adding Tracks to a Session

In this exercise, you will add four tracks to the radio advertisement session you created in previous exercises. You will then save the session for use in subsequent exercises.

Exercise Details

■   **Required Media:** None

■   **Exercise Duration:** 10 to 15 Minutes

Media Files

To complete the exercises in this book, you will be using various files included in the **PT Academy Media Files** folder. You can download the media files from your course learning module in ElementsED.com. Consult your instructor or visit nxpt.us/make-music for more details.

Getting Started

You will start by opening the Pro Tools session you saved at the end of Exercise 3. If that session is not available, you can use the provided Exercise04-Starter file in the 01. Starter Sessions folder.

Open the session and save it as Exercise 4:

1.   Open the session file that you created in Exercise 3: Storage Drive/Folder > Exercises-XXX > Exercise03-XXX.ptx.

    Alternatively, you can use the Exercise04 Starter file: PT Academy Media Files > 01. Starter Sessions > Exercise04-Starter.ptx.

2.   Choose **FILE > SAVE AS** and name the session Exercise04-XXX. Keep the session inside the original Exercises-XXX folder (or move it into Exercises-XXX if working from the starter file).

The session will open with the Edit and Transport windows displayed, as they were when you last saved it.

Creating and Naming Tracks

In this exercise, you will be working in the Edit window. Make sure the Edit window is displayed (**WINDOW > EDIT**), and then maximize or resize the window as needed to use your available screen space.

 On macOS systems, hold the OPTION key while clicking the Maximize button to make the window full-size without obscuring the menus at the top of the screen.

In the next series of steps, you will create tracks for the session, giving them appropriate descriptive names.

Verify Preferences for Audio tracks:

1. Choose **SETUP > PREFERENCES** to open the Preferences dialog box.

2. Select the **EDITING** tab at the top of the dialog box.

3. Disable the checkbox next to **New Tracks Default to Tick Timebase** in the **Tracks** section on the left side of the dialog box. (See Figure 4.28, left.)

4. Click on the **PROCESSING** tab at the top of the dialog box to switch to that page.

5. Disable the checkbox next to **Enable Elastic Audio on New Tracks** in the **Elastic Audio** section on the right side of the page.

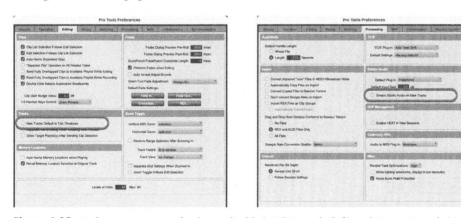

Figure 4.28 Preferences settings after being disabled; Editing tab (left) and Processing tab (right)

Create the tracks for the session:

1. Choose **TRACK > NEW** to open the New Tracks dialog box.

 Try using the keyboard shortcut for new tracks: COMMAND+SHIFT+N (Mac) or CTRL+SHIFT+N (Windows).

2. Configure the displayed row for *two mono Audio tracks* named Audio.

3. Click the plus sign at the right to add a second row; configure this row for *two stereo Audio tracks*.

4. Press the **TAB** key and rename this row Music.

5. Add a third row and configure it as a *stereo Instrument track*.

6. Press **TAB** and rename this row Beat Wave.

7. Add one more row, configured as a *stereo Master Fader* named Master.

Figure 4.29 New Tracks dialog box configured for this exercise (Classic color theme shown)

8. Click **CREATE** to add the tracks to your session.

Rename the tracks:

1. Double-click on the track nameplate of the first audio track. A dialog box will open, allowing you to rename the Audio 1 track.

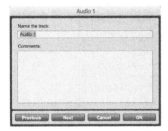

Figure 4.30 The track rename dialog box

2. Rename the track VO without closing the dialog box. This track will be used for the voice over.

3. Click the **NEXT** button at the bottom of the dialog box. The Name field will show the Audio 2 track.

4. Rename this track Hi Hat.

5. Click the **NEXT** button again to advance to the Music 1 track.

6. Rename the track Guitar.

7.   Click the **NEXT** button to move to the **Music 2** track.

8.   Rename the track **Drums**; then click **OK** to close the dialog box.

Reorder Your Tracks

After adding tracks, your Edit window should look like the image shown in Figure 4.31.

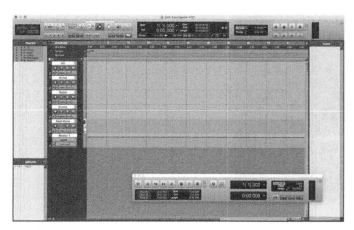

Figure 4.31 The Edit window with the tracks from this exercise (Classic color theme)

In this section of the exercise, you will change the order of the tracks in your session. The desired track order is as follows:

- VO

- Drums

- Hi Hat

- Guitar

- Beat Wave

Rearrange your tracks:

1.   **OPTION-CLICK** (Mac) or **ALT-CLICK** (Windows) on the nameplate of any selected track to deselect all of the tracks.

2.   Click on the **Drums** track nameplate and drag the track above the **Hi Hat** track.

3.   Drag other tracks as necessary to put the tracks in the order shown above.

Verify Your Work

Press **COMMAND+=** (Mac) or **CTRL+=** (Windows) to view your tracks in the Mix window. Your Mix window should look like the image shown in Figure 4.32.

Figure 4.32 The Mix window with the tracks from this exercise (Classic color theme)

Make sure that your tracks have the same names, track type icons, and number of pan controls as shown here. If your session does not look like the figure above, consult your instructor to make changes as needed.

Finishing Up

To complete this exercise, you need to save and close your session. Note that you will be reusing this session in Exercise 5, so it is important to save the changes you've made.

Finish your work:

1. Choose **FILE > SAVE** to update the session with your changes.

2. Choose **FILE > CLOSE SESSION** to close the session.

 You cannot close a Pro Tools session by closing the Mix and Edit windows. This common mistake leaves the session open with no active windows. Instead, you must choose CLOSE SESSION from the FILE menu.

That completes this exercise.

Techniques for Importing Audio

In the previous Lesson, you learned how to create and configure tracks of different types. In this Lesson, you will learn how to import audio files into your session and how to work with clips within Pro Tools.

This Lesson covers three basic import methods: using the **IMPORT > AUDIO** command under the **FILE** menu, dragging and dropping files into Pro Tools from an open Finder or Explorer window, and importing from a Workspace browser window.

Learning Targets

- Use the Import Audio command to import files from your system

- Import files by drag-and-drop from an open folder

- Search for files using a Workspace browser and import them to a session

TOPIC 5.1:
USING THE IMPORT COMMAND

Once you've created a session and added some tracks, it's time to get some audio onto the tracks. Although you will often record audio to your tracks, that's not the only option. You can also import audio files that you have on your computer.

In this section, we discuss one common way to bring external audio files into a Pro Tools session: using the Import command under the File menu.

Discussion: Importing Audio Files into Pro Tools

Importing audio is a part of many workflows. Uses range from importing a drum loop to a song to importing sound effects into a movie soundtrack. The process is fairly simple and straightforward. However, there are important details to be mindful of along the way.

Importing from the File Menu

Importing from the File menu gives you a few options. This process illustrates the difference between adding and copying audio in a session.

1. From the **FILE** menu, select the **IMPORT** submenu item.

2. From the Import submenu, choose **AUDIO**.

Figure 5.1 Choosing File > Import > Audio

 To activate the Import Audio command from the keyboard, press
Command+Shift+I on Mac or Ctrl+Shift+I on Windows.

The Import Audio dialog box will appear. (See Figure 5.2.) This dialog box will look slightly different on macOS than on Windows, but the functionality is the same.

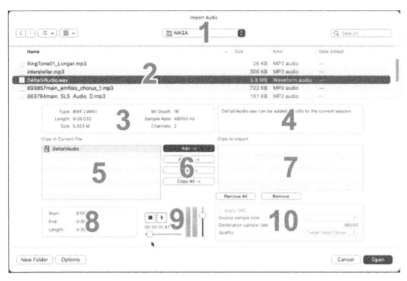

Figure 5.2 The Import Audio dialog box (macOS)

From top to bottom, the sections of the Import Audio dialog box include:

- **NAVIGATION (1)**—The top of the Import Audio dialog box (Mac) or left column (Windows) consists of standard navigation tools, similar to your computer's file browser. The appearance and features of this section will vary slightly between Mac and Windows systems.

- **FILE BROWSER (2)**—Like the navigation tools at the top of the dialog box, these will follow the conventions of your computer. In this section, you can further navigate within folders and select files to import. It's worth noting that although you can see non-audio files in this section, only audio files can be selected.

- **FILE PROPERTIES (3)**—Once a file is selected, the file properties section will show important information, including type, length, file size, sample rate, bit-depth, and number of channels.

- **COMMENTS (4)**—This section will give you valuable information relating to your different import options.

- **CLIPS IN CURRENT FILE (5)**— This area shows the whole-file clip (parent file) and any subset clips included in the file. Whole file clips are differentiated from subset clips by their icons.

  ⊞Whole File
  ⚙Subset

- **ADD/CONVERT/COPY CONTROLS (6)**—The **ADD CLIP** and **COPY CLIP** (or **CONVERT CLIP**) buttons will let you control how imported media files are treated (as discussed below). Clicking any of these buttons will populate the Clips to Import section.

- **CLIPS TO IMPORT (7)**—The Clips to Import section lists the audio clips that will import into your session when you click the **OPEN** button. This list can be adjusted with the **REMOVE** and **REMOVE ALL** buttons at the bottom of this section.

- **CLIP DETAILS (8)**—This section shows the start time, end time, and length of the clip selected in the Clips in Current File section.

- **AUDITION CONTROLS (9)**—These controls let you preview a selected clip from the Clips in Current File area. The horizontal slider adjusts the play position, and the vertical slider adjusts the volume.

- **SAMPLE RATE CONVERSION CONTROLS (10)**—When sample rate conversion is required, this section let's you adjust the parameters for the conversion.

> (i) If the controls shown here aren't appearing in your system, click the Options button in the lower left-hand corner of the Import Audio dialog box.

To import audio files:

1. Choose **FILE > IMPORT > AUDIO** as described above.

2. In the Import Audio dialog box, navigate to the desired location and select the file(s) that you want to import. Selected files will appear in the **Clips in Current File** section of the dialog box.

Figure 5.3 Selecting files in the Import Audio dialog box

3. Optionally audition any clips in the **Clips in Current File** section by selecting them individually and clicking the **PLAY** button in the **Audition Controls** area.

Figure 5.4 Auditioning the selected clip

4. Use the **ADD**, **COPY**, or **CONVERT** buttons to place the clips in the Clips to Import section:

    *   **ADD**—Click this button to place the selected clip(s) into the Clips to Import list. This will cause the session to reference (or link to) the audio file in its original storage location.

    *   **ADD ALL**—Click this button to place all clips from the Clips in Current File list into the Clips to Import list. This will cause the session to refer to all audio files in their original storage location.

 Clips that don't match your session sample rate will not play back at the correct pitch and speed when imported using Add or Add All. If a Convert button appears instead of the Copy button, your sample rates don't match.

 When adding files, if the audio files are later moved or otherwise become inaccessible, the session will no longer be able to play the referenced files.

    *   **COPY**—Click this button to place the selected clip(s) into the Clips to Import list. This will cause the file to be copied into the Audio Files folder for your session.

    *   **COPY ALL**—Click this button to place all clips from the Clips in Current File list into the Clips to Import list. This will cause all files to be copied into the Audio Files folder for your session.

    Audio files that are incompatible with your session – files using a different sample rate, or file format (MP3 files, for example) – must be converted. When an incompatible clip is in the Clips in Current File list, the **COPY** and **COPY ALL** buttons are replaced by **CONVERT** and **CONVERT ALL**.

    *   **CONVERT**—Click this button to place the selected clip(s) into the Clips to Import list. This will cause a new file to be created, matching the audio settings for your session.

    *   **CONVERT ALL**—Click this button to place all clips from the Clips in Current File list into the Clips to Import list. This will cause new files to be created for each source file, matching the audio settings for your session.

5. Click the **OPEN** button to accept the settings and import the clips into your session.

    If you're copying or converting files, a file browser will appear, allowing you to select the location for the new files. By default, this will be your session's Audio Files folder.

6. Click **OK** or **OPEN** in the file browser to accept the selected location.

    Next, the Audio Import Options dialog box will display. (See Figure 5.5.)

7. Select the desired import destination—you can import to a new track or to the Clips List.

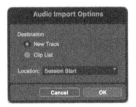

Figure 5.5 The Audio Import Options dialog box

- **NEW TRACK**—Choosing this option will create a new track for each imported clip and place the clip on the track. The clips will also be represented in the Clips List.

- **CLIP LIST**—Choosing this option will place the imported clips in the Clips List only. They won't be audible in your mix until they are placed on a track.

If you choose to import to New Track, you can use the Location menu to select where to place the clips on your session's timeline.

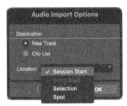

Figure 5.6 The Location menu of the Audio Import Options dialog box

- **SESSION START**—Places the clips at the beginning of your session's timeline.

- **SONG START**—Places the clips at the beginning of the first measure (Bar 1).

- **SELECTION**—Places the clips at the start of an Edit selection (or at the Edit cursor).

- **SPOT**—Opens the Spot dialog box, letting you type in a location for the clips.

 Using the Spot option when importing files is similar in many ways to using Spot mode. Spot mode is discussed in Lesson 6 of this course.

8. Click the **OK** button in the Audio Import Options dialog box to import the clips into your session.

TOPIC 5.2
IMPORTING FROM A FILE BROWSER

You can import any audio files from your computer into your session using a drag-and-drop process, as long as Pro Tools supports the audio file type. You've already learned about two audio file types that Pro Tools supports natively: What are they? What other audio file formats do you think Pro Tools will support? Can you think of any audio file types that Pro Tools might not support?

Activity: Import Files with Drag and Drop

■   Open the Media Files folder inside the ACTIVITY 5.2 folder and examine the contents.

■   Open the Activity 5.2.ptx session.

■   Drag some files into the session from the open Media Files folder. Where can you place the files to have them import? What types of files can you import to each location?

■   Do any messages appear when you drag certain files into Pro Tools? Why do you think this might happen?

■   What was the result of dragging files to different locations in your session?

Discussion: Importing Audio from an Open Folder

To import an audio file using the drag-and-drop method, you'll need to open a folder from your computer's file browser and position it so that the Pro Tools Edit window is also visible.

To import audio from a file browser:

1.   Open your computer's file browser (Mac Finder or Windows Explorer) and navigate to the folder that contains the file that you want to import.

2.   Drag the file from the open folder into the Pro Tools Edit window. You have a few options for this that will give you different results:

   •   If you drag the file into the Clips List, a new clip will be added to the Clips List only—no tracks will be created.

   •   If you drag the file into the Tracks List, a new track will be created, and the clip will be placed at the beginning of the timeline.

   •   If you drag a file onto an existing track, an outline will display showing where that file will be placed once you release the mouse.

Mono files cannot be placed on stereo tracks, and stereo files cannot be placed on mono tracks. If you drag a stereo audio file onto the first of multiple mono tracks, two separate mono clips will be created on the first two mono tracks.

- If you drag a file to a blank area in the Edit window (below the existing tracks), an outline will display showing where the file will be placed. When you drop the file, a new Audio track will be created, with a clip placed on it. The track name will follow the name of the imported file.

 Whether you're using the File > Import menu or dragging from a file browser window, you can import multiple audio files at the same time.

Added or Copied?

When you drag a file from a browser into Pro Tools, the file may or may not be copied into your Audio Files folder. Here are the rules:

- If the file does *not* require conversion—in other words, if the sample rate and file format are compatible with the session—Pro Tools will add the file, referencing it in its original location.

- If the file *does* require conversion (due to sample rate or file format), Pro Tools will create a new copy of the file to match the audio settings for the session. This file will be placed in the Audio Files folder.

While this default behavior is useful in conserving disk space, it is sometimes helpful to have all of your session's audio in the Audio Files folder. Here are two ways that you can influence this:

- Hold the **OPTION** key (Mac) or **ALT** key (Windows) while dragging a file into Pro Tools. Pro Tools will force-copy the file into the session's Audio Files subfolder, even if no conversion is necessary.

- Open the Preferences dialog box (**SETUP > PREFERENCES**), select the **PROCESSING** tab, and check the box next to **AUTOMATICALLY COPY FILES ON IMPORT**. With this setting activated, Pro Tools will always copy files into the Audio Files subfolder when importing, even if no conversion is necessary.

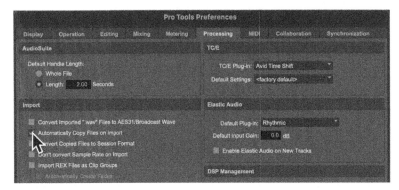

Figure 5.7 Activating the "Automatically Copy Files on Import" preference

TOPIC 5.3:
IMPORTING WITH A WORKSPACE BROWSER

Searching for files to import can be difficult and time consuming. If you search for "vocal" in a Mac Finder window, for example, you may find PDF files, videos, emails—everything with the word "vocal" in it! As an alternative, you can use search functions that are customized for Pro Tools from within a Workspace browser window.

In this unit, you will explore how to locate audio files in a Workspace browser. You can search for media by file type, by location, by size, and more.

Activity: Explore Workspace Browsers

- Open the Activity 5.3.ptx session. This session has several existing tracks in it.

- Open a Workspace browser window (**WINDOW > NEW WORKSPACE > DEFAULT**).

- Search for a file containing the name Drum-C5U3 and drag it out of the Workspace browser into the Clip List area.

- Search for a file containing the name Guitar-C5U3 and drag it out of the Workspace browser into the Track List area.

Discuss what you learn. What happened to the first audio file you imported? Can you place it onto a track? What happened to the second audio file? What observations can you make about the track that the file is on? What do you hear during playback?

Discussion: Searching in a Workspace Browser

Workspace browsers are similar to your computer's file browser, but they are designed specifically for use with Pro Tools. Within a Workspace browser, you can quickly find audio files, sessions, and other Pro Tools-related files without the distractions that commonly come with using a generic file browser.

Opening a Workspace Browser

To open a new Workspace browser:

1. From the **WINDOW** menu, select **NEW WORKSPACE**. A submenu will appear.

2. In the submenu, choose **DEFAULT**. A new Workspace browser window will appear.

To open a new Workspace browser from the keyboard, press Option+I (Mac) or Alt+I (Windows).

Understanding the Workspace Browser

At a basic level, Workspace browsers are divided into two main sections (or panes) in the lower portion, with the browsing tools located across the top of the window.

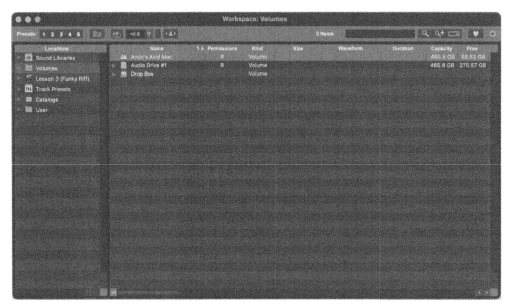

Figure 5.8 A Workspace browser window showing the browsing tools across the top and the two display panes underneath

The Locations Pane

The Locations pane (left-hand side of the browser window) allows you select an area to search for files.

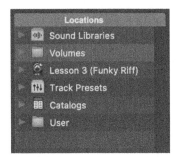

Figure 5.9 The Locations pane in a Workspace browser

Several options are available in the Locations pane:

- **SOUND LIBRARIES**—Provides access to sound libraries that are installed for use with Pro Tools.

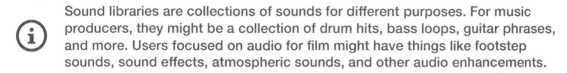 Sound libraries are collections of sounds for different purposes. For music producers, they might be a collection of drum hits, bass loops, guitar phrases, and more. Users focused on audio for film might have things like footstep sounds, sound effects, atmospheric sounds, and other audio enhancements.

- **VOLUMES**—Provides access to all of your attached storage drives (including your internal drive).

- **SESSION**—Provides access to the individual audio files imported or recorded into your session.

- **TRACK PRESETS**—Provides access to saved Track Presets, which can be recalled to quickly add a stored track or set of tracks to a session.

(i) The topic of Track Presets is beyond the scope of this course.

- **CATALOGS**—Provides access to user-created Catalogs that contain pointers to commonly used folders and favorite sounds.

(i) The topic of Catalogs is also beyond the scope of this course.

- **USER**—Provides quick access to your Desktop, Documents folder, and User folder.

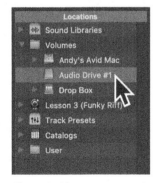

Figure 5.10 Accessing Audio Drive #1 under the Volumes location

When you select an area in the Location pane, its contents will be visible in the main area of the browser.

The Browser Pane

The Browser pane (the main area of a Workspace browser window) displays the contents of any selected drive or folder, or the results of any search. Valuable information is shown in this area, in addition to file names. For example, in the Waveform column, you will see a graphic representation of the audio's waveform; in the Tempo column, you'll see the tempo that the audio was originally recorded at.

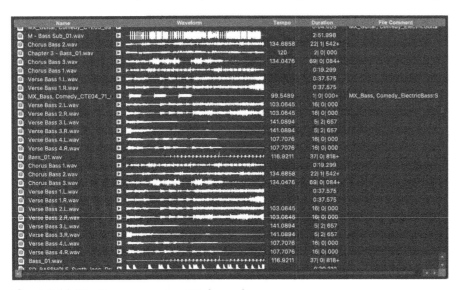

Figure 5.11 The Browser pane in a Workspace browser

 If the browser does not provide enough space to view all the columns that you want to see, you can resize it or use the scroll bar at the bottom to navigate through the columns to the left or right.

Searching with a Workspace Browser

Workspace browsers provide two primary search modes: simple search and advanced search.

Simple Search Mode

You can type into the search field in the upper-right corner of a Workspace browser to start a simple search. The Browser pane will immediately begin to populate with search results.

Figure 5.12 Searching for "Bass" using the simple search method

While the search is in progress, an **X** with a spinning circle around it will appear to the right of the search field. As the search progresses, additional items may be added in the Browser pane.

Figure 5.13 A search in progress

To stop a search in progress, click on the **X** button. The spinning circle will disappear, and no additional search results will be added to the Browser pane.

To clear the search, click the **X** button one more time. The results will be cleared, and the button will return to its default state (magnifying glass icon).

Advanced Search Mode

To search with more precision, you can use Advanced Search mode. The Advanced Search options will help you filter your results so that you can quickly find exactly what you're looking for.

Here's a typical workflow using Advanced Search mode:

1. Type the key word into the search field. The Workspace browser will immediately start searching and populating the Browser pane with results.

2. Click the **ADVANCED SEARCH** button, which appears as a magnifying glass with a plus sign (**+**).

Figure 5.14 Starting an Advanced Search

The Advanced Search Settings pane will display, with a single row visible. From left to right, the row will display the search criterion type (in this case it will read Any Text Column) followed by the search criterion (**Contains**), and then the value you typed in the search field.

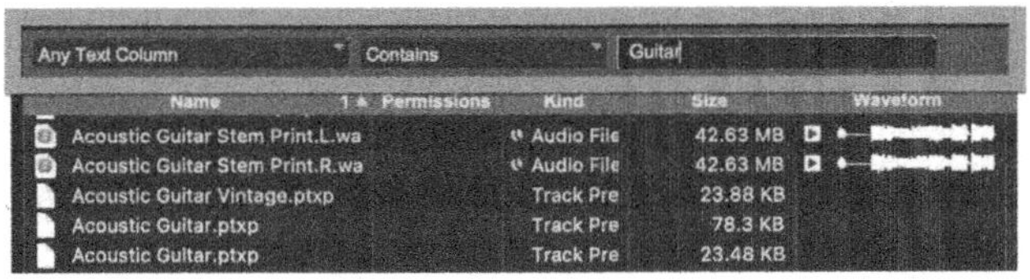

Figure 5.15 A single row in the Advanced Search Settings pane

At this point, your results will be identical to the Simple Search workflow, but the Advanced Search Settings pane will give you new ways to filter your search:

3. Click the **ADD ROW** button, indicated by a plus (**+**) sign, to add another criterion to your search. A new row will appear below the current row.

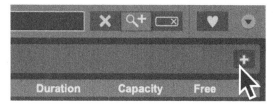

Figure 5.16 Adding an Advanced Search row

4. Change the filters as needed. For example, to show only audio files, you would set the search criterion to Kind – Is – Audio File.

5. You can further refine your search by adding more rows. For example, if you wanted to show only stereo audio files, you'd add a new row and set the columns appropriately:

- Column 1: # Channels

- Column 2: Equal to

- Column 3: 2

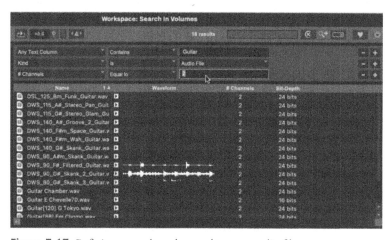

Figure 5.17 Refining a search to show only stereo audio files

Previewing Audio

Once the Browser pane shows the search results, you can preview the files before you commit to importing them. It is here where the Workspace browser really shines.

At the top of the Workspace browser are tools that will assist you in previewing your audio.

Figure 5.18 Preview controls in a Workspace browser

Preview Button

On the leftmost side of the preview controls, the **PREVIEW** button will start and stop playback of an audio file selected in the Browser pane.

Figure 5.19 The Workspace browser's Preview button

 While audio is being previewed, the Preview button will be colored green. Otherwise, the button will be grey (with a green Play triangle icon).

Preview Volume

Next to the Preview button is a volume display, showing the level of the audio playback. You can change the preview volume by clicking and dragging on the fader icon to the right of the display. The small meter to the right of the control indicates the output level of a previewed audio file as it plays.

Figure 5.20 The Workspace browser's Preview Volume controls

Audio Files Conform to Session Tempo

To the right of the volume controls is a metronome icon, called the **AUDIO FILES CONFORM TO SESSION TEMPO** button. You can enable or disable this option by clicking the button—if the button is colored green, the option is enabled; if it's gray, it's disabled.

Figure 5.21 The Workspace browser's Audio Files Conform to Session Tempo button (disabled)

Clicking the **AUDIO FILES CONFORM TO SESSION TEMPO** button will ensure that any musical file you preview will be played at the tempo of your current session, regardless of its original tempo!

 Not all audio files are musical, so not all files should change to match the tempo of your session. Keep an eye of this button if you are importing sound effects so that they don't accidentally get sped up or slowed down.

To preview an audio file, you can:

1. Select the file that you want to preview.

2. Click the **PREVIEW** button.

Here's another way to preview a file:

1. Make sure that the Waveform column is visible.

2. Click the **WAVEFORM PREVIEW** button (small triangle to the left of the waveform).

To preview a long file from midway through the file, you can click at the desired location in the waveform display. This is especially useful if the audio file begins with silence.

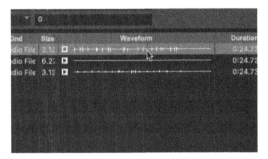

Figure 5.22 Previewing from a point within a file

 Regardless of how you preview a file, the preview will follow the selected Preview options, as set at the top of the browser.

Importing from a Workspace Browser

Once you've found a file you want to use within a Workspace browser, you can import it by drag and drop.

To import audio from a Workspace browser:

1. Click on the file that you want to import in the Browser pane of the Workspace browser. Your cursor will appear as a small hand icon. (See Figure 5.23.)

Name	1 ▲	Permissions	Kind	Size	Waveform
🗎 Lesson 3 - Arpeggio.wav			◉ Audio File	6.83 MB ▶	─────
🗎 Lesson 3 - Bass.wav			◉ Audio File	3.13 MB ▶	┼┼┼┼
🗎 Lesson 3 - Hat.wav			◉ Audio File	3.13 MB ▶	─────
🖐 Lesson 3 - Kick.wav			◉ Audio File	3.13 MB ▶	┼┼┼┼
🗎 Lesson 3 - Overheads.wav			◉ Audio File	6.27 MB ▶	─────
🗎 Lesson 3 - Pad.wav			◉ Audio File	6.83 MB ▶	─────
🗎 Lesson 3 - Room.wav			◉ Audio File	6.27 MB ▶	─────
🗎 Lesson 3 - Snare.wav			◉ Audio File	3.13 MB ▶	┼┼┼┼

Figure 5.23 Ready to import a Kick drum pattern

2. Drag the file into your Edit window and drop it in one of the following locations:

    - The Clips List: A new clip will be added to the Clips List and no tracks will be created.

    - The Tracks List: A new track will be created, and the clip will be placed at the start of the track.

    - An existing track: The new clip will be placed on the track at the dropped location.

    - The blank area below the tracks: A new Audio track will be created with a clip placed at the dropped location. The track name will follow the name of the imported file.

Added or Copied?

Importing audio from the Workspace follows the same rules as importing from an open folder:

- If the file does *not* require conversion, Pro Tools will add the file, referencing it in its original location.

- If the file requires conversion (due to sample rate or file format), Pro Tools will create a new file copy to match the audio settings for the session. The new file will be placed in your Audio Files folder.

Holding Option (Mac) or Alt (Windows) while importing from a Workspace browser will force-copy the file, placing the copy in the Audio Files folder.

ⓘ The Pro Tools preference "Automatically Copy Files on Import" also applies to files imported from the Workspace browser. With this preference activated, Pro Tools automatically creates a new file in the session's Audio Files folder.

LESSON 5 CONCLUSION

This Lesson explored various ways to import audio into your Pro Tools sessions. You were introduced to importing audio from the File menu and learned the difference between adding and copying audio files. You learned how to import from an open folder on your computer and examined how to use a Workspace browser. You also learned the modifier key that you can hold to force-copy audio files when importing from an open folder or from a Workspace browser.

Discussion: Summary of Key Concepts

In this Lesson, you learned:

- How to import audio using the **FILE > IMPORT > AUDIO** command

- How to use the audition controls in the Import Audio dialog box

- The difference between the **ADD** button and the **COPY** button in the Import Audio dialog box

- Why the Import Audio dialog box might display a **CONVERT** button instead of the **COPY** button

- What can cause imported audio to play back at the wrong pitch and speed

- How to import audio from an open folder on your system

- How to force-copy audio files on import

- How to access a Workspace browser window

- How to use simple search and advanced search modes in a Workspace browser

- Different ways to audition audio files from within a Workspace browser

- How to import files from a Workspace browser into Pro Tools

Essential Keyboard Commands and Shortcuts

Below is a summary of modifier behaviors and shortcut operations that you should know from this Lesson.

- Press **OPTION+I** (Mac) or **ALT+I** (Windows) to open a new Workspace browser window.

- Hold **OPTION** (Mac) or **ALT** (Windows) to force-copy a file when dragging it into Pro Tools from a file browser or Workspace browser window.

Activity: Lesson 5 Knowledge Check

This quiz will check your knowledge on material covered in the Techniques for Importing Audio lesson.

1. The Import command in Pro Tools is found under the _____ menu.

2. True or False? The **ADD** button in the Import Audio dialog box will place a copy of the imported file in your session's Audio Files folder.

3. The _____ button in the Import Audio dialog box will create a new file at the correct sample rate if the file you want to import does not match your session.

4. Which of the following conditions can cause an audio file to import at the wrong pitch and speed?

    Converting the file from AIFF to WAV or vice versa

    Importing the file at the wrong bit depth

    Holding the Option modifier while importing the file

    Importing a file at the wrong sample rate

5. Which of the following locations can you use to drop an audio file when dragging it into your session from an open folder on your computer? (Select all that apply.)

    Tracks List

    Existing track

    Empty space below all tracks

    Clips List

    Groups List

6. True or False? Dragging an audio file into Pro Tools from an open folder in your computer's file browser will always copy the file into the session's Audio Files folder.

7. A Workspace browser can be opened from the _____ menu.

8. What is the purpose of the Locations pane in a Workspace browser?

9. Match the Workspace browser control to its name.

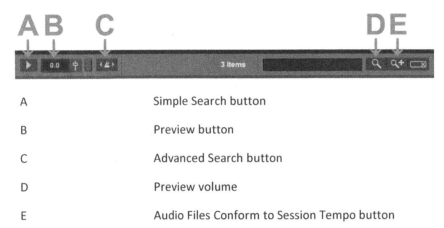

A	Simple Search button
B	Preview button
C	Advanced Search button
D	Preview volume
E	Audio Files Conform to Session Tempo button

10. How can you audition a file in a Workspace browser that starts with a long period of silence, to skip to the portion with meaningful content?

Importing Audio

In this exercise tutorial, you will import audio files into the session you saved in Exercise 4. You will import audio files to the Clip List and directly to new tracks and place the clips at the proper locations.

Exercise Details

- **Required Media:** Beach FX_01.wav, Fire.wav, Drums_04.wav, Hi Hat_03.wav, GTR_01.wav

- **Exercise Duration:** 10 to 15 Minutes

Downloading the Media Files

To complete the exercises in this book, you will use files included in the **PT Academy Media Files** folder available through the course learning module on ElementsED.com.

To download the media files, click on the **Access Files** link in the sidebar after logging in to your account. Consult your instructor or visit **nxpt.us/make-music** for more details.

Getting Started

You will start by opening the Pro Tools session you saved at the end of Exercise 4. If that session is not available, you can use the provided **Exercise05-Starter** file in the **01. Starter Sessions** folder.

Open the session and save it as Exercise 5:

1. Open the session file that you created in Exercise 4 (**Storage Drive/Folder > Exercises-XXX > Exercise04-XXX.ptx**).

   Alternatively, you can use the Exercise05 Starter file (**PT Academy Media Files > 01. Starter Sessions > Exercise05-Starter.ptx**).

   The session will open with the Mix and Transport windows displayed, as it was when last saved.

2. Press **COMMAND+=** (Mac) or **CTRL+=** (Windows) to toggle to the Edit window.

3. Choose **FILE > SAVE AS** and name the session Exercise05-XXX, keeping it inside the original session folder. (Move the session into your Exercises-XXX folder if working from the starter file.)

Importing Audio to the Clip List

In this part of the exercise, you will import audio files to the Clip List for use on existing tracks. You will then drag the audio onto the appropriate tracks in your session.

Import audio files to the Clip List:

1. Choose **FILE > IMPORT AUDIO** and navigate to the Media Files folder: PT Academy Media Files > 02. Exercise Media.

2. Select the following audio files by clicking on the Drums file, then **COMMAND-CLICKING** (Mac) or **CTRL-CLICKING** (Windows) on each of the other two files.

   - Drums_04.wav

   - GTR_01.wav

   - Hi Hat_03.wav

3. Copy the files into your session by clicking the **COPY** or **COPY FILES** button and then clicking **OPEN** or **DONE** to import the audio. A dialog box will open, prompting you to select a save location.

(i)   Be sure you choose the button to *Copy* files, not the button to *Add* files.

4. Save the files in the Audio Files folder for your session (the default) by clicking **OPEN** (Mac) or **USE CURRENT FOLDER** (Windows). A progress bar will appear as the audio is copied to your session.

5. When the Audio Import Options dialog box appears, choose the option to import to the **Clip List**. (See Figure 5.24.) Click **OK**. The files will appear in the Clip List (right side of the Edit window).

Figure 5.24 Audio Import Options dialog box set to import to the Clip List (Classic color theme shown)

Place the imported audio files on existing tracks:

1. Select the **GRABBER** tool (hand icon) in the Edit window toolbar.

2. Click in the blank space below the clips in the Clip List to deselect the clips you imported.

3. Select only the Drums_04 clip in the Clip List and drag it anywhere on the Drums track.

4. Next, select the Hi Hat_03 clip in the Clip List and drag it anywhere on the Hi Hat track.

5. Finally, select the GTR_01 clip and drag it anywhere on the Guitar track.

Position the Drum and Hi Hat clips on the tracks:

1. Using the Grabber tool, drag the Drums_04 clip to the very start of the Drums track.

2. Repeat the process with the Hi Hat_03 clip, dragging it to the start of the Hi Hat track.

3. Click the **MUTE** button (**M**) on the Guitar track to silence the track for now. You'll come back to this in the next exercise.

4. Click the **GRID** button in the Edit window toolbar (underneath the Spot button) to put the session into Grid mode.

5. Choose **FILE > SAVE** to save your work in progress.

Importing Audio to Tracks

In this part of the exercise, you will import additional audio files, placing them directly onto new Audio tracks. You will then rename the Audio tracks with descriptive names for the session.

1. Choose **FILE > IMPORT > AUDIO** and again navigate to the 02. Exercise Media folder.

2. Copy the following files into your session (select the files and click the **COPY** or **COPY FILES** button):

    *   Beach FX_01.wav

    *   Fire.wav

3. Click **OPEN** or **DONE** to import the audio and proceed to the prompt to choose a save location.

4. Choose the default save location (Audio Files folder), as before. A progress bar will appear as the audio is copied to your session.

    Once again, the Audio Import Options dialog box will appear.

5. This time, choose the option to import to New Track. (See Figure 5.25.)

6. Set the **LOCATION** pop-up to Spot. This will cause the Spot dialog box to appear, allowing you to set the import location.

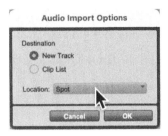

Figure 5.25 The Audio Import Options dialog box configured to import to new tracks

7. Click **OK**. The Spot dialog box will appear.

8. Set the **TIME SCALE** selector at the top to Min:Secs. Then set the **START** field to 0:01.050.

Figure 5.26 The Spot dialog box

9. Click **OK** to proceed. Two new tracks will appear in your session, with each of the audio clips aligned to the specified Min:Secs location.

Rename the tracks:

1. Double-click on the track nameplate of the Beach FX_01 track and shorten its name to Beach FX. Then click the **NEXT** button and rename the Fire track to Fire FX.

2. Click **OK** when finished.

3. Mute the Fire FX track for now. You will return to this track in a later exercise.

4. Double-click on the **ZOOMER** tool icon in the Edit window toolbar to fit the entire session timeline within the Edit window display.

5. Re-activate the **GRABBER** tool when done.

Finishing Up

You have now imported the music and sound effects for the radio advertisement. To complete this exercise, you will need to verify your work and save and close the session. You will be reusing this session in subsequent exercises, so it is important to save the work you've done.

You may also want to listen to your work before exiting.

Review and save your work:

1. Press **ENTER** or **RETURN** to place the cursor at the beginning of the session.

2. Verify that your session looks like Figure 5.27 below. If not, review the earlier steps and consult your instructor to make changes as needed.

Figure 5.27 The Edit window showing completed work for this exercise

3. Press the **SPACEBAR** to play back the session and confirm your results.

4. Press the **SPACEBAR** a second time when finished.

5. Choose **FILE > SAVE** to save the session.

6. Choose **FILE > CLOSE SESSION** to close the session.

ⓘ Remember that you cannot close a Pro Tools session by closing its windows. You must choose CLOSE SESSION from the FILE menu.

Editing Fundamentals

You've created a session, made your tracks, and imported some audio to work with. The next step in the production process is editing—the adjusting, tweaking, and moving of the elements in a session to a point where it's ready to be mixed. In this Lesson, we focus on the basics of the editing process.

Learning Targets

- Play from any place on the session timeline using Counters and Rulers
- Navigate in the Edit window
- Differentiate between different scrolling options
- Understand the behavior of the playback cursor
- Recognize the functions of the Edit tools
- Understand the different Edit modes

TOPIC 6.1:
GETTING AROUND THE TIMELINE

In this unit, you will explore how to navigate a session using the counters and rulers in the Edit window. As you work through this unit, consider the following: Why might you need to navigate to different locations in a session? How many different ways can you move around your session? What options might be the quickest? When should you use one method over another?

Activity: Scrolling and Playback Behaviors

- Open the Activity 6.1.ptx session. This session includes several long tracks and opens with the Edit window displayed and only a portion of the available audio visible.

- Use the scroll bar at the bottom to scroll from start to end. What does the counter area at the top center of the Edit window display?

- Press the spacebar. Where does playback begin? What do you see on screen?

- Allow playback to continue until the audio ends. Did the display scroll during playback? When does scrolling occur? Do you think you can change this behavior?

- Stop playback and click somewhere on a track with the Selector tool. What does the counter area show now?

- Press the spacebar again. Where does playback start this time? Stop playback when finished.

Discuss what you've learned or observed. What is the effect of clicking at different locations on a track? How might this be useful?

Discussion: Configuring the Session for Navigation

To edit efficiently, you'll need to be able to quickly make selections and control playback in different ways. So far in this course, we've touched upon some of these ways—now let's review and expand on them. We'll start by configuring the Edit window to simplify navigation.

Configuring the Counters

The counters and indicators at the top of the Edit window show the location of the timeline insertion (Edit cursor), and the beginning of any selected area. In Figure 6.1 below, the Edit cursor is at Bar 3. If we were to start playback at this point, it would begin at measure three.

Figure 6.1 The playback cursor at the beginning of measure three (3|1|000)

The counter display does more than show location; you can type in a value to move the cursor to that spot.

Main Counter

The large, singular value shown in the image above is what is known as the Main Counter. The Main Counter can be set to any one of various timescales.

To change the timescale of the Main Counter:

1. Click the Main Counter selector (small triangle icon on the right). A pop-up menu will appear.

Figure 6.2 Timescale menu for the Main Counter

The timescale options in Pro Tools Artist include the following:

*   Bars|Beats (Bars and Beats)
*   Min:Secs (Minutes and Seconds)
*   Timecode
*   Samples

2. Choose the desired timescale from the list. The Main Counter will change accordingly.

(i)   **Changing the Main Counter's timescale will also change the Edit selection's timescale and will show the corresponding ruler, if it is not already visible.**

Another way to change the Main Counter is to click on the name of any displayed timebase ruler (Bars|Beats, Min:Secs, Timecode, or Samples). The ruler will become highlighted, and the Main Counter's timescale will change accordingly.

Sub Counter

In the Counter section, you can optionally display a second timescale. This is called the Sub Counter. This can be useful, for example, if you're working on a music project. You might want to be able to track time in **Bars and Beats** with the Main Counter and **Minutes and Seconds** with the Sub Counter.

To display the Sub Counter:

1. From the Main Counter pop-up menu, choose **SHOW SUB COUNTER** at the bottom.

Figure 6.3 Showing the Sub Counter

2. Like the Main Counter, the Sub Counter can be set to different timescales. You can set the timescale by clicking the selector (triangle icon) to the right of the Sub Counter.

The Main and Sub Counters are similar. However, the Main Counter's timescale also determines the timescale for the Edit Selection fields. Also, the ruler corresponding to the Main Counter's timescale will always be shown. This ruler is known as the Main Timebase Ruler.

 The settings for the Main and Sub Counters in the Edit window toolbar mirror the counters in the Transport window; changing the timescale for a counter in one window will also change it in the other.

Configuring the Rulers

Along with a session's counters, the rulers are also useful for navigating the session's timeline.

Showing and Hiding Rulers

Pro Tools provides two basic ways to show or hide rulers to suit the needs of your session:

■ From the **VIEW** menu, select the **RULERS** submenu. Displayed rulers are indicated with a check mark. Click on an unchecked ruler's name to show it, or click a checked ruler's name to hide it.

■ Click on the **RULER VIEW SELECTOR** on the left side of the main timebase ruler. (See Figure 6.4.) A menu will appear, with shown rulers indicated by a green check mark. Click a menu item to show or hide the corresponding ruler.

Figure 6.4 Managing rulers from the Ruler View selector

 In either method, one menu is grayed out and cannot be unchecked. This is the main timebase ruler, which cannot be hidden.

Rearranging Rulers

You can easily reorder rulers by clicking on the name of a ruler that you want to move and dragging vertically to a new location. A yellow line will indicate the new position as you drag.

 Reordering rulers in the Edit window will not affect the order of the rulers in the View > Rulers submenu or the Ruler View Selector menu.

TOPIC 6.2:
SELECTING A PLAYBACK POINT

One of the great features of DAWs is the ability to navigate instantly to any location in your work. With Pro Tools, you can do this in several ways. In this unit, you will learn how to jump to a new position by typing in a location, by clicking in a ruler, and by using Transport controls. You will also learn about selections—and the difference between a Timeline selection and an Edit selection.

Discussion: Navigating and Controlling Playback

In the previous section, you learned how to configure the counters and rulers in the Edit window. Setting up properly will help you quickly make selections and control playback. In this section, you'll learn some specific techniques that you can use for navigation and playback.

Typing a Location

To choose a playback position, you can simply type a number in the Main or Sub Counter fields at the top of the Edit window. Just enter the location to move to and press the **RETURN** key (Mac) or **ENTER** key (Windows). The Edit cursor will move to that position, and playback can now start from that point.

 You can also navigate from the Transport window using a similar process.

You can also make selections from the counters. To do so, type values into both the Start and End fields in the Counters area. (You can also use the Length field to specify duration.)

When you press **RETURN** (Mac) or **ENTER** (Windows), the designated area will become selected (highlighted) in the ruler and on any tracks that contained the Edit cursor.

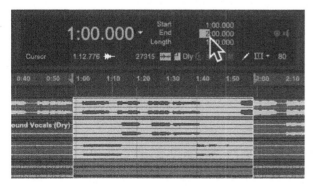

Figure 6.5 Selecting an area on the timeline using the Edit Location fields in the Counters area

Using Rulers to Set Location

The rulers in the Edit window can also be used to position the playback start point. Just click on a ruler at the point in time where you want playback to begin. The Edit cursor will jump to that location. A small blue arrow icon will appear on the Main Timebase ruler indicating the Edit cursor location. Playback will start at this point when you click the Play button or press the Spacebar.

You can similarly make a selection on the timeline by clicking and dragging across a range from a ruler. A selected area will appear on the timeline. This area will determine your playback range.

(i)   Drag the blue arrow icons on either side of the selected area to adjust the beginning or ending of the selection.

(i)   The Shift key is useful for making and extending selections in Pro Tools. Shift-clicking enables you to set or change the start or end point of a selection.

Go to Zero and Go to End Shortcuts

Two shortcuts that have been mentioned already in this course bear repeating:

- To move the Edit cursor to the beginning of your timeline (aka, *Go to Zero*), press the **RETURN** key (Mac) or the **ENTER** key (Windows).

- To move the Edit cursor to the end of your timeline (aka, *Go to End*), hold the **OPTION** key (Mac) or the **ALT** key (Windows), and press **RETURN** (Mac) or **ENTER** (Windows).

Timeline and Edit Selections

When you make a selection in the rulers, you're making a Timeline selection. Another kind of selection, called an Edit selection, is made when you select a range of time on one or more tracks.

By default, a session's Timeline and Edit selections will be linked. You can enable and disable this behavior under **OPTIONS > LINK TIMELINE AND EDIT SELECTION**. You can also turn this on and off from the Edit window toolbar using the **LINK TIMELINE AND EDIT SELECTION** button.

Figure 6.6 The Link Timeline and Edit Selection button

For this course, make sure the **LINK TIMELINE AND EDIT SELECTION** button is enabled (blue).

When you make an Edit selection on a track with Link Timeline and Edit Selection activated, you will also make a corresponding Timeline selection in the rulers.

 You'll learn about the Selector and Grabber tools later in this Lesson. These tools can be used to make Edit selections on your tracks.

Loop Playback

The selected area on your session's timeline will determine the playback range. Playback will begin at the start of the selection and stop at the end of the selection. When an area is selected, you can also use Loop Playback mode. With this mode active, your selected area will repeat until you stop playback.

To use Loop Playback:

1. Select the area on your timeline that you want to hear.

2. Do one of the following:

   • From the **OPTIONS** menu, choose **LOOP PLAYBACK**.

   • Right-click on the **PLAY** button in either the Transport window or the Edit window toolbar. From the menu that appears, choose **LOOP**.

   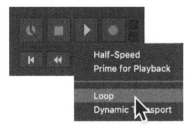

   Figure 6.7 Activating Loop Playback from the right-click menu

   The Play button will display a looping arrow.

   Figure 6.8 Play button showing a looping arrow with Loop Playback active

3. Click the **PLAY** button or press the **SPACEBAR** to start playback. Once the end of the selected area is reached, playback will seamlessly start from the beginning again.

TOPIC 6.3:
SCROLLING AND ZOOMING IN THE EDIT WINDOW

In this unit, you will explore different ways of zooming in and out in the Edit window. You will also learn about the Edit window scrolling modes. These techniques can be useful to help you focus on what you want to see at any given time as you work.

Activity: Auto-Scroll Behaviors

- Open the Activity 6.3.ptx session. This session will open with the Edit window zoomed in on a section of a long track.

- Go to the OPTIONS menu and select EDIT WINDOW SCROLLING > NO SCROLLING.

- Begin playback and let it continue past the visible section of the audio.

- Stop playback. Make some observations about what happened. Could you see the audio that you are listening to? What are you now viewing on screen?

- Select OPTIONS > EDIT WINDOW SCROLLING again, and this time choose AFTER PLAYBACK.

- Play the same portion of the audio a second time and stop. What observations can you make about playback this time? How might this scrolling mode be useful?

- Repeat the process for each of the other scrolling modes: PAGE and CONTINUOUS.

- How does each of these modes affect what you are seeing during and after playback? Which option do you think would be the most useful?

Discussion: Scrolling and Zooming in Pro Tools

As your session gets bigger, knowing how to get around Pro Tools becomes more important. Navigating in the Edit window involves two general operations—scrolling and zooming.

Scrolling Operations

Scrolling in Pro Tools, on a basic level, isn't all that different from scrolling a webpage, except that you can scroll vertically and horizontally.

Horizontal Scrolling

At the bottom of the Edit window, you'll find a Horizontal scroll bar that allows you to shift your view earlier or later in time. You can also scroll earlier or later using the triangular buttons in the lower right corner of the window. (See Figure 6.9.)

Figure 6.9 Left-right scroll triangles at the bottom right side of the Edit window

Vertical Scrolling

Along the right edge of the Edit window, you'll find a Vertical scroll bar. This will allow you to shift your view up or down to view tracks at the top or bottom of the arrangement in a larger session.

In the lower right-hand edge of the window, you'll also see a pair of up-down triangles (when enough tracks are present). Clicking on the up-down triangle buttons will scroll your view up or down one track at a time.

 On a mouse with a scroll bar or scroll wheel, up-down gestures will scroll your Edit window up and down. Holding the Shift key while using up-down gestures will scroll your window left or right (earlier or later in the timeline).

Edit Window Scrolling (Auto-Scroll) Options

You have a few auto-scroll options to choose from. These determine how your Edit window scrolls during playback.

To set the scrolling behavior for the Edit window:

1.   From the **OPTIONS** menu, select the **EDIT WINDOW SCROLLING** submenu.

2.   Choose the desired behavior from the submenu. Available options include:

   • **No Scrolling:** When selected, Pro Tools will not auto-scroll during playback. This means that when your playback cursor moves off the right edge of the window during playback, you will no longer see what you're hearing.

   • **After Playback:** With this option selected, although Pro Tools will not scroll during playback, when you stop the transport, the Edit window will scroll to the point where playback stopped.

   • **Page:** In this mode, whenever the playback cursor reaches the right edge of the window, Pro Tools will immediately scroll later by one screen, putting the cursor at the left side. This option has the advantage of enabling you to always see what you're hearing.

 Page scrolling may not behave properly under particularly high zoom magnification settings.

- **Continuous:** In Continuous scrolling mode, the playback cursor is fixed in the middle of the Edit window. During playback, the playhead stays put, with the Edit window content scrolling past it.

 Of the four scrolling options available in Pro Tools Artist, Continuous scrolling requires the most processing power from your computer.

Zooming Operations

Zooming is also critically important—so much so that there is a dedicated Edit tool just for that purpose. Like scrolling, you can zoom horizontally and vertically.

Horizontal Zooming

Zooming out or in horizontally changes how much time you can see in your session. Zooming out shows more time in the Edit window, while zooming in will shows less time at greater detail. Pro Tools provides several methods that you can use to zoom in and out horizontally.

ZOOM CONTROLS—On the left side of Edit window toolbar you'll find a cluster of Zoom controls. These include two side-facing triangle buttons. Clicking the left triangle (Horizontal Zoom Out) will show more time on the timeline; clicking the right triangle (Horizontal Zoom In) will show less time on the timeline.

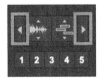

Figure 6.10 Zoom controls in the Edit window toolbar

 Clicking and dragging on either of these buttons will smoothly zoom in or out. (Drag left to zoom out and right to zoom in.)

SCROLL BAR BUTTONS—You can also zoom in and out using the plus and minus buttons in the lower right-hand corner of the Edit window, next to the horizontal scroll bar. Click the minus button to zoom out and show more of your timeline; click the plus button to zoom in and show more detail.

Figure 6.11 Edit window zoom controls

EDIT FOCUS MODE KEYS—Lastly, you can use Edit Keyboard Focus mode to zoom in and out. In this mode, press the **R** key to zoom out and the **T** key to zoom in.

Activating Edit Focus Mode

The zoom functions associated with the R and T keys require Edit Keyboard Focus mode to be active. To put your system into Edit Keyboard Focus mode, click the **a-z** button in the upper right-hand corner of the Edit window's tracks area.

When active, the button will be illuminated in yellow, as shown here.

Figure 6.12 Activating Edit Keyboard Focus mode

Vertical Zooming

Vertical zooming can be useful for seeing more detail in your audio files. Again, Pro Tools provides several ways that you can do this.

 Vertical zooming will change the display size of your audio waveforms; however, it will not change the amplitude of the audio. This function simply gives you the ability to see low-amplitude waveforms more clearly.

ZOOM CONTROLS—The two buttons in the center of the Zoom controls cluster are the Audio Zoom In/Out button on the left and the MIDI Zoom In/Out button on the right. Here, we focus on audio zooming, but the effects are similar for both buttons.

Figure 6.13 Vertical Zoom tools in the Edit window

Click the top half of the Audio Zoom In/Out button to zoom in vertically on your audio clips, making the audio waveform appear taller. Click the bottom half of this button to zoom out vertically.

Clicking the top or bottom of the button will incrementally zoom your audio up or down. For a smooth zoom, click and hold either button and drag up or down.

SCROLL BAR BUTTONS—In the upper right-hand corner of your tracks area, above the vertical scroll bar, you'll see miniature Audio Zoom In/Out and MIDI Zoom In/Out buttons. You can click the top and bottom of each of these buttons to zoom in and out vertically.

Figure 6.14 Vertical zoom tools in the Edit window

The Zoomer Tool

In addition to the zoom controls already discussed, Pro Tools has a dedicated Zoomer tool. In the Edit window toolbar, the Zoomer tool is shown as a magnifying glass icon.

Figure 6.15 The Zoomer tool in the Edit tools cluster area of the Edit window toolbar

To zoom in and out with the Zoomer tool:

1. Click the Zoomer tool button to activate it.

 Press Function Key F5 to activate the Zoomer tool from the keyboard.

2. Do one of the following:

    • To zoom in, position the Zoomer tool anywhere in the tracks area; a magnifier with a plus sign will display. Each click will incrementally zoom in on your timeline.

    • To zoom out, position the Zoomer tool anywhere in the tracks area and hold the **OPTION** key (Mac) or **ALT** key (Windows); a magnifier with a minus sign will display. Each click will incrementally zoom out on your timeline.

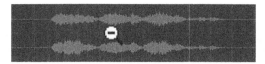

Figure 6.16 Using the Option or Alt modifier to zoom out with the Zoomer tool

You can do a few more things with the Zoomer tool:

- Double-click on the Zoomer tool button to zoom your session all the way out, showing the longest displayed track in its entirety. This is a quick way to see your entire timeline.

- Click and drag over an area with the Zoomer tool. A marquee box will indicate the selected range. Release the mouse to zoom in on the selected area.

- Hold the **CONTROL** key (Mac) or **START** key (Windows) while you click and drag left or right anywhere in a track to smoothly zoom in or out.

- Hold the **CONTROL** key (Mac) or **START** key (Windows) while you click and drag up or down on any track to smoothly zoom the track's waveforms up or down.

TOPIC 6.4:
PLAYING BACK YOUR SESSION

Now that you are armed with techniques for navigating, scrolling, and zooming, it's time to start looking at playback options. In this unit, we explore common playback behaviors and functions available in Pro Tools.

Activity: Session Playback and Cursor Behavior

- Open the Activity 6.4.ptx session. The Edit window will display with some tracks in it.

- Click on the Bars|Beats ruler at Bar 2 or on the Minutes:Seconds ruler at 2 seconds.

- Take note of the flashing cursor at the clicked location. This is the Edit cursor.

- Press spacebar to begin playback.

- Take note of the cursor scrolling across the screen. This is the playback cursor.

- Note where the flashing Edit cursor is during playback.

- Stop playback. Note where the Edit cursor is after playback.

- Go to the OPTIONS menu and enable INSERTION FOLLOWS PLAYBACK.

- Start playback and note where the Edit cursor is during playback.

- Stop playback and note where the Edit cursor is after playback.

- Start and stop playback again. Note what happens to the Edit cursor.

Discuss what you observed. What effect does the Insertion Follows Playback option have on Pro Tools' playback behavior? When might you want this behavior? When might you not want this?

Discussion: Playback Behavior

Pro Tools lets you configure and control many aspects of playback behavior. You can change what happens as you start and stop Pro Tools. You can also quickly navigate to either the playback cursor or the Edit cursor location.

Playback Cursor versus Edit Cursor

The playback cursor is a vertical line that moves across your screen during playback and recording. Pro Tools also provides an Edit cursor (sometimes called the Insertion cursor), which remains stationary during playback. This blinking cursor is an important visual indication, showing precisely where you are parked on the timeline.

Insertion Follows Playback

The Insertion Follows Playback option determines what effect playback will have on the Edit cursor location.

- When Insertion Follows Playback is disabled (default), the Edit cursor remains parked when you start and stop playback. This means that when you start the transport again, playback will start from the same position.

- When Insertion Follows Playback is enabled, the Edit cursor will move to the point where a playback pass ends. This means that when you start the transport again, playback will pick up where it left off previously. This is sometimes called *tape transport* mode, since it behaves like a tape deck would.

Pro Tools provides three ways to enable or disable Insertion Follows Playback:

- From the **OPTIONS** menu, select **INSERTION FOLLOWS PLAYBACK** to toggle the behavior on/off. When enabled, the menu item is marked with a check mark.

- Click the **INSERTION FOLLOWS PLAYBACK** button in the Edit window toolbar. When enabled, the button will be colored blue, as shown below.

Figure 6.17 Enabling the Insertion Follows Playback button in the Edit window toolbar

- Press the **N** key in Edit Keyboard Focus mode.

 When working with selections, be sure to disable INSERTION FOLLOWS PLAYBACK. If it is enabled, Pro Tools will drop the selection after any playback pass.

Locating the Playback Cursor and the Edit Cursor

PLAYBACK CURSOR—As you work, you will occasionally find that your playback cursor has moved off screen. To quickly scroll to the playback cursor, you can click on the Playback Cursor Locator. This blue triangle icon will appear on the main timebase ruler whenever the playback cursor is off-screen.

- When the playback cursor is earlier on the timeline, the triangle icon will display on the left side of the ruler. (See Figure 6.18.)

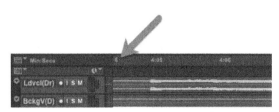

Figure 6.18 Playback Cursor Locator indicating that the playback cursor is to the left of the visible area

■ When the playback cursor is later on the timeline, the triangle icon will display on the right side of the ruler.

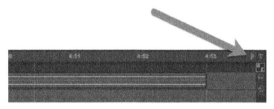

Figure 6.19 Playback Cursor Locator indicating that the playback cursor is to the right of the visible area

Clicking the Playback Cursor Locator will scroll to the playback cursor at any time during playback.

EDIT CURSOR—Clicking the Playback Cursor Locator will scroll to the Edit cursor when the transport is in stop. You can also quickly scroll to the Edit cursor at any time using either the LEFT ARROW or RIGHT ARROW keys. This works whether the transport is rolling or in stop.

When you have an Edit selection, you can scroll to the start of end of the selection using the arrow keys:

■ Press the LEFT ARROW key to scroll to the start of the Edit selection.

■ Press the RIGHT ARROW key to scroll to the end of the Edit selection.

> When you have a selection on a track (an Edit selection), the Left/Right Arrow keys will center the start or end of the selection on screen, respectively. With no selection, the Edit cursor represents a "selection" that starts and the ends at the same point, so both keys do the same thing.

TOPIC 6.5:
THE EDIT TOOLS

Pro Tools has a wide variety of Edit tools and features. You've already been introduced to the first of these, the Zoomer tool. In this unit, we introduce the remaining Edit tools: the Trim tool, the Selector, the Grabber, the Scrubber, and the Pencil tool.

Discussion: Edit Tool Functions

Selecting the proper Edit tool will allow you to work quickly while arranging and editing your clips.

The Trim Tool

The Trim tool enables you to adjust the boundaries of clips in your session. You can use this tool to remove content at the start or end of a clip.

To use the Trim tool:

1. Click the Trim tool button in the Edit window toolbar to activate it.

Figure 6.20 Choosing the Trim tool

 To activate the Trim tool from the keyboard, press Function key F6.

 On Mac computers, the Function keys may need to be reassigned to be available in Pro Tools. From the Apple menu, choose System Preferences. Then choose **Keyboard** and enable *Use F1, F2, etc. Keys as Standard Function Keys.*

2. Position your cursor near the start (left) or the end (right) of the clip that you want to trim. The cursor will become a bracketed icon.

Figure 6.21 The Trim tool positioned at the start of a clip

The Trim tool must be positioned within a clip to be active.

3.   Click and drag left or right to trim the clip. The clip boundary will adjust accordingly.

The Trim tool's direction is based on which end of the clip your cursor is closest to. In the front half of the clip, the tool will trim the clip start; in the back half, it will trim the clip end.

 You can reverse the direction of the Trim tool by holding Option (Mac) or Alt (Windows) before you click. This will to flip the direction of the Trim tool bracket.

Note that Pro Tools provides non-destructive editing. This means that when you remove audio content from the timeline, the audio data is not permanently deleted. To recover trimmed material, for example, you can simply click and drag with the Trim tool in the opposite direction. This will restore the removed content.

The Selector Tool

Next to the Trim tool is the **SELECTOR** tool. This tool lets you click to position the Edit cursor. You can also click and drag to create a selection.

To use the Selector tool to make a selection:

1.   Click on the Selector tool button in the Edit window toolbar to activate it.

Figure 6.22 Choosing the Selector tool

 To activate the Selector tool from the keyboard, press Function key F7.

2.   Click and drag over the area that you want to select. This creates an Edit selection.

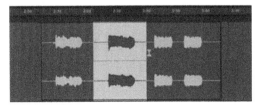

Figure 6.23 Selecting the second phrase in a clip

Edit selections can used for a number of purposes. For example, if you wanted to eliminate the selected area, you could press the **DELETE** key and the selected content would be removed.

In addition to selecting a range, you can use the Selector tool to select an entire clip or your entire track:

- Double-clicking within a clip with the Selector tool will select the entire clip.

- Triple-clicking in a track with the Selector tool will select all clips on that track.

The Grabber Tool

After the Selector tool, you'll find the **GRABBER** tool. You can use this tool to select a clip and drag it left or right (earlier or later) in the timeline. You can also drag clips up and down to move them to other tracks.

To use the Grabber tool:

1. Click on the Grabber tool button in the Edit window toolbar to activate it.

Figure 6.24 Choosing the Grabber tool

 To activate the Grabber tool from the keyboard, press Function key F8.

2. Click on a clip and drag it to a new location on the timeline (or to a different track in your session).

(i) You can select multiple clips and move them with the Grabber tool, moving the clips *and* any spaces between them. Click on the first clip, then Shift-click on the last clip; all clips and space in between will become selected.

Here's a handy little tip: Hold the **OPTION** key (Mac) or **ALT** key (Windows) while moving a clip to make a duplicate copy of the clip. This lets you create a copy of the clip in a new location while leaving the source clip in its original position.

(i) Double-clicking an audio clip with the Grabber tool will open the Clip Name dialog box, enabling you to rename the clip.

The Scrubber Tool

The Scrubber tool can be used to "scrub" slowly across a track in the Edit window to find a moment on the timeline. The audio from the track will audition as you scrub, letting you locate an edit point by ear.

To use the Scrubber tool:

1.   Click the Scrubber tool button to activate the tool.

Figure 6.25 Activating the Scrubber tool

   To activate the Scrubber tool from the keyboard, press Function key F9.

2.   Click on a track in the Edit window and drag left or right to begin playback in either direction.

ⓘ   For more precise scrubbing, zoom in horizontally on your tracks. The greater the zoom level, the more control you will have over the scrubbing behavior.

ⓘ   If you position your cursor on the boundary between two adjacent tracks in the Edit window, you can scrub the two tracks at once.

The Pencil Tool

The Pencil tool is commonly used for MIDI production and for editing automation. Both of these topics are discussed later in this book. For now, just know that you can activate the Pencil tool by clicking on the associated button in the Edit window toolbar.

Figure 6.26 Activating the Pencil tool

   To activate the Pencil tool from the keyboard, press Function key F10.

TOPIC 6.6:
THE EDIT MODES

You'll choose your Edit tools—Trim, Selector, Grabber, and so on—based on what you want to do to a clip. Another choice that you must make is which Edit *mode* to use. Your Edit mode choice will determine how your Edit tools affect your track content.

Discussion: Activating the Proper Edit mode

The Edit mode buttons are shown in the top left corner of the Edit window. The basic Edit modes are SHUFFLE, SLIP, SPOT, and GRID. The currently active mode is indicated by a highlight color.

Shuffle Mode

Shuffle mode is quite powerful for arranging clips. In this mode, clips on a track will snap to each other as you drag them with the Grabber tool. Adjacent clips will swap places if you drag one on top of another. This lets you assemble clips back-to-back and easily rearrange the order of clips on a track.

Another effect of Shuffle mode is that it closes up any gap that would ordinarily be left when you delete a clip or selection. This lets you remove unwanted audio—like coughs, *um's* and *uh's*, or background noises in a voiceover—without leaving an awkward silence behind.

To activate Shuffle mode:

■   Click the Shuffle button in the Edit window toolbar. The Shuffle mode button will highlight in red.

Figure 6.27 Activating Shuffle mode

The images below show an example of using Shuffle mode to rearrange the order of clips on a track.

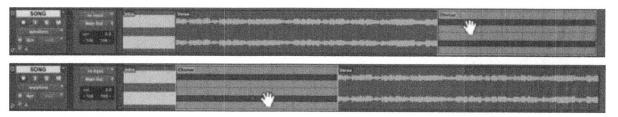

Figure 6.28 Reordering the clips on the Song track: before (top) and after (bottom)

Any edit you make on a track in Shuffle mode will affect the location of any clips later in the timeline. This behavior makes Shuffle mode unsuitable for work involving tracks that must stay in sync with one another.

Slip Mode

Slip mode is the most flexible of the Edit modes. In this mode, you can make edits and move clips around without any constraints.

To Activate Slip mode:

■ Click the Slip button in the Edit window toolbar. The Slip mode button will highlight in green.

Figure 6.29 Activating Slip mode

Slip mode lets you do the following:

■ Use the Grabber tool to drag clips forward or backward in time to any location. This can be used to fine-tune the position of clips.

■ Use the Selector tool to make an Edit selection that starts and ends at any point.

■ Use the Trim tool to adjust the beginnings and ends of clips with a high degree of flexibility.

Spot Mode

Spot mode is most commonly used in post-production work. Spot mode lets you specify a location for a clip by typing in a numeric time value.

To use Spot mode:

1. Click the Spot button in the Edit window toolbar. The Spot mode button will highlight in orange.

Figure 6.30 Activating Spot mode

2. Click on a clip with the Grabber tool. The Spot dialog box will display. (See Figure 6.31.)

3.   Enter the desired location in the Spot dialog box.

Figure 6.31 Typing a numeric location in the Spot dialog box

4.   Click **OK**. The clip will instantly move to the specified location.

Grid Mode

Grid mode constrains any selections or clip movements that you make, aligning them to timing intervals on a grid. This is especially useful in music production when using a bar and beat-based grid.

Using Grid Mode

The basic process for using Grid mode involves both activating the mode and setting the grid size. Activating Grid mode is done on the far left side of the toolbar; setting the grid size is done toward the right side.

To use Grid mode:

1.   Click the Grid button on the left side of the Edit window toolbar. The Grid mode button will highlight in blue.

Figure 6.32 Activating Absolute Grid mode

2.   Click on the **GRID VALUE SELECTOR** to the right of the Counters area to configure the spacing of the grid increments. (See Figures 6.33 and 6.34.)

Figure 6.33 The Grid Value Selector to the right of the Counters area

Figure 6.34 Using the Grid Value Selector to set the grid to 1/4 notes

The grid spacing will be represented in the Edit window by vertical grid lines.

3. (Optional) Show or hide the grid lines by clicking the **Show Grid Lines** button (the word **Grid** to the left of the Grid Value Selector). When this button is green, the grid lines will display.

Figure 6.35 Showing/hiding the grid lines with the Show Grid Lines button

When working in Grid mode, the Edit tool behaviors will be constrained as follows:

- **Grabber tool**—As you drag a clip earlier or later on the timeline, the start of the clip will jump from grid line to grid line. For example, if the grid value is set to one bar, any clip that you drag will snap to the start of the nearest measure.

- **Selector tool**—As you make a selection, the start and end of the selection will snap to the nearest grid lines. To make a 1-bar selection with the grid value set to one bar, you would select one increment. (With set the grid value to quarter notes, you would select four increments.)

- **Trim tool**—As you make adjustments to the beginning or the end of a clip, the clip boundary will trim to the nearest grid line.

Absolute Grid Mode versus Relative Grid Mode

What we commonly call Grid mode is more precisely named *Absolute* Grid mode. A second Grid mode option is available called *Relative* Grid mode.

In Absolute Grid mode, moving a clip will cause the clip start to snap to the grid, regardless of where the clip was previously positioned. So for example, when using a 1/4 note grid, if you move a clip that originally started ahead of the beat (or behind the beat), it will align to start right on the beat.

In Relative Grid mode, moving a clip will maintain its offset, while the clip moves in grid increments. In this case, dragging a clip that is ahead of the beat on a 1/4 note grid will allow you to move it forward or backward in 1/4 note steps, keeping it ahead of the beat by the original amount.

To activate Relative Grid mode:

1. Click and hold on the Grid button on the left side of the Edit window toolbar. A menu will display showing the two available grid mode options.

2. Select Relative Grid mode. The Grid mode button will highlight in purple, and the button will display REL GRID.

Figure 6.36 Relative Grid mode active in the Edit Modes section of the toolbar

Accessing the Edit Modes with Function Keys

Changing your Edit modes is frequently done in many kinds of workflows, so doing it quickly can be a real timesaver. Here are some shortcuts:

■   Press the F1 key to activate SHUFFLE mode.

■   Press the F2 key to activate SLIP mode.

■   Press the F3 key to activate SPOT mode.

■   Press the F4 key to activate GRID mode. Press repeatedly to toggle between Absolute Grid mode and Relative Grid mode.

LESSON 6 CONCLUSION

In this Lesson, we introduced techniques that you can use to navigate and get around your session. We also discussed how to control playback and how to enable auto-scrolling in the Edit window during playback. Along the way, you learned about the differences between the playback cursor and the Edit cursor. You also learned techniques for scrolling the Edit window to each cursor when they are off-screen. Lastly, we covered the various Edit tools and Edit modes available in Pro Tools and described what they each can be used for.

Discussion: Summary of Key Concepts

In this Lesson, you learned:

- How to configure the Counters and Rulers in your session

- How to use the Counters and Rulers to set a location or playback point on your session's timeline

- How to scroll vertically and horizontally in the Edit window

- How to zoom in and out in the Edit window

- The differences between the available Edit Window Scrolling options

- How to change scrolling and playback behavior

- How to quickly locate the playback cursor when it is off-screen

- How to activate and use the Edit tools—the Trim, Selector, Grabber, Scrubber, and Pencil tools

- How to activate and use the Edit modes—Shuffle, Slip, Spot, and Grid

Essential Keyboard Commands and Shortcuts

Below is a summary of modifier behaviors and shortcut operations that you should know from this Lesson.

- To move the Edit cursor to the start of a session, press the **RETURN** key (Mac) or **ENTER** key (Windows).

- To move the Edit cursor to the end of a session, hold **OPTION** (Mac) or **ALT** (Windows) while pressing **RETURN** (Mac) or **ENTER** (Windows).

- To zoom out horizontally, press the **R** key in Edit Keyboard Focus mode.

- To zoom in horizontally, press the **T** key in Edit Keyboard Focus mode.

- To zoom out with the Zoomer tool, hold the **OPTION** key (Mac) or the **ALT** key (Windows).

■ To zoom all the way out and show the longest shown track in its entirety, double-click on the Zoomer tool.

■ To smoothly zoom in or out using the Zoomer tool, hold the **CONTROL** key (Mac) or **START** key (Windows) while dragging left or right in a track.

■ To smoothly zoom the waveforms up or down for a track using the Zoomer tool, hold **CONTROL** (Mac) or **START** (Windows) while dragging up or down in a track.

■ To enable or disable Insertion Follows Playback, press the **N** key in Edit Keyboard Focus mode.

■ To scroll the Edit window to the Edit cursor or the start of a selection, press the **LEFT ARROW** key.

■ To scroll the Edit window to the Edit cursor or the end of a selection, press the **RIGHT ARROW** key.

■ To flip the direction of the Trim tool, press the **OPTION** key (Mac) or the **ALT** key (Windows).

Activity: Lesson 6 Knowledge Check

This quiz will check your knowledge of material covered in the Editing Fundamentals lesson.

1. Rulers can be shown or hidden from which menu?

2. What shortcut can you use to immediately place the playback cursor at the beginning of the session?

3. Which scrolling option causes the screen to scroll by one screen at a time, each time the playback cursor reaches the end of the screen?

4. True or False? The Insertion Follows Playback option will allow you to easily play the same section over and over in succession.

5. Match the Edit tool to its description.

Trim tool	Plays audio as the mouse is dragged across a clip
Selector tool	Draws MIDI notes or mix automation data
Grabber tool	Defines an area on a track for playback or editing
Scrubber tool	Adjusts clip boundaries
Pencil tool	Selects and moves clips

6. What happens when you double-click on a clip with the Selector tool?

7. What happens when you hold **OPTION** (Mac) or **ALT** (Windows) while dragging a clip with the Grabber tool?

8. Match the Edit mode to its description.

Slip mode	Causes clips to snap to the nearest grid increment
Shuffle mode	Allows you to move clips freely
Spot mode	Allows you to type a location for a clip into a dialog box
Grid mode	Causes clips to snap end-to-end

9. What is the difference between Slip mode and Grid mode?

10. Name and describe the two types of Grid mode that are available in Pro Tools.

Spotting and Trimming Audio

In this exercise tutorial, you will configure your radio ad session to display the required rulers, spot the previously imported guitar clip to its proper time location, and trim off excess audio from the hi-hat clip. When finished, you will save your work for future use.

Exercise Details

- **Required Media:** None

- **Exercise Duration:** 10 to 15 Minutes

Downloading the Media Files

To complete the exercises in this book, you will use files included in the **PT Academy Media Files** folder that you previously downloaded from the course learning module on ElementsED.com.

To re-download the media files, click on the **Access Files** link in the sidebar after logging in to your account. Consult your instructor or visit **nxpt.us/make-music** for more details.

Getting Started

You will start by opening the Pro Tools session you saved at the end of Exercise 5. If that session is not available, you can use the provided **Exercise06-Starter** file in the **01. Starter Sessions** folder.

Open the session and save it as Exercise 6:

1. Open the session file that you created in Exercise 5: **Storage Drive/Folder > Exercises-XXX > Exercise05-XXX.ptx**.

   Alternatively, you can use the Exercise06 Starter file (PT Academy Media Files > 01. Starter Sessions > Exercise06-Starter.ptx).

2. Choose **FILE > SAVE AS** and name the session **Exercise06-XXX**, keeping it inside the original session folder. (Move the session into your **Exercises-XXX** folder if working from the starter file.)

The session will open with the Edit and Transport windows displayed, as it was when last saved.

Configuring Rulers

In the first part of the exercise, you will configure the Edit window to display the required rulers.

Show the desired rulers:

1. Click on the **RULER VIEW SELECTOR** on the left side of the Bars|Beats ruler. A pop-up menu will appear.

Figure 6.37 Ruler View Selector menu

2. Enable each of the following, if not already shown:

   • Min:Secs ruler

   • Markers ruler

   • Tempo ruler

3. Press **ESCAPE** when finished to close the menu.

Spotting Audio on Tracks

In this part of the exercise, you will position the guitar clip that you previously placed in the session.

Spot audio clips:

1. Click on the **SPOT** button on the left side of the Edit window toolbar to activate Spot mode.

Figure 6.38 Spot mode active

2. Click on the **GTR_01** clip with the Grabber tool; the Spot dialog box will display.

3. Set the **Time Scale** at the top of the dialog box to **MIN:SECS**.

4. Configure the **Start** location in the Spot dialog box to 0:01.118 and click **OK**. The clip will move to start at the specified location.

Figure 6.39 Spot dialog box configured for the GTR_01 clip

5. Click the **GRID** button in the Edit window toolbar (underneath the Spot button) to put the session into Grid mode.

6. Choose **FILE > SAVE** to save your work in progress.

Trimming Unwanted Noise

The next thing you need to do is to trim the start and end of the clip on the Hi Hat track to remove noise and bleed on the track. To do this, you will use the Trim tool.

Remove noise at either end of the clip:

1. Activate **SLIP** mode on the left side of the Edit Window Toolbar.

2. Click on the Trim tool in the toolbar to activate it.

Figure 6.40 Activating the Trim tool

3. Click in the front part of the **Hi Hats_03** clip and drag to adjust the trim point. Trim up to the start of the first major transient in the clip (the first hi hat strike).

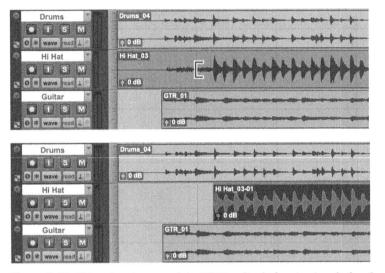

Figure 6.41 Trimming the start of the Hi Hat clip: before (top) and after (bottom)

4. Scroll the window to view the end of the Hi Hat clip.

5. Click in the end part of the clip and drag to adjust the trim point. Trim back to the end of the decay on the last hi hat strike.

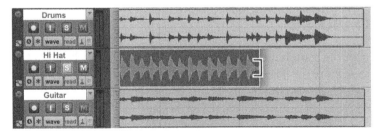

Figure 6.42 Trimming the end of the Hi Hat clip

Finishing Up

To complete this exercise tutorial, you will need to save your work and close the session. You will be reusing this session in Exercise 7, so it is important to save the work you've done.

You may also want to listen to your work before exiting.

Review and save your work:

1. Press **ENTER** or **RETURN** to place the cursor at the beginning of the session.

2. Press the **SPACEBAR** to play back the session and confirm your results.

3. Press the **SPACEBAR** a second time when finished.

4. Choose **FILE > SAVE** to save the session.

5. Choose **FILE > CLOSE SESSION** to close the session.

ⓘ Remember that you cannot close a Pro Tools session by closing its windows. You must choose CLOSE SESSION from the FILE menu.

Getting Ready to Record

The things you've learned thus far are important skills in becoming a strong Pro Tools user. Sooner or later though, you'll need to start recording performances. For this, you will need an appropriate input source for the material you wish to record. You will also need to make sure you have adequate space on your computer or on an external drive to store your recordings. In a music session, you may also want to configure the session tempo and meter to match the piece you are recording.

Learning Targets

- Recognize characteristics of different types of microphones

- Capture audio from different input sources

- Prepare the recording space for best results

- Set the session tempo and meter

TOPIC 7.1:
GETTING AUDIO INTO YOUR SYSTEM

Recording audio is straightforward enough—the goal is to acquire a signal as accurately as possible, with minimal noise. In fact, that's been the aim since the earliest days of recording, and the basic process has remained essentially the same throughout the decades.

In this unit, you will explore the idea of signal flow. What happens first on a track? What happens last? Why is the order of operations important? You will also learn how to configure a system for recording. How do you get audio into the system? How can you control record levels? Lastly, you'll consider what to do after recording. How can you keep the record takes that were good and discard the takes that were bad?

Discussion: Audio Components and Signal Flow

Recording audio can take on many different forms, from using one or two microphones for a podcast or dialogue recording, all the way up to recording full symphony orchestras. Understanding the signal flow behind the recording process is a critical first step. Let's take a look at where the signal flow begins.

Microphone Basics

One of the most commonly used input devices is the microphone.

Microphones and speakers are closely related and are both forms of *transducers*—devices that convert one form of energy into another. With speakers, an electrical signal is applied to an electromagnet (called a voice coil), which then moves the speaker cone in and out. The speaker vibration creates variations in air pressure that we perceive as sound.

If you reverse that process, you have a microphone. In microphones, changes in air pressure create vibrations to a component within the microphone. The movement of that component creates an electrical signal.

The electrical signal is then transmitted through the microphone cable to your recording medium.

However, the voltage coming from microphones is unusably low. To increase the signal level to something useful, we use *preamplification*. Preamplification can be applied a few different ways. Here are two examples:

■ **Audio Interface:** Many audio interfaces have built-in microphone preamps, solving the voltage problem. If an interface has 3-pin XLR microphone connections, it's a safe bet that it has an integrated mic preamp. The preamp can be adjusted using the gain control on the audio interface.

■ **USB:** USB microphones are arguably the simplest solution for boosting the signal. USB mics will include not only a built-in microphone preamp, but also a built-in audio interface, converting the analog sound to digital audio.

Types of Microphones

There are different microphone types: dynamic, condenser, and ribbon microphones. Let's take a look at the pros and cons of each type.

Dynamic Microphones

A *dynamic* mic works by moving a coil of wire around a magnet (or moving a magnet around a coil of wire), pushing electrons in the wire and creating an electrical current, similar to how an electrical generator works.

When sound causes the diaphragm to move, the coil interacting with the magnetic field generates a small electrical current, which is then sent to a microphone preamp to boost the signal.

Dynamic Microphones have a few advantages:

- They are generally less expensive than other kinds of microphones. Two of the most popular dynamic microphones, the Shure SM57 and SM58, are only about $100 USD.

- They have a simple design and tend to be very sturdy. Not only can they withstand the occasional knocks and drops, but they are also well-suited to record loud sounds like guitars and drums and are commonly used in live music stage performances.

Classic examples of dynamic microphones, the Shure SM57 and SM58, are not only relatively affordable, but they are among the most popular microphones today.

Figure 7.1 The Shure SM57 and SM58 dynamic microphones

Dynamic microphones have some downsides, though; they are generally not the most sensitive type of microphone and will not capture all the nuances of a performance, particularly in the higher frequencies.

Condenser Microphones

Condenser microphones are also commonly found in recording studios. Condenser microphones contain two metal plates that are oppositely charged and separated by a small gap. One metal plate is attached to the diaphragm, while the other has a fixed position. As vibrations cause the diaphragm to move, the relative distance between the two plates changes, producing capacitance, which generates an electrical signal.

Condenser microphones are typically a bit more expensive than dynamic microphones. They also tend to be more delicate due to their more complex construction, meaning you should not put one too close to a kick drum or guitar amp. However, they can record sound in greater detail and over a larger frequency range.

The *Neumann U87*, perhaps the most coveted microphone in the world, is a great example of a condenser microphone.

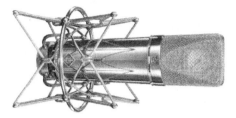

Figure 7.2 The Neumann U87 condenser microphone

One important characteristic of condenser microphones is that they need *power* in order to function. Electrical current must be supplied to the two metal plates, typically from an external source. This is commonly provided by the microphone preamp or audio interface, and is known as *phantom power*. If you're using a condenser microphone, make sure that phantom power is turned on for that connection.

 Condenser microphones can cause noise when they are plugged in due to their circuitry powering up. Turn down your studio monitors before connecting these kinds of microphones to your preamp or interface.

Ribbon Microphones

A *ribbon* microphone is generally the most expensive kind of microphone you can buy. In a ribbon microphone, an extremely thin strip of metal is suspended between two magnets. As sound hits the ribbon and causes it to move, its vibration in the magnetic field generates an electrical current.

If you need to capture sound with very high quality and accuracy, it's hard to beat a good ribbon microphone. The ribbon design can capture detail and clarity from very low to very high frequency ranges. These mics also provide a good reproduction of the area around the microphone, making them very effective recording tools in professional recording spaces and concert halls.

Ribbon microphones are typically on the higher end of the price range (the Royer R-121 for example, is over $1,000 USD). And the thin ribbon—the core of the microphone's design—is very delicate. It can be torn by wind or rough handling, rendering the microphone useless.

Figure 7.3 The Royer R-121 ribbon microphone

 Although most modern ribbon microphones won't be damaged if phantom power is turned on, there are some that *will*. (This is also true for dynamic mics.) As a general rule, if a microphone doesn't need phantom power, don't turn it on.

Large Diaphragm Versus Small Diaphragm

When you're shopping for microphones—condenser mics, in particular—you'll find that there are two different types: *large diaphragm* and *small diaphragm* microphones. As a general rule, a large diaphragm microphone has a diaphragm of 1 inch or more in diameter. On the other hand, a small diaphragm microphone has a diaphragm of ½ inch or less in diameter.

Small diaphragm microphones tend to be smaller than large diaphragm microphones, but their differences go beyond size:

- **Large diaphragm** microphones have a higher signal level and lower noise. They are generally less sensitive than small diaphragm microphones, but although they don't record as accurately, they have a pleasing warmth in the low frequencies, making them a popular choice for recording vocals.

- **Small diaphragm** microphones tend to be more technically accurate in recording a performance. The small vibrating area is far more responsive, especially to the initial attack (or transient) of sounds and higher frequency ranges. Small diaphragm microphones are better for recording all the details of a performance, and are commonly used for drums, guitar, piano, and other instruments.

Polar Patterns

Last, but certainly not least as it pertains to your microphone choices, is the microphone's *polar pattern*. The polar pattern is a representation of the directional sensitivity of the microphone. Microphones use different polar patterns that characterize their sensitivity to sound arriving from different directions. The three most common polar patterns are *omnidirectional, cardioid,* and *figure 8.*

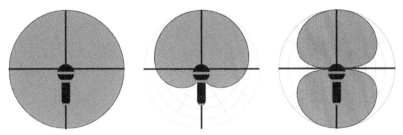

Figure 7.4 Microphone polar patterns: omnidirectional, cardioid, and figure 8 (left to right)

A microphone with *omnidirectional* polarity is sensitive to sound in all directions. This design typically gives you the most natural sound and is resistant to plosives (the pop sound that microphones will often pick up with hard P's, B's, and other consonants).

The most common polar pattern is called *cardioid*. The name is derived from the heart (cardio) shape of the pattern. This kind of microphone is most sensitive to sound in front of it, making it more directional than other microphones. Sounds behind or to the side of the mic will not be picked up as well. For that reason, cardioid microphones are commonly used in live performances. Unlike omnidirectional microphones though, cardioid microphones are susceptible to plosives.

The last pattern, called *figure 8* (or sometimes *bidirectional*), is equally sensitive to sounds in front of it and behind it, but not on the sides. Ribbon microphones, as a result of their design, tend to have this polarity. Figure 8 microphones give a clear recording of a performer, plus the ambience of the recording space.

Other Analog Input Devices

At times you might need to connect devices that use line level signals to your system. These could include musical equipment like keyboard synthesizers or drum machines, or consumer devices such as CD or DVD players. In such cases, you'll want to use an input on your interface labeled for Line In. This will typically be a 1/4-inch jack. (Some interfaces will use a combo jack with a Line/Instrument switch.)

If you want to record a guitar or bass amplifier directly into Pro Tools, look for a line level output on the amp and connect that to a line input on your audio interface.

Alternatively, you can connect an electric guitar or bass directly into an interface without going through an amp. Instruments like guitars and basses have an output signal that is a bit stronger than microphone level and a bit lower than line level signals. Many audio interfaces include direct injection (or DI) inputs for this purpose. These inputs may be labeled Instrument, Inst, or simply DI.

Digital Inputs

Many audio devices have digital outputs that can be connected to corresponding digital inputs on your system. Keeping a signal in the digital realm will minimize noise levels and signal degradations that can accompany Digital-to-Analog (D/A) and Analog-to-Digital (A/D) conversions.

Three common digital audio formats that you might encounter in a recording situation include:

- S/PDIF—Uses RCA (also called *coaxial*) or TOSLINK fiber optic connections. A single S/PDIF connection carries two channels of information.

- AES/EBU—Uses XLR cables and is a professional digital format. A single AES/EBU connection carries two channels of information.

- ADAT—Uses a TOSLINK fiber optic cable. A single ADAT connection carries 8 channels of audio information.

> The audio quality of these formats is virtually identical, but if you have a choice, AES/EBU or ADAT formats are generally preferable, as they do not include any copy protection encoded into the audio signal.

TOPIC 7.2:
YOUR RECORDING SPACE

Recording spaces come in all shapes and sizes. The importance of the room design will vary depending upon the kind of recording work you are doing. If you're only recording instruments or devices that are plugged directly into an audio interface, pretty much any room will do the trick. Recording with microphones, though—that's another story.

Activity: Listen to Sample Recordings

■ Open the Activity 7.2.ptx session. The Edit window will display with audio on a single track.

■ Play the session to hear the audio. You will hear several takes of the same recording.

■ Which recording sounds better? Why? How would you characterize each take?

Discuss your observations. What conclusions can you make about the impact of the recording environment on the sound quality of the recording?

Discussion: Configuring Your Recording Environment

Your recording environment includes more than the physical location where recording will take place. Other key considerations include the hardware used to hold and protect your microphone, room treatments used to control unwanted noise, and the distance from the microphone to the source you are recording.

Isolating the Microphone

When you see vocalists recording in a studio, you won't see them holding the microphone in their hands. This is for two reasons: First, when a singer holds a microphone, the distance between the sound source (the singer) and the microphone can easily vary; this will then result in an inconsistent recording. Secondly, holding a microphone can produce handling noise, which will impact the recording.

Microphone Stands

Using a microphone stand prevents handling noise. Mic stands come in a variety of shapes and sizes, from desktop to standalone. Frequently, microphone extensions called boom arms are attached to a basic microphone stand. These not only extend the height of a microphone stand, but they also give more flexibility with microphone placement.

Microphone Clips and Shock Mounts

In basic setups, microphones are attached to the stand with a solid plastic microphone clip. However, these clips can transmit vibrations from the stand to the microphone, and this will be picked up as noise.

Additional isolation is often used in the form of a shock mount. This device suspends the microphone using elastic cords or springs.

Figure 7.5 A microphone fitted with a shock mount

Pop Filters

Unwanted vibrations could also come from the performer, in the form of powerful bursts of air called plosives. These normally occur when we pronounce hard consonants like **B** or **P** sounds. Such plosives can be picked up by microphones as noticeable *pops*.

Pop filters are designed to minimize plosives by dispersing the air from the performer's mouth before it reaches the mic. Pop filters are inexpensive and easy to use; just clip one to your microphone stand and position the circular barrier between the performer and the microphone.

Figure 7.6 A pop filter for a microphone

 To prevent the microphone from picking up playback audio from Pro Tools, performers can listen to playback using headphones. Closed-back headphones work best in these situations.

Sound Absorption

Sound, like light, can be reflected. The sounds you are recording also produce sound reflections that bounce off nearby walls. These reflections, in turn, are picked up by the microphone. Generally speaking, you'll want these reflections to be minimized. This is where sound absorption panels applied on walls and other surfaces can help.

Sound absorbers are not tremendously expensive, but they can be a bit difficult from a logistical perspective. Sometimes it's just not practical to put sound-absorbing foam on your walls or to hang absorption panels everywhere. Less intrusive alternatives include small sound-absorbing panels that can be attached to a microphone stand.

The Proximity Effect and Your Recording Space

If you're recording too close to a microphone, something called the proximity effect can occur. This is a disproportionate increase in low frequencies as a sound source gets closer to a directional microphone. Sometimes, this can be desirable: For example, if you're doing a voiceover for a documentary, a rich, warm low end is a great sound. However, the proximity effect can also create a "muddy" recording. To prevent this, simply move the microphone further from the sound source.

(i) Microphones with omnidirectional polarity are not affected by proximity.

(i) Moving the mic further from the sound source will also affect the reflections being recorded: you'll get less of the source and more of the room sound. So sound absorption becomes more important.

TOPIC 7.3:
SETTING TEMPO AND METER

Once you're ready to begin recording from a technical perspective, you may have a few other details to consider. This is especially true when recording music.

In this section, we go through a pre-session checklist to prepare for recording to a metronome click.

Discussion: Configuring the Session Tempo and Meter

If you're working on a music project, it's quite common to have performers playing to a click track—a track with a steady metronome pulse indicating the tempo. For the click track to work correctly, you'll need to set up your song's meter and tempo first.

Tempo

Tempo is the speed at which beats are played. In music, tempo is measured in beats per minute, or BPM. By default, Pro Tools uses a tempo of 120 BPM. However, you can change this as needed.

Tempo and the Tempo Ruler

In the MIDI controls section of either the Edit window or Transport window, you'll see a button showing a conductor holding a baton. This is the **TEMPO RULER ENABLE** button.

Figure 7.7 Activating the Tempo Ruler Enable button

The Tempo Ruler Enable button determines how your session will derive its tempo:

- When active (blue), the tempo settings applied in the Tempo ruler will be in effect. This is called **TEMPO MAP MODE**. In this mode, your session could start at a tempo of 120 BPM, and then change tempo at measure 3 to 100 BPM. This mode is required for a session that includes tempo changes.

- When inactive (grey), your session will be in **MANUAL TEMPO MODE**. In this mode, the tempo will simply be the value that is set in the Tempo field. Any tempo settings applied to the Tempo ruler will be disregarded. Manual Tempo mode provides a quick way to experiment with tempo after you've created a tempo map.

Setting Tempo

When the Tempo ruler is disabled (or before tempo changes have been added to the Tempo ruler), the Tempo field in the MIDI controls section will let you set the tempo for the session:

1.   Click in the Tempo field. It will become highlighted in green.

Figure 7.8 Clicking the Tempo field in the MIDI Controls section

2.   Type a tempo value and press the **RETURN** key (Mac) or **ENTER** key (Windows).

When the Tempo ruler is enabled, you can create tempo events in the Tempo ruler itself:

1.   Click the plus (**+**) button to the right of the word Tempo in the Rulers area of the Edit window.

Figure 7.9 Adding a tempo event to the Tempo ruler

2.   In the **TEMPO CHANGE** dialog box, specify the location where your tempo event will take effect. (In the image below, the location is set to Bar 11, Beat 1, Tick 000.) In the **BPM** field, type the desired tempo.

Figure 7.10 The Tempo Change dialog box

3.   Click the **OK** button. The tempo change will be applied.

Tap Tempo

Sometimes you might not know the numeric value of the tempo you need. In this case, you can highlight the tempo or BPM field and repeatedly tap the **T** key on your keyboard, in tempo. As you tap, Pro Tools will quickly calculate the tempo from your keystrokes.

Meter

A song's meter (or *Time Signature*) determines the number of beats in a measure (the first number), and the note value that gets one beat (the second number). Most songs that you hear on the radio have a **4/4** meter, meaning that there are four beats in a measure and a quarter note gets one beat. However, other meters are commonly used as well. Setting the meter correctly will ensure that the click provides the right beat.

The default meter in Pro Tools is **4/4**.

To change the meter:

1. In the MIDI controls section of the Edit or Transport window, double-click the **METER** value.

Figure 7.11 Double-clicking the Meter value in the MIDI Controls section

Alternatively, you can click the plus (**+**) button to the right of the word **Meter** in the Rulers area of the Edit window.

Figure 7.12 Setting the meter from the Meter ruler

2. In the Meter Change dialog box that appears, choose the location for your meter change. (See Figure 7.13.) Then type in the Meter you want, and finally choose your click value.

Figure 7.13 The Meter Change dialog box

 The check box in the upper left-hand corner, labeled Snap To Bar, will cause the meter change to be applied on Beat 1 of the bar. You can safely leave this box checked in most cases to help align the meter change correctly.

3.   Click the **OK** button to create the meter change event.

Tempo and Meter Rulers

Once you've made your tempo and meter changes, you can view them on the Meter and Tempo rulers. Initial meter and tempo settings will be shown at the far left of the ruler. In Figure 7.14, the starting tempo is 120 BPM and the starting meter is 4/4 time—the Pro Tools defaults.

Figure 7.14 Tempo and Meter rules shown in the Edit window

As another example, Figure 7.15 shows a tempo change at **Bar 3** from **120 BPM** down to **100 BPM**.

Figure 7.15 Tempo change at Bar 3

LESSON 7 CONCLUSION

Getting good quality audio into your Pro Tools system involves several stages before the DAW itself. In this Lesson, you learned how different types of microphones impact the input signal. You also learned how to get various different types of signals into a track and reviewed some options that can be used to improve the audio captured by a microphone. Lastly, you learned how to set the meter and tempo for your session.

Discussion: Summary of Key Concepts

In this Lesson, you learned:

- The different types of microphones, and their individual strengths and weaknesses

- The differences between different input sources—microphones, line-level signals, instrument-level signals, and digital signals—and how to get them into your DAW

- How a microphone's polar pattern affects its ability to record the sounds around it

- How to prepare your recording space for best results

- How to set the tempo and meter for your music recording sessions

Essential Keyboard Commands and Shortcuts

Below is a summary of modifier behaviors and shortcut operations that you should know from this Lesson.

- Press the **T** key repeatedly with the tempo field highlighted to derive tempo using the Tap Tempo function.

Activity: Lesson 7 Knowledge Check

This quiz will check your knowledge of material covered in Lesson 7, Getting Ready to Record.

1. What component in a recording signal flow is used to increase the signal level coming from a microphone going onto a Pro Tools track?

    a. A microphone preamp

    b. A microphone cable

    c. A pop filter

    d. A shock mount

2. The most rugged type of microphone is _____. The most delicate and easily damaged type is _____.

    a. Condenser

    b. Dynamic

    c. Ribbon

3. The _____ microphone type requires phantom power.

4. The _____ microphone polar pattern works best to record sound from the front and reject sound from the back. The _____ polar pattern works best to record sounds from front and back, rejecting sounds from the sides.

    a. Omnidirectional

    b. Cardioid

    c. Figure 8

5. Give an example of a device that might use a line-level signal.

6. What is the purpose of a shock mount for a microphone?

7. What inexpensive device can you use to reduce plosives when recording vocals? What microphone polar pattern is most sensitive to plosives?

8. How are sound absorption panels useful in a recording space? What problem sounds can they reduce?

9. The _____ button in the Transport window can be used to switch between Manual Tempo mode and Tempo Map mode (to add tempo changes to your session).

    a. Wait for Note

    b. Metronome

    c. Tempo Ruler Enable

    d. Countoff

10. How can you add a tempo change to your session? How can you add a meter change?

Configuring Tempo and Meter

In this exercise, you will configure your radio ad session to allow working in Grid mode and set Pro Tools to match the rhythmic characteristics of the music you previously imported. To do this, you will display the Meter ruler, confirm the meter for the session, and set the tempo for the session. When finished, you will be able to make musical selections in meaningful rhythmic units.

Exercise Details

- **Required Media:** None

- **Exercise Duration:** 10 Minutes

Getting Started

You will start by opening the Pro Tools session you completed in Exercise 6. If that session is not available, you can use the provided Exercise07-Starter file in the **01. Starter Sessions** folder.

Open the session and save it as Exercise 7:

1. Open the session file that you created in Exercise 6: Storage Drive/Folder > Exercises-XXX > Exercise06-XXX.ptx.

    Alternatively, you can use the Exercise07 Starter file: PT Academy Media Files > 01. Starter Sessions > Exercise07-Starter.ptx.

2. Choose **FILE > SAVE AS** and name the session Exercise07-XXX, keeping the session inside the original folder. (Move the session into your Exercises-XXX folder if working from the starter file.)

Playing a Grid Selection

In this part of the exercise, you will activate Grid mode and experiment with playing back Grid-based material. When the session meter and tempo match the musical material, the grid will correspond to the bars and beats in the performance; when they don't, the grid will correspond to random musical locations.

Experiment with playback in Grid mode:

1. Before making any changes, play through the session one time to get familiar with the musical material. Stop playback when finished.

2. Click on the **GRID** button on the left side of the Edit Window Toolbar to activate Grid mode. The button will light blue when active.

Figure 7.16 Activating Grid mode

3. Use the **GRID VALUE SELECTOR** on the right side of the Edit Window Toolbar (to the right of the Counters area) to set the grid size to **1 Bar**.

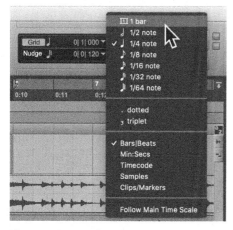

Figure 7.17 Setting the grid value

4. Click on the **HORIZONTAL ZOOM IN** button on the toolbar to zoom in a level for a better view.

Figure 7.18 Clicking on the Horizontal Zoom In button on the Edit window toolbar

5. Make a selection on the **Drums** track from **Bar 5** to **Bar 7**. The selection will snap to bar boundaries as you drag. (Note that you will need to drag at least half way across each bar to select it.)

Figure 7.19 A two-bar selection on the Drums track

6. Choose **OPTIONS > LOOP PLAYBACK** to activate Loop Playback mode. A looping arrow will display on the Play button in the Transport window.

7. Start playback and take note of the results. You should hear that playback does not begin on a beat and it does not loop smoothly. This is because the beats in the performance do not match the beats represented in the Pro Tools Bars|Beats ruler.

8. Stop playback when finished.

Configuring the Session

Next you will configure the session meter and tempo and confirm your settings by playing back Grid-based material at the new tempo. The music in this session uses a tempo of 123 beats per minute in 4/4 time.

Set the meter and tempo:

1. Choose **VIEW > RULERS > METER** to display the Meter ruler, if not already shown.

2. Verify that the Meter ruler shows **4/4** at the head of the ruler. If not, click the plus (**+**) button on the Meter ruler and enter the correct meter in the resulting dialog box. (See Figure 7.20.)

Figure 7.20 The Meter Change dialog box configured for 4/4 timing

Click OK to accept the meter and close the dialog box.

3. Take note of the tempo displayed at the head of the Tempo ruler. This will be the default tempo of 120 BPM.

4. Double-click on the red tempo event at the start of the Tempo ruler. (See Figure 7.21.) The Tempo Change dialog box will open.

(i) **Alternatively, you can press Return (Mac) or Enter (Windows); then click the plus (+) button on the Tempo ruler to open the Tempo Change dialog box at Bar 1.**

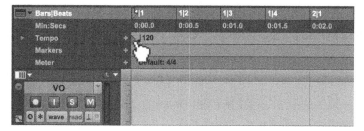

Figure 7.21 The red tempo event on the Tempo ruler; double-click to modify the tempo

5. Change the session tempo in the dialog box to **123 BPM** and click **OK**. The red tempo event will update to reflect the change.

Figure 7.22 Tempo configured properly in the Tempo Change dialog box

The red triangle at the head of the Tempo ruler is a special kind of tempo event, known as the Song Start Marker. This marker is actually diamond-shaped, with half of the diamond hidden behind the head of the ruler.

6. If needed, re-create your selection on the Drums track from Bar 5 to Bar 7.

7. Press the **SPACEBAR** to start playback again. Notice the results. Playback should now start on the downbeat of the measure, and the selection should loop smoothly.

8. Stop playback when finished.

Finishing Up

You have now configured your radio ad session to match the musical content used in the ad. To complete this exercise tutorial, you will need to save your work and close the session. You will be reusing this session in Exercise 8, so it is important to save the work you've done.

You may also want to listen to the results from different locations before exiting.

Review and save your work:

1. (Optional) Audition results from different locations:

   • Use the **SELECTOR** tool to place the cursor at a different location in the session, such as at Bar 8.

   • Press the **SPACEBAR** to play back the session and listen to the results. You should hear playback begin on the beat. Press the **SPACEBAR** a second time when finished.

   • Repeat the process, positioning the cursor to a new bar and listening again. (Try listening from Bar 10, Bar 14, Bar 18, or other locations of your choice.)

2. When finished, press **ENTER** or **RETURN** to place the cursor at the beginning of the session.

3. Choose **FILE > SAVE** to save the session.

4. Choose **FILE > CLOSE SESSION** to close the session.

 Remember that you cannot close a Pro Tools session by closing its windows. You must choose CLOSE SESSION from the FILE menu.

Recording Audio

Recording audio is an area where Pro Tools really shines, and its flexibility has helped Pro Tools earn its place as a leader in the audio field. This Lesson will start you on the road to recording great takes!

Learning Targets

- Create a click track
- Prepare tracks for recording audio
- Complete a basic record pass
- Identify and manage audio clips after recording

TOPIC 8.1:
CONFIGURING A METRONOME

You're almost ready to start recording. Before proceeding, you will often need to set up the session so that musicians can keep time during the recording.

Activity: Using the Metronome

- Open the Activity 8.1.ptx session. This session contains music tracks without a click track.

- Begin playback.

- Toggle the Metronome button in the Transport window on and off. What effect does this have?

- Stop playback and choose **TRACK > ADD CLICK TRACK** to add a new click track to the session.

- Begin playback again, and again toggle the Metronome on and off. What effect does this have now?

Discuss what you've observed. What conclusions can you draw about using a metronome in Pro Tools?

Discussion: Using a Metronome Click

Many music-recording scenarios require the use of a metronome click. If you've taken the time to set your meter and tempo, you're almost done—all you need to do is to create a click track.

Creating a Click Track

The click track provides the metronome click for the performers. This steady pulse helps musicians keep consistent time.

To create a click track:

- From the **TRACK** menu, choose **CREATE CLICK TRACK**.

The click track is an Aux Input track with a plug-in on it called Click II. This simple plug-in plays short click sounds (beeps, beats, or notes) to indicate tempo.

Setting Click and Countoff Options

Once a click track is set up, you can configure how it will behave. You can make changes from the **CLICK/COUNTOFF OPTIONS** dialog box.

To open the Click/Countoff Options dialog box, do either of the following:

■ From the SETUP menu, choose CLICK/COUNTOFF.

■ Double-click the Metronome button in the MIDI controls section in the Edit window or Transport window.

Figure 8.1 Double-clicking the Metronome button

The Click/Countoff Options dialog box will appear. Here, you can choose when your click will play.

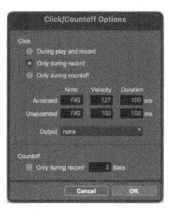

Figure 8.2 The Click/Countoff Options dialog box

The Click/Countoff Options dialog box is divided into three sections. At the top, you can select the conditions for playing the click:

■ **During Play and Record:** This option plays the click sound during playback and during recording. Since click tracks are typically needed only during recording, this is not a common choice.

■ **Only During Record:** This is the most common option. During playback, the click will be silent. The click sound will be heard only when one or more tracks is in the process of recording.

■ **Only During Countoff:** Countoff plays a set number of beats before recording starts, allowing musicians to adjust to the tempo in advance. With this option chosen, the click will be heard *only* during the countoff—once recording begins, the click track will be silent.

The middle section of the dialog box is largely unused. It allows you to choose an external sound module to provide the click sound. If you're using a click track, this section can be ignored.

At the bottom of the dialog box, you can set how many measures (bars) of countoff the musicians will hear. If you use a countoff, it is recommended to select the Only During Record option here.

To use a click track, there's one more step: enabling the metronome to play the click sound. Pro Tools provides two ways to activate the metronome:

■ From the **OPTIONS** menu, you can choose **CLICK** to toggle the metronome sound on or off.

■ In the Transport controls, you can click the **METRONOME** button to toggle the metronome sound on or off. When active, this button will display in blue.

Figure 8.3 Activating the Metronome

TOPIC 8.2:
PREPARING YOUR TRACKS

Before starting a record pass, you need to take a few steps to prepare the record tracks.

Discussion: Configuring Tracks for Recording

To get started, you will need to verify (1) that your microphones (or other sound sources) are routed correctly and (2) that the tracks are named appropriately. You also need to make sure you have enough storage space on your record drive for the audio you plan to capture.

Setting I/O for Recording to an Audio Track

Before you can record to a track, you need to identify where the signal is coming from and where it's going.

For this, you need to use the **I/O** view. If needed, enable this view in the Edit window (or Mix window) by selecting **VIEW > EDIT WINDOW VIEWS > I/O** (or **VIEW > MIX WINDOW VIEWS > I/O**).

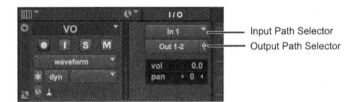

Input Path Selector
Output Path Selector

Figure 8.4 The I/O view in the Edit window

To configure the I/O for a track:

1. Click the **INPUT PATH SELECTOR** (top selector in the I/O view), and choose the input that corresponds to your audio source.

   ⓘ Each record track should have a different input selected. For example, if the lead vocalist is recording through the *Mic 1* input, a background singer would need to use another track with a different input (*Mic 2*, for example).

2. Click the **OUTPUT PATH SELECTOR** (bottom selector in the I/O view), and choose the output that corresponds to the connection you'll use to monitor your session as you record.

3. (Optional) Adjust the volume level on a track-by-track basis in the Edit or Mix window.

   • In the Mix window, adjust the Volume fader on a track up or down.

   • In the Edit window, click and hold on the Volume indicator and drag the pop-up fader up or down. (See Figure 8.5.)

Figure 8.5 Changing a track's monitoring volume in the Edit window

4. (Optional) Change the pan setting on a track-by-track basis. Panning will shift the output of the track left or right.

Figure 8.6 Changing a track's panning in the Edit window

Setting Default Inputs and Outputs

If you've set your Playback Engine device properly but aren't seeing the inputs or outputs that you're expecting, the problem might lie in the I/O Setup dialog box. This dialog box can get quite involved and is discussed in detail in later courses in the Avid Learning Series.

To get you started though, here's how to create the default inputs and outputs you need:

1. Go to the **SETUP** menu.

2. Choose **I/O**. The *I/O Setup* dialog box will appear.

3. In the **INPUT** tab, click the **DEFAULT** button.

4. In the **OUTPUT** tab, click the **DEFAULT** button.

5. In the **BUS** tab, click the **DEFAULT** button.

6. Click the **OK** button. The I/O Setup dialog box will close, and your inputs and outputs will be set to their default settings for your audio device.

To quickly reset your volume to unity (0.0) or your pan to center (0), hold OPTION (Mac) or ALT (Windows) while clicking on the volume or pan controls.

 It is very important to avoid having a recording microphone pick up the signal from the monitor speakers. If this happens, you run the risk of feedback, which can quickly damage your speakers and your hearing.

 To avoid feedback, turn off or turn down your speakers and instead monitor playback through closed-back headphones.

The Importance of Track Names

One of the most important steps in the recording process is the naming of your tracks. Why?

In Pro Tools, when you record onto a track (Audio or MIDI), the names of the recorded clips and files are based on the name of that track.

For example, if you record to a track named Lead Vocal, the name of the first recorded clip (and its corresponding audio file) will be Lead Vocal_01. The number at the end of the clip indicates that this is the first clip recorded on the track. Subsequent recordings on this track will be named Lead Vocal_02, Lead Vocal_03, Lead Vocal_04, and so on.

Changing the name of the track *after* recording will not change the name of the clips or files.

The names of the files in your session's Audio Files folder and the clips in the Clips List are vitally important as you continue your production process. Recording to tracks using generic names like Audio 1, Audio 2, and so on may very well cause confusion later, as you face a long list of clips whose names give no clue as to what they contain. Therefore, the best practice for a recording session is to descriptively name your tracks prior to recording.

Managing Storage: The Disk Usage Window

In Pro Tools, your storage drive holds all your recordings—when the drive is full, you won't be able to record any longer. Also, higher sample rates and bit-depths will consume your drive space at a faster rate.

Pro Tools gives you visibility into how much available space you have, in the form of the Disk Usage window. To access this window, choose **WINDOW > DISK USAGE**.

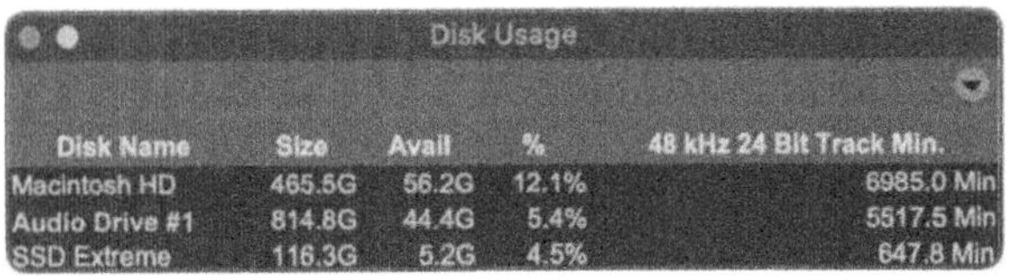

Figure 8.7 The Disk Usage window

This window provides valuable information on your system:

■ **Disk Name:** The names of the various drives that are connected to your computer. Bear in mind that in a basic recording situation, your audio is recorded to the Audio Files subfolder of your session, so it's important to know which drive is holding your session.

■ **Size:** The total size of each drive connected to your computer.

■ **Avail:** The available space on each drive connected to your computer.

■ **%:** The percentage of space remaining available on each drive.

■ **Track Min.:** The number of minutes of recording possible on each drive, at your current sample rate and bit depth. This number is calculated for mono recordings.

The last thing you want is to run out of disk space in the middle of a recording session, so it's a good idea to quickly check the Disk Usage window before beginning to record.

■ Estimate the amount of time you need to record on all of your tracks for the duration of the session, including multiple takes. Remember that stereo tracks require twice the disk space of mono tracks.

■ Compare this number to the Track Min number in Disk Usage to ensure you have adequate drive space before beginning the project.

For example, to record 8 mono tracks and 1 stereo track for a three-minute song, you will need 30 mono track minutes. If you need to record three takes of the song, you will need at least 90 track minutes of available storage.

TOPIC 8.3:
BASIC RECORDING

With setup complete, you're now ready to record!

Discussion: Making a Recording

To get started recording, follow these steps:

1. Avoid feedback situations—if you're recording with a microphone in the same room as your monitor speakers, turn your speakers down or off. Consider using closed-back headphones for monitoring.

2. Verify that signal is reaching your destination track. Click the Input Monitor button (labeled I). Once active, the track will have a live input, and you'll hear your incoming signal.

Figure 8.8 Activating the Input Monitor feature for the Lead Vocal track

3. Watch the meter on the track to gauge the signal level. Adjust the sound source or the gain control on your audio interface to get a strong signal without clipping (red light at the top of the meter). To start out, target having levels peak in the light green section of the meter, but not in the yellow range.

ⓘ Any volume and pan changes you make will affect the track's output only, not its input. If you're recording a loud signal that is clipping your input, you'll need to bring down the level of your sound source (instrument, microphone, and so on) rather than the track's volume fader in Pro Tools.

4. Once you're happy with the incoming level of the track, disable input monitoring.

5. Click the Record Enable button to arm the track for recording. (See Figure 8.9.) When a track is armed, its input will be active (similar to input monitoring), so take care to avoid feedback situations.

Figure 8.9 Record-enabling the Lead Vocal track

Note that the In and Out points in the rulers area will switch from blue (playback) to red (record) whenever any track in your session is record-enabled.

6. Position the Edit cursor where you want recording to begin (or select the area where you want to record).

7. Click the **RECORD** button in the Transport controls. The Record button will begin to flash.

8. Click the **PLAY** button or press the **SPACEBAR**. Recording will begin.

 To start recording immediately without first record-arming the transport, press Command+Spacebar (Mac) or Ctrl+Spacebar (Windows). Alternatively, you can press Function key F12 or press the [3] key on the numeric keypad.

9. Click the **STOP** button when you want to stop recording. A new clip will be shown in the track.

TOPIC 8.4:
AFTER RECORDING

After you've finished a recording, you may have some housekeeping to do. Have you captured a good take? Are you finished recording on that track? What should you do with any bad takes you've recorded? Mostly how you proceed is up to you, but there are a few good habits to get into.

Discussion: Post-Recording Activities

Immediately after recording a take, you'll want to listen to it. If it is a keeper, you can disarm recording on the track. From there, you may want to do some work to organize the clips in your Clips List.

Playing Back

When you're done recording on a track, it's generally a good idea to put the track into a playback-only mode. This will safeguard against accidentally recording over what you've just done!

Disarm the Track

Before continuing, click on the Record Enable button at the head of the track to disarm it.

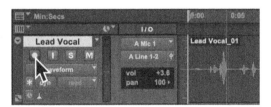

Figure 8.10 Disarming the Lead Vocal track

Play the Track

At this point, you can play back as normal. Use the Selector tool to position your Edit cursor at the desired position on your timeline, and then click the Play button (or press the Spacebar) to hear your newly completed recording.

Managing Clips

Once you've completed recording, you'll find that you have new clips in your Clips List. At times, you may need to identify the clips from the Clips List and/or manage the clips in your session.

Whole File Clips and Subset Clips

When you complete a basic recording pass, you create a clip on your timeline that starts with the first sample of the recorded audio file and ends at the last sample of that file. Put another way, the clip on your timeline represents an entire audio file recorded to your storage drive. This is called a *whole-file* clip.

Any edited clip that *doesn't* represent a complete file is called a *subset* clip. For example, if you use the Trim tool to remove the beginning or end of a whole-file clip, the result no longer represents the entire file. This is now a subset clip.

Identifying whole-file clips and subset clips is an important part of media management. Whole-file clips appear in the Clips List in a **bold** font. For example, the image below includes four whole-file clips:

- Acoustic Guitar Stem Print

- Acoustic Rhythm Guitar

- Break.02_03

- Crash

Figure 8.11 Whole-file and subset clips in the Clips List

Clips that are in plain text (not bold) are subset clips. Clip names also indicate a relationship between the clips. For example, Crash is a whole file clip, with Crash-02 being a subset clip related to it. The whole-file clip is sometimes referred to as the *parent file*.

When you edit a whole-file clip, Pro Tools adds a hyphen (-) to the subset clip name, followed by two digits to indicate the edit number. For example, if you start with a whole-file clip named Crash, and then trim that clip, you'll get a new subset clip named Crash-01. If you create additional subset clips from the same clip, they'll be appended with -02, -03, and so on.

Mono and Stereo Clips

By now, you know that the track width (mono or stereo) determines the kind of clip that can be put on that track. A mono track can only hold mono clips, and a stereo track can only hold stereo clips.

Stereo clips are easily identified in your Clips List in two ways. First, the clip name is appended with (Stereo) in the list. Secondly, there is a small disclosure triangle to the left of the clip name.

In the image below, the Drums_01 clip and the Keys_01 clip are stereo clips—all of the others are mono.

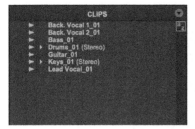

Figure 8.12 Mono and stereo clips in the Clips List

If you click on a stereo clip's disclosure triangle, you'll see the two mono clips that comprise that stereo clip. The mono clip names indicate the channel: a clip with a .L extension indicates the left channel, and a clip with a .R extension indicates the right channel.

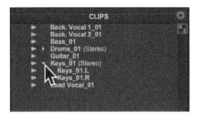

Figure 8.13 Showing the mono clips that comprise a stereo clip

Renaming Clips

As you've already learned, Pro Tools names recorded clips based on the tracks they are recorded on. Even so, from time to time you'll want to rename a clip.

To rename an audio clip:

1. Do one of the following:

    *   Using the Grabber tool, double-click on the clip.

    *   Right-click on the clip and select **RENAME** from the pop-up menu.

    These operations work in both the Edit window and the Clips List.

    The **NAME** dialog box will appear. The dialog box will vary slightly between a subset clip and a whole-file clip. (See Figure 8.14.)

2. Enter a new name for the clip.

3. In the case of a whole-file clip, select whether to rename the clip only or to rename the clip (in the session) and the parent file (on disk). The image on the right in Figure 8.14 shows these options.

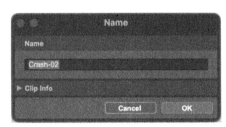

Figure 8.14 The Name dialog box for subset clips (left) and for whole-file clips (right)

4. Click **OK** to commit the change.

Removing Clips and Deleting Files

You can easily remove unwanted clips from your session. However, Pro Tools draws a distinction between removing a clip from the session only, and deleting the audio file from your storage drive.

To remove an unwanted clip:

1. Do one of the following:

    • Right-click the clip that you want to remove (either in the Edit window's tracks area or in the Clips List), and choose **CLEAR** from the pop-up menu.

    • Select the clip(s) that you want to delete in the Clips List, then click on the Clips List pop-up menu (small circular icon in the upper right-hand corner of the Clips List) and choose **CLEAR**.

> **(i)** You can select a range of clips in the Clips List by selecting the first clip then holding Shift while selecting the last clip. You can add or remove individual clips by holding Command (Mac) or Ctrl (Windows) while clicking additional clips.

    The resulting dialog box will vary based on whether you are removing subset clips or whole-file clips.

2. Click the **REMOVE** button for subset clips, or select from the available options for whole-file clips:

    • **DELETE**—Selected whole-file clips *and* their associated audio files will be permanently deleted.

    • **MOVE TO TRASH**—Selected whole-file clips will be removed from your session and their associated audio files will be moved to your computer's Trash or Recycle bin.

    • **REMOVE**—Selected clips will be removed from your session, but no audio files will be deleted or moved to the Trash/Recycle bin. (Audio files will remain in your session's Audio Files folder.)

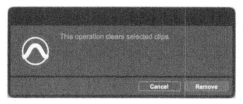 

Figure 8.15 The Clear dialog box for subset clips (left) and for whole-file clips (right)

The selected clips will be removed from the Clips List and any audio files associated with whole-file clips will be affected as described above for the selected option.

In some cases, Pro Tools will display an additional dialog box before completing the selected action:

■   If you attempt to clear a clip that is used in your session (including in your Undo History or your clipboard), you'll be prompted to proceed or cancel.

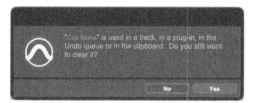

Figure 8.16 Dialog box regarding a clip that is in use

■   If you try to delete a parent file that is being used by any subset clips in your session, Pro Tools will present a warning that it cannot delete that file. If you'd like to remove the clip from your Clips List while leaving the audio file on your storage drive, click the **YES** button.

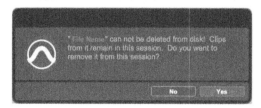

Figure 8.17 Dialog box regarding a parent file that is still needed by the session

LESSON 8 CONCLUSION

The recording process is simple when you break it down to its component parts. This Lesson described how to create a click track, how to check your available drive space, and how to complete an audio recording.

Discussion: Summary of Key Concepts

In this Lesson, you learned:

- What a click track is and what it is used for

- The process used to prepare your session for recording

- How to complete a basic record pass

- How to identify and manage your recorded clips after recording

Essential Keyboard Commands and Shortcuts

Below is a summary of modifier behaviors and shortcut operations that you should know from this Lesson.

- To reset volume to unity (0.0) or pan to center (0), hold **OPTION** (Mac) or **ALT** (Windows) and click the volume or pan control.

- To start the transport in record mode, press **COMMAND+SPACEBAR** (Mac) or **CTRL+SPACEBAR** (Windows). Alternatively, press Function key **F12** or press the **[3]** key on the numeric keypad.

- To select a range of clips in the Clips List, select the first clip in the range, then hold **SHIFT** and select the last clip in the range.

- To add or remove individual clips from a selection, hold **COMMAND** (Mac) or **CTRL** (Windows) while clicking on a clip.

Activity: Lesson 8 Knowledge Check

This quiz will check your knowledge of material covered in the Recording Audio lesson.

1. What kind of track is created when you choose the TRACK > CREATE CLICK TRACK command?

    a. Audio track

    b. Basic Folder track

    c. Aux Input track

    d. Instrument track

2. With a click track added to your session, what button in the Transport window can you use to toggle the click sound on and off?

    a. Wait for Note

    b. Metronome

    c. Tempo Ruler Enable

    d. Countoff

3. True or False? You can open the Click/Countoff Options dialog box under the OPTIONS menu.

4. The display area that you can use to select inputs and outputs for a track is called the _____ view. This display area can be shown in the Edit window using the _____ menu.

5. Which of the following keyboard shortcuts can you use to begin recording, once a track has been record-armed? (Select all that apply.)

    a. Function key F12

    b. Command+= (Mac) or Ctrl+= (Windows)

    c. Option+R (Mac) or Alt+R (Windows)

    d. The [3] key on the numeric keypad

6.   True or False? If the input level is clipping on a track, you can turn down the track's fader to reduce the level and avoid clipping.

7.   Where are recorded audio files stored by Pro Tools?

   a. In the session's Audio Files folder

   b. Embedded in the Pro Tools session file

   c. Within the Global Tracks folder on your storage drive

8.   What aspect of your session determines the names used for your recorded files?

   a. The session name

   b. The track number

   c. The track type

   d. The track name

9.   Refer to the Image: How many whole-file clips are shown?

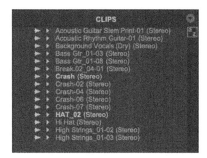

   a. Zero

   b. Two

   c. Five

   d. Fifteen

10.   True or False? With a whole-file clip selected, you can use the Clear dialog box to either (1) remove the clip from your session only or (2) remove the clip and delete the associated audio file from disk.

Recording Audio

In this exercise, you will be recording the voiceover (VO) for your radio advertisement. You have two options available to complete this exercise.

Option 1: Live Recording. For this option, you will first connect a microphone to Pro Tools and then record yourself or a classmate speaking the script for the ad.

 This exercise does not include detailed instructions for routing audio from a microphone into Pro Tools. See Topic 8.2 for basic setup information. Consult your instructor for additional help as needed.

Option 2: Bus Recording. If live recording is not possible or practical in your school, you can instead record from an existing bus in the included starter session by routing the bus to the input of the VO track.

Exercise Details

- **Required Media:** None

- **Exercise Duration:** 15 Minutes

Downloading the Media Files

To complete the exercises in this book, you will use files included in the **PT Academy Media Files** folder that you previously downloaded from the course learning module on ElementsED.com.

To re-download the media files, click on the **Access Files** link in the sidebar after logging in to your account. Consult your instructor or visit nxpt.us/make-music for more details.

Option 1: Live Recording from a Microphone

To record live input from a microphone, complete the steps in this section. (To record from a bus in the starter session instead, skip forward to Option 2 on page 225.)

Option 1, Part 1: Getting Started

You will start by opening the Pro Tools session that you created in Exercise 7. If that session is not available, you can use the provided Exercise08-Starter file in the 01. Starter Sessions folder.

Open the session and save it as Exercise 8:

1. Launch Pro Tools and choose **FILE > OPEN SESSION** (or choose **OPEN FROM DISK** from the Dashboard).

2. Navigate to the session file that you created in Exercise 7: Storage Drive/Folder > Exercises-XXX > Exercise07-XXX.ptx.

   Alternatively, you can use the Exercise08 Starter file: PT Academy Media Files > 01. Starter Sessions > Exercise08-Starter.ptx.

3. Select and open the session. The session will open displaying eight tracks in the Edit window.

4. Choose **FILE > SAVE AS** and name the session Exercise08-XXX, keeping it inside the original session folder. (Move the session into your Exercises-XXX folder if working from the starter file.)

5. Toggle the display to the Mix window by choosing **WINDOW > MIX** or by pressing **COMMAND+=** (Mac) or **CTRL+=** (Windows).

Option 1, Part 2: Preparing to Record

To get started, you will need to route audio from a connected microphone to the VO track. You will also need to set the input level going to the track.

Route the signal to the audio input of the VO track:

1. Locate the **AUDIO INPUT PATH SELECTOR** for the VO track. This will be the top selector in the I/O section. (See Figure 8.18.)

2. Click on the **AUDIO INPUT PATH SELECTOR** and select **INTERFACE > INPUT 1 (MONO)** (or the corresponding input where your microphone is connected).

Figure 8.18 Audio Input Path selector for the VO track in the Mix window

3. Record-enable the track by clicking on the **RECORD ENABLE** button so that it begins flashing red.

Figure 8.19 VO track after being record-enabled

Set the input level for the track:

1. Test the input level by having the announcer (yourself or a classmate) talk into the microphone in the same manner that you will use when recording. (Keep the speaking distance and volume consistent while setting levels.)

    Try using the first line or two of the voiceover script as you set the level: "Summer's here and it's time for some fun in the sun. But don't hit the dunes unprepared." Have the announcer repeat the lines as needed.

2. Keep an eye on the track meter as you set levels. Adjust the gain on your audio interface or make other adjustments to get a strong input signal with consistent levels around two-thirds of the way up the meter while the announcer speaks.

 Be careful not to push the meter into the top half of the orange zone, as this could lead to irreversible clipping in the recorded audio file.

Option 1, Part 3: Recording the Voiceover

With the input routed and the level set, you will now record the voiceover for the commercial. You will want to have the announcer practice the script a few times to determine proper pacing.

Practice the script:

1. Review the voiceover script below.

   Summer's here and it's time for some fun in the sun. But don't hit the dunes unprepared! Spicoli's Surf Shop has the coolest beach gear so you don't get baked by the sun. Our gnarly accessories include swimming apparel, sun block, boogie boards, flip flops, and oversized beach towels with sand-free technology. So keep the sand at the beach and the waves within reach. Stop by Spicoli's Surf Shop today!

2. Toggle the display to the Edit window by choosing **WINDOW > EDIT** or by pressing **COMMAND+=** (Mac) or **CTRL+=** (Windows).

3. Use the **HORIZONTAL ZOOM OUT** button on the toolbar to zoom out as needed to see 30 seconds on the Min:Secs ruler. (You can also use the R key in Edit Focus mode to zoom out.)

   You may also want to resize the side columns (Tracks List and Clips List) to allow more screen real estate for your tracks area.

Figure 8.20 Showing 30 seconds on the Min:Secs ruler

4. Press the **SPACEBAR** to begin playback and have the announcer read the script aloud to get a sense of the proper pacing.

   Keep an eye on the Min:Secs ruler and the Sub Counter display at the top of the Edit window as you practice. The voiceover should start around 2-3 seconds into the session and end shortly before reaching the 30-second mark (0:30.000).

   ⓘ This is a 30-second radio spot, so the announcer will not have much time to complete the script. Practice keeping a brisk pace without sounding rushed.

5. Press the **SPACEBAR** when finished to stop playback.

6. Repeat the process as needed to refine the announcer's timing.

Record the voiceover:

1. If needed, choose **WINDOW > TRANSPORT** to display the Transport window; then disable the **COUNT OFF** button, if active (lit green). (See Figure 8.21.)

2. With the **VO** track record-enabled, record-arm the Transport window. The Record button will flash red when active.

Record button (active)   Count Off button (inactive)

Figure 8.21 The Transport window with countoff disabled and the session in Record Ready mode

3. When ready, click the **PLAY** button or press the **SPACEBAR** to begin recording.

4. Have the announcer read the script while keeping an eye on the Sub Counter and/or Min:Secs ruler to complete the script within 30 seconds.

5. When finished, click the **STOP** button or press the **SPACEBAR** a second time to stop recording.

6. If needed, repeat the above process to record additional takes until you are satisfied with the results.

7. Go to the "Finishing Up" section on page 228 to complete this exercise.

Option 2: Bus Recording from a Starter Session

To record the VO part from a bus in the starter session, complete the steps in this section. (If you've completed the recording in Option 1 using a microphone, skip forward to "Finishing Up" on page 228.)

Option 2, Part 1: Getting Started

You will start by opening use the provided Exercise08-Starter file.

Open the session and save it as Exercise 8:

1. Launch Pro Tools and choose **FILE > OPEN SESSION** (or choose **OPEN FROM DISK** from the Dashboard).

2. Navigate to the starter session in the download media folder: PT Academy Media Files > 01. Starter Sessions > Exercise08-Starter.ptx.

3. Select and open the session. The session file will open displaying eight tracks in the Edit window.

4. Choose **FILE > SAVE AS** and navigate to your **Exercises-XXX** folder.

5. Name the session **Exercise08-XXX** (where **XXX** is your initials) and click **SAVE**.

6. Maximize the Edit window as needed to utilize the available space on your desktop. (On Mac, hold the **OPTION** key while clicking the Maximize button to enlarge the window without obscuring the menus.)

7. Use the **HORIZONTAL ZOOM OUT** button on the toolbar to zoom out as needed to see 30 seconds on the Min:Secs ruler. (You can also use the R key in Edit Focus mode to zoom out.)

   You may also want to resize the side columns (Tracks List and Clips List) to allow more screen real estate for your tracks area.

Figure 8.22 Showing 30 seconds on the Min:Secs ruler

8. Toggle the display to the Mix window by pressing **COMMAND+=** (Mac) or **CTRL+=** (Windows).

9. Maximize the Mix window as needed to utilize the available space (again holding **OPTION** on Mac).

Option 2, Part 2: Preparing to Record

To get started, you will need to route audio from the Scratch VO bus to the VO track for recording.

Route the signal to the audio input of the VO track:

1. Locate the **AUDIO INPUT PATH SELECTOR** for the VO track. This will be the top selector in the I/O section of the track. (See Figure 8.23.)

2. Click on the **AUDIO INPUT PATH SELECTOR** and select **BUS > SCRATCH VO (MONO)** to record the voiceover from existing audio included in the session.

 Audio Input Path selector

Figure 8.23 Audio Input Path selector for the VO track in the Mix window

3.   Record-enable the track by clicking on the **RECORD ENABLE** button so that it begins flashing red.

Figure 8.24 VO track after being record-enabled

Option 2, Part 3: Recording the Voiceover

With the input routed, you will now record the voiceover for the commercial.

To record the voiceover:

1.   If needed, choose **WINDOW > TRANSPORT** to display the Transport window; then disable the **COUNT OFF** button, if active (lit green). (See Figure 8.25.)

2.   With the **VO** track record-enabled, record-arm the Transport. The Record button will flash red.

Record button (active)   Count Off button (inactive)

Figure 8.25 The Transport window with countoff disabled and the session in Record Ready mode

3. Toggle the display to the Edit window by pressing **COMMAND+=** (Mac) or **CTRL+=** (Windows).

4. When ready, click the **PLAY** button or press the **SPACEBAR** to begin recording.

5. Let the script complete. Keep an eye on the Sub Counter display at the top of the Edit window and/or the Min:Sec ruler as you record. The voiceover should end shortly before reaching the 30-second mark (0:30.000).

6. When finished, click the **STOP** button or press the **SPACEBAR** a second time to stop recording.

Finishing Up

To complete this exercise tutorial, you will need to save your work and close the session. You will be reusing this session in Exercise 9, so it is important to save the work you've done.

You may also want to listen to your work before exiting.

Review and save your work:

1. Click the **RECORD ENABLE** button on the VO track to take the track out of record mode.

2. Press **ENTER** or **RETURN** to place the cursor at the beginning of the session.

3. Press the **SPACEBAR** to play back the session and hear your results.

4. Press the **SPACEBAR** a second time when finished.

5. Choose **FILE > SAVE** to save the session.

6. Choose **FILE > CLOSE SESSION** to close the session.

> (i) Remember that you cannot close a Pro Tools session by closing its windows. You must choose CLOSE SESSION from the FILE menu.

Getting Started with MIDI

The term MIDI (short for Musical Instrument Digital Interface) represents a protocol that enables keyboards, synthesizers, and other musical devices to interact with each other. Invented in the early 1980s, MIDI technology transformed the music industry. The protocol has become an essential tool for music creation of all kinds.

For this Lesson, we limit the discussion to the basics of what MIDI is and how it's commonly used on tracks in Pro Tools. Advanced MIDI operations are discussed in the next Lesson.

Learning Targets

■ Understand the basics of MIDI

■ Set up MIDI in Pro Tools

■ Learn about the MIDI controls in the Edit and Transport windows

■ Import and record MIDI

TOPIC 9.1:
MIDI BASICS

In order to understand MIDI, we need to go back to the early days of music technology.

Discussion: MIDI History and Background

In the late '70s and early '80s, many different electronic music manufacturers built new, powerful sound-making tools—primarily synthesizers. However, each was designed using proprietary technology. This meant that a keyboard made by one manufacturer would be incompatible with a sound module made by another; therefore, the two could not be used together.

The MIDI Protocol

At the 1981 convention for the National Association of Music Merchants (NAMM), two manufacturers proposed a way to connect musical devices that would allow electronic instruments made by different companies to easily communicate. The idea was enthusiastically supported by several other manufacturers.

Three years later, the MIDI specification was unveiled at the 1984 NAMM convention. Soon, virtually all music manufacturers worldwide had adopted this revolutionary standard.

Digital Sheet Music

One key characteristic of MIDI is that it has *no sound* by itself—it is *only* information that controls an instrument. MIDI data provides instructions for sound-producing devices in much the same way that sheet music provides instructions for musicians.

If a piece of music is placed before a tuba player, they will read the printed notes, tempo, dynamics, and so on. When they play the music, they translate it into sound produced through their tuba. If the same music were put in front of a saxophone player, they would translate it into sound through their sax. The printed music that guides both players has no sound on its own—MIDI works the same way.

MIDI data comprises different types of information. These can include:

- **MIDI Channels:** Most MIDI data is assigned to one of 16 MIDI channels. Channels allow for each piece of MIDI information to be directed differently. This is what allows a DAW to send a single stream of MIDI data that controls multiple sounds discretely.

- **Note Data:** Individual notes can be recorded and played back with specific pitch, timing, duration, and velocity. All this information is stored numerically.

- **Continuous Controllers:** MIDI can store non-note data, like volume, pitch change, and expression. These values can change smoothly over time, allowing sounds to change over the course of a performance or over the course of a single, held note.

- **Other:** MIDI also stores messages that affect a song more globally, such as tempo, meter, and key.

How Sound is Created with MIDI

Through the years, different kinds of MIDI setups have evolved. Let's take a look at some common configurations.

Keyboard Controllers and Sound Modules

In its early days, MIDI was primarily used to connect keyboard controllers with sound-creating modules. This connection was made with a five-pin DIN connector.

Figure 9.1 A MIDI 5-pin cable

The connection was easy enough—one end of the cable was connected to the MIDI keyboard's **MIDI Out** port, and the other was connected to a synthesizer module's **MIDI In** port.

Other Controllers

Over the years, MIDI controllers have taken on new forms, moving beyond the keyboard style. Alternative controllers like the Akai EWI (Electronic Wind Instrument), the Moog Theremini, and drum pad controllers like the M-Audio Trigger Finger enable performers to record MIDI data in different ways.

Figure 9.2 Alternate controllers: Moog Theremini (top left), Akai EWI (bottom left), M-Audio Trigger Finger (right)

Virtual Instruments

Today, hardware sound modules are not as common as they once were. MIDI controllers are still used, but they now typically control software synthesizers commonly called virtual instruments. These typically operate as plug-ins inside a DAW such as Pro Tools.

With the advent of virtual instruments, the way that MIDI controllers are connected has also changed. Although the traditional 5-pin cable is still around, today it is common for MIDI controllers to connect to computers via USB connections.

TOPIC 9.2:
MIDI AND INSTRUMENT TRACKS

As discussed above, MIDI isn't audible on its own. A common misconception is that MIDI and audio are directly related. This misunderstanding can cause inefficiency and frustration in getting MIDI to work.

Discussion: Virtual Instrument Configurations

Two common ways that MIDI is used in Pro Tools include (a) through a *MIDI track* and *Aux Input track* combination and (b) through an *Instrument track*.

MIDI plus Aux Input Track Workflow

Years ago, setting up virtual instruments in Pro Tools required using a MIDI track (to record and play back MIDI data), as well as an Aux Input track (to host the virtual instrument plug-in). This method can still be used today, although it is uncommon. The description below provides a quick overview of the process.

 The images in this section show the Edit window, but these workflows could easily be accomplished in the Mix window as well.

The first step is to create a MIDI track. In Figure 9.3, we've created a MIDI track named Piano.

Figure 9.3 A MIDI track in the Edit window

The next step is to create an *Aux Input* track for the virtual instrument. In Figure 9.4 we've added an Aux Input named Piano VI and then added the Xpand!2 virtual instrument using an Insert selector on the track.

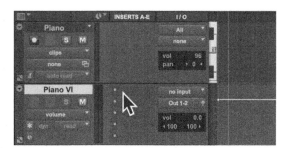 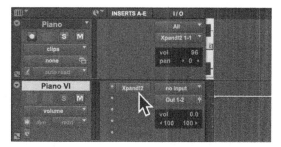

Figure 9.4 Clicking on Insert A of the Aux Input track (left); the Xpand!2 virtual instrument placed on Insert A (right)

Next, we connect the MIDI track's output to the virtual instrument, using the MIDI track's **OUTPUT SELECTOR** (bottom selector in the I/O section).

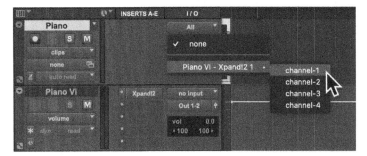

Figure 9.5 Routing the MIDI output from the Piano track to channel 1 of the Xpand!2 plug-in on the Piano VI track

The above steps can be used to configure a basic MIDI signal flow and the associated the audio signal routing that are required for playback through a virtual instrument. However, today there is an easier way.

Instrument Track Workflow

Instrument tracks are real timesavers for MIDI production, combining the power of a MIDI track and an Aux Input track into a single track. The setup steps are also simplified.

1. From the New Tracks dialog box, create a Stereo Instrument track with an appropriate name.

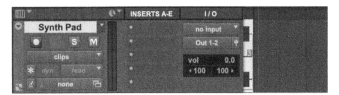

Figure 9.6 An Instrument track named Synth Pad in the Edit window, with Inserts A-E and the I/O view displayed

2. Use the top insert selector on the Instrument track to add a virtual instrument, such as Xpand!2. (Select **Multichannel Plug-in > Instrument > Xpand!2**.) (See Figure 9.7.)

> ⓘ To display the INSERTS A-E view in the Edit window, use the Edit Window View selector or select View > Edit Window Views > Inserts A-E.

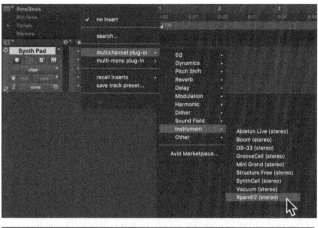

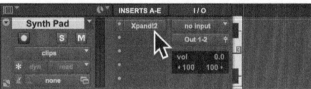

Figure 9.7 Selecting the Xpand!2 plug-in from Insert A (top); the Xpand!2 plug-in on the track (bottom)

Once a virtual instrument is added to an Instrument track, the MIDI Output on the track will automatically route to the plug-in.

Checking Your Work

The signal flow behind using MIDI for a virtual instrument is as follows:

- MIDI data routes through a MIDI or Instrument track (from a MIDI clip on the track or from a connected MIDI controller).

- The *MIDI Output* routes to a virtual instrument, which exists as a plug-in on an *Insert*.

- The virtual instrument responds to the MIDI data by creating audible sound.

- The *Audio Output* of the virtual instrument is routed to monitor speakers.

On an Instrument track, you can view the MIDI I/O and the MIDI meter in the Instrument view.

To display the Instrument view in the Edit window:

- Click the Edit Window View selector and choose **INSTRUMENT**.

 Alternatively, you can select View > Edit Window Views > Instrument to display the Instrument view from the main menus.

The Instrument view includes the following controls:

- **MIDI INPUT SELECTOR (1)** — This controls where the MIDI signal is coming from.

- **MUTE BUTTON (2)** — This will mute all MIDI data.

- **MIDI OUTPUT SELECTOR (3)** — This determines where MIDI data is going to, such as a virtual instrument (VI).

- **MIDI VOLUME (4)** — This displays the MIDI volume level for the track.

- **MIDI PAN (5)** — This displays the MIDI Pan position for the track.

- **MIDI VELOCITY METER (6)** — Shows how energetically each MIDI note is played.

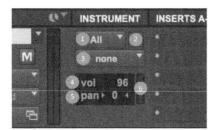

Figure 9.8 The Instrument view in the Edit window

To test your MIDI setup, you can record-enable the MIDI or Instrument track and play some notes on a connected MIDI controller. If you see activity in the MIDI meter, then you know that MIDI data is getting to the track. If you hear sound from the virtual instrument, then you know the virtual instrument is receiving the MIDI data and generating audio output.

If you don't have a MIDI keyboard handy, you can also test your setup using the mini keyboard on a track.

1. On the MIDI or Instrument track, click the **TRACK VIEW SELECTOR** (which will initially read Clips).

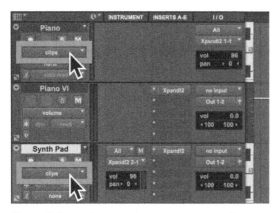

Figure 9.9 Track View selectors on MIDI and Instrument tracks

2. Choose the **Notes** view from the pop-up menu.

3. In Notes view, click on any note on the mini keyboard to the left of the track's playlist area. This will trigger the associated note, allowing you to audition playback.

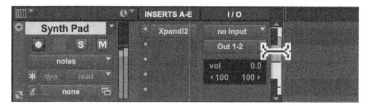

Figure 9.10 Auditioning a note on an Instrument track

If everything is set up properly, MIDI data will be created, the data will be sent to the virtual instrument, and the instrument will sound.

As yet another alternative, you can use the built-in virtual MIDI keyboard in Pro Tools (**WINDOW > MIDI KEYBOARD**) to test your setup. The virtual MIDI keyboard is introduced later in this lesson.

 For information on using the virtual MIDI keyboard, see Topic 9.4 toward the end of this lesson.

TOPIC 9.3:
MIDI CONTROLS

In Lesson 2, we explored the Edit window toolbar, including the MIDI Controls section. Now that we're starting to work with MIDI, we'll take a closer look at these tools and where they fit into a MIDI workflow.

Discussion: Functions in the MIDI Controls Section

The MIDI Controls section is available in the Edit window toolbar and in the Transport window. The available controls and their layout is the same in both locations.

Figure 9.11 The MIDI Controls section in the Edit window toolbar

Count Off Controls

A *count off* (also commonly called a "count-in") is a specific number of clicks played in tempo prior to starting a recording. This gives a musician the tempo information that they need so that they can play "in time" with the session. A typical count off will provide one or two bars of a metronome click.

In the MIDI Controls section, you'll find a **COUNT OFF** button that can be used to enable or disable the count off function. When the **COUNT OFF** button is active, the words will be shown in a green box. Clicking on this button will toggle its state.

Figure 9.12 Count Off display in the MIDI Controls section

You can change the count off settings from the **CLICK/COUNTOFF OPTIONS** dialog box, which you can access from the **SETUP** menu. You can also access this dialog box by double-clicking on the Count Off value displayed in the Edit window toolbar or in the Transport window.

The Count Off function can be enabled or disabled by pressing the [8] key on the numeric keypad of an extended keyboard.

Meter

As discussed in Lesson 5, the meter determines how many beats are in one measure, and which note increment gets the beat. For example, in 4/4 meter, there are 4 beats in a measure, and a quarter note gets one beat. In 5/8 meter, there are five beats in a measure, and an eighth note gets a beat.

Figure 9.13 Meter display in the MIDI Controls section

Double-clicking the meter value in the MIDI Controls section will open the Meter Change dialog box, allowing you to specify a meter for the session.

 The default meter in a Pro Tools session is 4/4.

Tempo

Also introduced in Lesson 5, tempo refers to the speed of the beats in a musical piece. Tempo is measured in beats per minute, or BPM.

Tempo works differently depending upon whether a session is in Manual Tempo mode or Tempo Map mode (following the Tempo Ruler). In Manual Tempo mode, you can easily change the tempo by selecting the tempo value and pressing the **T** key on your computer's keyboard in tempo.

Figure 9.14 Tempo controls in the MIDI Controls section

The default tempo for a Pro Tools session is 120 BPM.

Wait For Note

Normally, recording begins when the Record button is active and the Play button (or spacebar) is pressed. However, when you're working alone and your MIDI keyboard isn't close to your Pro Tools system, you can use the Wait for Note function to start a record pass.

When enabled, the **WAIT FOR NOTE** button will be colored blue. In this state, recording will not begin until a MIDI event is received (for example, when the first note is played on a keyboard).

Figure 9.15 The Wait for Note button in the MIDI Controls section

 Enabling Wait for Note will automatically disable Count Off.

If you use the Wait For Note feature frequently, you can enable a shortcut for this function. From the Preferences dialog box (**SETUP > PREFERENCES**), select the MIDI tab and enable the **USE F11 KEY FOR WAIT FOR NOTE** setting. This lets you activate or deactivate Wait For Note using Function key **F11**.

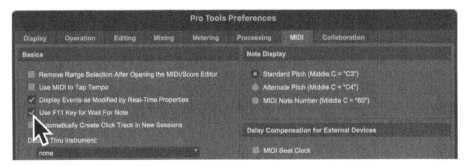

Figure 9.16 Enabling the F11 key for Wait For Note in Pro Tools Preferences

Metronome

The **Metronome** button is an easy way to enable or disable your click track. When enabled, the Metronome button will be colored blue. In this mode, the click track will be audible, following the settings in the Click/Countoff Options dialog box.

Figure 9.17 The Metronome button in the MIDI Controls section

If you need to make changes to the way your click behaves, you can easily access the **Click/Countoff Options** dialog box by double-clicking the **Metronome** button.

 The metronome click can be enabled or disabled by pressing the [7] key on the numeric keypad.

MIDI Merge

Normally, when you record MIDI over existing MIDI data, the new MIDI will replace the existing MIDI on the track. This behavior can be changed using the **MIDI Merge** button.

Figure 9.18 The MIDI Merge button in the MIDI Controls section

When MIDI Merge mode is enabled, the MIDI Merge button will be colored blue. When you record over existing MIDI data in this mode, the new data will be added into the existing data on the track. This is especially useful for things like MIDI drum recording, allowing for new drum parts to be added without recording over previously created drum parts.

 MIDI Merge mode can be enabled or disabled by pressing the [9] key on the numeric keypad.

Tempo Map Mode

As discussed in Lesson 5, Pro Tools can work in either Manual Tempo mode or Tempo Map mode. In Manual Tempo mode, the tempo in the tempo field is applied for the entire session. If you want to have the tempo change at any point during the session, you need to switch to Tempo Map mode. This is done using the **TEMPO RULER ENABLE** button.

Figure 9.19 Tempo Ruler Enable button in the MIDI Controls section

When active, the Tempo Ruler Enable button will be colored blue. In this mode, tempo changes can be applied in the Tempo ruler for your session.

 Workflows involving tempo maps are discussed in other courses in the Avid Learning Series.

TOPIC 9.4:
IMPORTING AND RECORDING MIDI

Now that we have set up our tracks, let's turn to the topic of acquiring MIDI data for a session.

Activity: Recording MIDI Drums

- Open the Activity 9.1.ptx session.

  The session with open showing the Drum VI track in the Edit window, along with a click track. It will also have the Transport window open and the onscreen MIDI Keyboard displayed.

- Record-arm both the Drum VI track and the session (Transport window). Ensure that MIDI Merge mode is enabled in the Transport window.

- Start the transport by clicking the **PLAY** button or by pressing the spacebar. (Make sure the **COUNT OFF** button is active in the Transport window.)

- After the count off, begin pressing the **A** key on your computer keyboard on every beat (1, 2, 3, 4) to create a kick drum pattern. Continue for 4 bars; then stop the transport.

- With the track still record-enabled, record-arm the transport again and start a second record pass.

- After the count off, begin pressing the **W** key on your computer keyboard on every other beat (Beats 2 and 4) to create a snare drum pattern. Continue for 4 bars; then stop the transport.

- Record-arm the transport again and start a third record pass.

- After the count off, begin pressing the **S** key on every 8th note (1, *and*, 2, *and*, 3, *and*, 4, *and*) to create a hi-hat pattern. Continue for 4 bars; then stop the transport.

- Repeat the process as desired, experimenting with different keys and patterns for additional parts.

Discuss what you've observed. How might you remove a part that you added if you weren't happy with the performance? How might you replace the entire recording if you wanted to start over?

Discussion: Acquiring MIDI Data

You can get MIDI data onto your tracks in a number of different ways. Here we'll look at two options: importing MIDI clips and recording MIDI notes.

Importing MIDI Clips

Importing MIDI into your session is similar to importing audio, but differs in one significant way—unlike imported audio clips, imported MIDI isn't referred to from a separate location on disk. Instead, the MIDI clips become part of the session file itself. This is because MIDI files are very small compared to audio files.

Pro Tools provides several ways that you can import a Standard MIDI File into your session.

To import by drag-and-drop, do one of the following:

- From your computer's file browser, navigate to a MIDI file that you want to import. (MIDI files will have a *.mid* file extension.) Drag the MIDI file from an open folder into your session's Edit window.

- From a Pro Tools Workspace browser, navigate to a MIDI file that you want to import. Drag the MIDI file from the Workspace browser into your session's Edit window.

To import from the menus:

1. From the **FILE** menu, select **IMPORT > MIDI**.

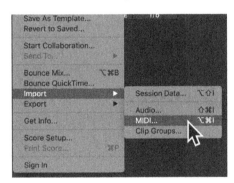

Figure 9.20 Importing MIDI from the File menu

A file browser will appear.

2. Navigate to the MIDI file that you want to import and click the **OPEN** button.

Regardless of which method you use, the **MIDI IMPORT OPTIONS** dialog box will appear.

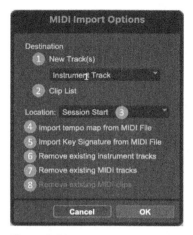

Figure 9.21 MIDI Import Options dialog box

The features in this dialog box include the following:

■ **NEW TRACK(S) (1)**—Choosing this option will import the MIDI to new tracks as needed. You can also choose whether to use Instrument or MIDI tracks from the associated menu.

■ **CLIP LIST (2)**—Clicking this radio button will import the MIDI data to the Clips List only.

■ **LOCATION (3)**—When importing to new tracks, this option lets you choose where on the timeline the MIDI clips will start. Available choices include **Session Start**, **Song Start**, **Selection**, and **Spot**.

■ **IMPORT TEMPO MAP FROM MIDI FILE (4)**—When checked, the tempo settings from the imported MIDI will overwrite the tempo settings in your session. When unchecked, the session's tempo settings will be unchanged.

■ **IMPORT KEY SIGNATURE FROM MIDI FILE (5)**—When checked, the key signature settings from the imported MIDI will overwrite the key signature settings in your session. When unchecked, your session's key signature settings will be unchanged.

■ **REMOVE EXISTING INSTRUMENT TRACKS (6)**—When checked, any Instrument tracks in your session will be permanently deleted. When unchecked, Instrument tracks in your session will be unchanged.

■ **REMOVE EXISTING MIDI TRACKS (7)**—When checked, any MIDI tracks in your session will be permanently deleted. When unchecked, MIDI tracks in your session will remain unchanged.

■ **REMOVE EXISTING MIDI CLIPS (8)**—When checked, any MIDI clips in your session will be permanently deleted. When unchecked, MIDI clips in your session will remain unchanged.

After choosing the appropriate settings in the MIDI Import Options dialog box, click the **OK** button to complete the import.

Recording MIDI

The process of recording MIDI is similar to audio recording in many respects, but with some additional flexibility.

 Before you start recording MIDI, you might want to set up a click track. Remember to use the Metronome button to enable the click.

Basic MIDI Recording

The first thing to address is how MIDI data gets into a track. MIDI tracks have their **MIDI INPUT SELECTOR** in the I/O section. On Instrument tracks, however, this selector is located in the **INSTRUMENT** section. In either case, the MIDI Input selector is set to **ALL** by default.

The **ALL** setting lets the track accept MIDI data from any port on any channel. This is convenient for basic MIDI recording. With **ALL** selected as the input, you can play any MIDI device connected to your computer and record to any record-enabled MIDI or Instrument track, without any further configuration.

To record MIDI data:

1.   Create a MIDI or Instrument track.

2.   (Optional) Verify that the track's MIDI input is set to **ALL**.

3.   Activate the track's **RECORD ENABLE** button to arm the track for recording.

4.   Click the **RECORD** button in the Transport window (or in the Edit Window Toolbar).

5.   Click the **PLAY** button or press the spacebar to start the transport. Recording will begin (after a count off, if enabled). As you play your MIDI instrument, MIDI data will record to the target track.

6.   When you're finished, stop the transport.

After recording MIDI, you'll see a MIDI clip on the track, similar to an audio clip. The MIDI clip will display MIDI note data within the clip rather than an audio waveform.

Recording with MIDI Merge

When you record over the top of an existing MIDI clip, you can choose between MIDI Merge mode and MIDI Replace mode. In MIDI Merge mode, instead of overwriting existing clips and MIDI data when you record, new MIDI data will be added to any MIDI data that already exists on the track.

A classic use of MIDI Merge mode is for recording a MIDI drum pattern. With MIDI Merge enabled, you can record a kick drum part first, then stack a snare drum part on top of it, then layer in hi-hats, cymbals, toms, hand claps, and so on. Although you might only play one part per pass, you'll end up with a single clip that contains all of the notes that you played, combined.

The steps to use MIDI Merge mode recording are as follows:

1. Record a first pass of your MIDI performance (for example, a Kick drum pattern).

2. Click the **MIDI MERGE** button in the MIDI Controls area of the Transport window or Edit Window Toolbar to enable MIDI Merge mode. The button will turn blue when active.

Figure 9.22 MIDI Merge mode enabled in the Transport window

3. Record a second pass of MIDI. The notes you play will be added to the existing part.

4. Repeat with subsequent passes, as needed, to add more parts.

With MIDI Merge recording, whenever you play, you'll add MIDI data to the clip. If you don't play anything during a pass, nothing new will be recorded, leaving the original MIDI unchanged. If you record something you don't like, you can use the **UNDO** command to undo just that record pass, keeping the MIDI from previous passes intact.

When you're finished recording with MIDI Merge mode, you'll have a clip that includes all the notes that you've played from all passes you've kept.

Recording with the Virtual MIDI Keyboard

To record MIDI data in Pro Tools, you can use an external MIDI keyboard or an alternate MIDI controller such as a drum pad. If you don't have a hardware MIDI controller, you can use the onscreen, virtual MIDI Keyboard. With this option, you can use your computer's keyboard as your MIDI controller.

To open the onscreen MIDI keyboard:

■   From the **WINDOW** menu, choose **MIDI KEYBOARD**. The virtual MIDI keyboard will appear. (See Figure 9.23.)

 To open and close the onscreen MIDI Keyboard from your computer keyboard, press Shift+K.

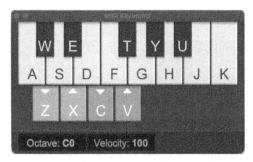

Figure 9.23 The Pro Tools onscreen MIDI Keyboard

This window is pretty simple, but let's break it down:

■ **A-K Keys:** The black and white piano keys of the MIDI Keyboard allow you to play notes. The physical layout of these keys on your computer keyboard is similar to a piano's keyboard, so when you press the A key, a C note will play; when you press the S key, a D note will play, and so on.

■ **Z and X Keys:** The range of the onscreen MIDI Keyboard is one octave (from one C to another). You can shift the octave of the keyboard down an octave by pressing the Z key, or you can shift up an octave by pressing the X key. The current octave is displayed in the lower left-hand corner of the screen, indicating the starting pitch of the currently targeted octave.

■ **C and V Keys:** These keys give you control over the MIDI velocity of the notes that you play. You can decrease the velocity by pressing the C key, or increase it by pressing the V key.

 MIDI velocity is discussed in Lesson 10 of this course book.

The recording process is identical to recording from an external MIDI controller:

1. Click on the track's **RECORD ENABLE** button to arm the MIDI or Instrument track for recording.

2. Click the **RECORD** button in the transport controls.

3. Click the **PLAY** button. Recording will begin (after the count off, if enabled).

4. Begin playing using the keys on your computer keyboard.

5. Stop the transport when finished.

Pro Tools' onscreen MIDI Keyboard makes recording MIDI easy and portable!

LESSON 9 CONCLUSION

In this Lesson, we talked about the basics of MIDI—from how MIDI functions to how to record MIDI data into Pro Tools. There's certainly more to talk about in the wide world of electronic music, but if you understand the concepts in this Lesson, you're off to a strong start.

Discussion: Summary of Key Concepts

In this Lesson, you learned:

- The basics of MIDI—what it is and what it can do

- How to set up MIDI in Pro Tools in two different ways: using a **MIDI** track in combination with an **AUX INPUT** track, or simply using an **INSTRUMENT** track

- The function and purpose of each of the MIDI controls in the Edit or Transport windows

- The basics of importing and recording MIDI

Essential Keyboard Commands and Shortcuts

Below is a summary of modifier behaviors and shortcut operations that you should know from this Lesson.

- To use the Tap Tempo function, select the tempo value displayed in the Transport window and press the **T** key on your computer's keyboard at the desired tempo.

- To enable the Wait for Note option, press Function key **F11** (when enabled in Preferences).

- To display the onscreen MIDI Keyboard, press **SHIFT+K**.

- To enable or disable the Metronome button, press the **[7]** key on the numeric keypad.

- To enable or disable the Count Off button, press the **[8]** key on the numeric keypad.

- To enable or disable the MIDI Merge button, press the **[9]** key on the numeric keypad.

Activity: Lesson 9 Knowledge Check

This quiz will check your knowledge on material covered in Lesson 9, Getting Started with MIDI.

1. True or False? MIDI on its own makes no sound.

2. Software synthesizers that operate as plug-ins inside of Pro Tools are known as _____.

3. What two track types support MIDI clips in Pro Tools?

4. What kind of track is commonly used with a MIDI track for hosting a virtual instrument?

5. What view on an Instrument track lets you click a note on the mini keyboard to trigger the virtual instrument and audition playback, as shown in the image?

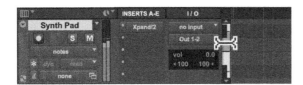

    a. Waveform view

    b. Clips view

    c. Notes view

    d. Blocks view

6. Refer to the Image: What is the name of the control outlined below?

    a. Wait for Note

    b. MIDI Merge

    c. Tap Tempo

    d. Tab to Transients

7.   What unit is Tempo measured in?

8.   True or False? When you import MIDI into Pro Tools, the MIDI file can either be referenced from its original location or copied into the MIDI Files folder within your session folder.

9.   Which MIDI record mode lets you record a MIDI drum performance in layers, adding the kick drum, snare drum, hi hats, and toms, each during a separate record pass?

   a. MIDI Replace mode

   b. MIDI Merge mode

   c. Percussive Record mode

   d. Record Safe mode

10. Which of the following options can be used to record MIDI data to a MIDI or Instrument track? (Select all that apply.)

   a. An external MIDI keyboard

   b. An external MIDI drum pad controller

   c. The Pro Tools onscreen MIDI Keyboard

   d. A microphone connected to an audio interface

Recording MIDI

In this exercise, you will start by adding a click track to your session and activating the metronome. Then you will assign the Xpand!2 virtual instrument to the existing **Beat Wave** track and record a MIDI performance on the track. Lastly, you'll import MIDI clips to use in your session.

Exercise Details

■   **Required Media:** BeatWaves.mid

■   **Exercise Duration:** 20 to 25 Minutes

Downloading the Media Files

To complete the exercises in this book, you will use files included in the **PT Academy Media Files** folder that you previously downloaded from the course learning module on ElementsED.com.

To re-download the media files, click on the **Access Files** link in the sidebar after logging in to your account. Consult your instructor or visit **nxpt.us/make-music** for more details.

Getting Started

You will start by opening the Pro Tools session you completed in Exercise 8. If that session is not available, you can use the provided **Exercise09-Starter** file in the **01. Starter Sessions** folder.

Open the session and save it as Exercise 9:

1.   Open the session file that you created in Exercise 8: **Storage Drive/Folder > Exercises-XXX > Exercise08-XXX.ptx**.

     Alternatively, you can use the Exercise09 Starter file: **PT Academy Media Files > 01. Starter Sessions > Exercise09-Starter.ptx**.

2. Choose **FILE > SAVE AS** and name the session Exercise09-XXX, keeping the session inside the original folder. (Move the session into your Exercises-XXX folder if working from the starter file.)

3. Click the **MUTE** button (**M**) on each of the existing tracks to temporarily mute them.

 Press OPTION (Mac) or ALT (Windows) while clicking the Mute button on any unmuted track to mute all of the tracks at once.

Configure Tracks

In this part of the exercise, you will add a click track to your session and configure the click settings. Then you will assign the Xpand!2 virtual instrument plug-in to the **Beat Wave** track. Lastly you will select an appropriate preset in Xpand!2 for the MIDI part you will be adding to the session.

Create a click track for the session:

1. Choose **TRACK > CREATE CLICK TRACK**. An Aux Input track named Click 1 will be added to your session.

2. Open the Transport window, if not already displayed, by choosing **WINDOW > TRANSPORT**.

3. Click on the **TRANSPORT WINDOW POP-UP** menu and verify that **MIDI CONTROLS** and **EXPANDED TRANSPORT** are enabled.

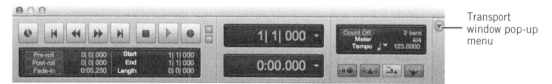

Transport window pop-up menu

Figure 9.24 MIDI Controls and Expanded Transport enabled in the Transport window

4. In the MIDI Controls section of the Transport window, verify that the **METRONOME** (click) button is enabled (blue). Turn off the **WAIT FOR NOTE** button, if active.

Assign a virtual instrument to the Instrument track:

1. Choose **WINDOW > MIX** or press **COMMAND+=** (Mac) or **CTRL+=** (Windows) to display the Mix window.

2. Click on **INSERT SELECTOR A** for the Beat Wave track and choose **MULTICHANNEL PLUG-IN > INSTRUMENT > XPAND!2 (STEREO)**. The Xpand!2 plug-in window will display.

3. Click on the **LIBRARIAN MENU** (displaying <factory default>) and select **04 ACTION PADS >
    18 SAMPLE HOLD PAD.** (Scroll down past +72 Take Off, where the numbering starts over at 01.)

Librarian menu

Figure 9.25 The Xpand!2 plug-in window

(i) You will have to scroll down past the "+##" presets to reach the 18 Sample Hold
     Pad preset.

4. When finished, close the Xpand!2 plug-in window.

Prepare to Record MIDI

In this part of the exercise, you will record a MIDI performance on the **Beat Wave** track. If you do not
have an available MIDI keyboard, you can use the onscreen MIDI keyboard (or skip this section and
proceed to "Importing MIDI Clips" on page 258).

Configure the session:

1. Do one of the following:

    • Verify that the MIDI device you will be using is powered on and connected to your system
       through an available MIDI In port or USB connection.

    • Choose **WINDOW > MIDI KEYBOARD** to display the onscreen virtual keyboard.

2. Choose **SETUP > PLAYBACK ENGINE** and verify that the H/W Buffer Size setting is set low, in order to minimize latency while recording.

(i) **For best results, use a H/W Buffer Size setting of 128 Samples or lower. Increase this setting only if Pro Tools displays frequent error messages during recording or playback.**

3. Press **COMMAND+=** (Mac) or **CTRL+=** (Windows) to toggle to the Edit window.

Make an 8-bar record-selection and activate count off:

1. Verify that the session is in **GRID** mode (blue Grid button on the left side of the toolbar), and set the grid to 1/4 notes (0|1|000) using the Grid Value pop-up selector on the right side of the toolbar.

Figure 9.26 Grid mode enabled (left); Grid value set to quarter notes (right)

2. Using the **SELECTOR** tool, make a selection on the **Beat Wave** track, extending from Bar 2 to Bar 10 (2|1|000 to 10|1|000).

(i) **Use the Start, End, and Length fields in the Counter area to verify your selection.**

3. Click the **COUNT OFF** button in the Transport window, if needed, so that it is highlighted in green.

Figure 9.27 Count Off button enabled in the Transport window (right side)

4. Record-enable the **Beat Wave** track and unmute the track.

5. Click the **RECORD** button in the Transport window to enable the session for recording. The Record button will flash red while the transport is stopped.

Record a MIDI Performance

In this section, you will record an 8-bar MIDI performance on the **Beat Wave** track. Review the instructions below before you begin, and practice the performance prior to recording.

Record the selection:

1.   If using the virtual MIDI Keyboard, press the **Z** key to transpose the keyboard down to octave **C2**.

Figure 9.28 The MIDI Keyboard window configured for octave C2

2.   When ready, click the **PLAY** button or press the **SPACEBAR** to start the count off. The count off will sound for two bars before the transport begins rolling.

3.   At the end of the two-bar count off, play the 8-bar pattern shown below. (See instructions below.)

Figure 9.29 8-bar musical pattern to record

For this recording, the timing does not need to be exact. You may want to release each note a little before the end of the bar to start the next note on time.

To play the pattern, do the following:

•   Play the **E2** key on your MIDI keyboard to begin the pattern. (Press **D** on your computer if using the virtual MIDI Keyboard.)

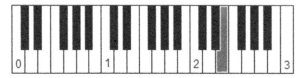

Figure 9.30 The E2 note on a standard piano keyboard

Hold the note steady for 4 bars; then release.

- Play the **A2** key on your MIDI keyboard to continue the pattern. (Press **H** on your computer if using the virtual MIDI Keyboard.)

Figure 9.31 The A2 note on a standard piano keyboard

Hold the note steady for 2 bars and release.

- Play the **E2** key again for the end of the pattern. (Press **D** on your computer if using the virtual MIDI Keyboard.) Hold the note steady for the final 2 bars.

When finished, your recording should look similar to Figure 9.32.

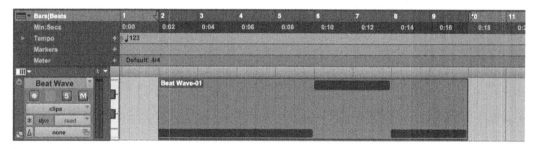

Figure 9.32 Desired result after completing the 8-bar recording

4. Review your results. If you are not happy with the recording, choose **EDIT > UNDO MIDI RECORDING** and try again.

5. **Challenge (optional):** Select the next nine bars on the **Beat Wave** track (from **10|1|000** to **19|1|000**) and record the 9-bar pattern shown below.

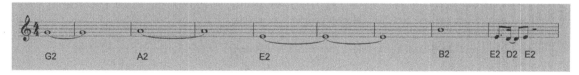

Figure 9.33 9-bar musical pattern to record

6. When finished, click the **RECORD ENABLE** button on the **Beat Wave** track to disable recording.

7. Next, disable the **COUNT OFF** and **METRONOME** buttons in the Transport window. Also close the MIDI Keyboard window if it is open.

Importing MIDI Clips

In this section, you will import MIDI clips from the BeatWaves.mid file provided with the PT Academy Media Files. You will use these clips to finish the performance on the Beat Wave track.

Import MIDI to the session:

1. Choose **FILE > IMPORT MIDI** and navigate to the Exercise Media folder: PT Academy Media Files > 02. Exercise Media.

2. Select the BeatWaves.mid file and click **OPEN**. The MIDI Import Options dialog box will appear.

3. In the MIDI Import Options dialog box, select **CLIP LIST** as the destination and click **OK**. (See Figure 9.34.) Two new clips will be placed in the Clip List (1st Wave-01 and 2nd Wave-01).

Figure 9.34 The MIDI Import Options dialog box with Clip List selected as the destination

Place MIDI clips on the Beat Wave track to finish the performance:

1. If you are not happy with initial 8-bar MIDI recording you completed in the previous section, you can replace it with the first MIDI clip you've imported:

   • Using the **GRABBER** tool, select just the 1st Wave-01 MIDI clip in the Clip List.

   • Drag the clip onto the Beat Wave track and position it to start at Bar 2.

2. If you did not complete the 9-bar challenge recording, or if you are not happy with the results, you can use the second MIDI clip you imported:

   • With the **GRABBER** tool, select just the 2nd Wave-01 clip in the Clip List.

   • Drag the clip onto the Beat Wave track and position it to start at Bar 10.

Finishing Up

To complete this exercise, you will need to save your work and close the session. You will be reusing this session in Exercise 10, so it is important to save the work you've done.

You should also listen to your progress thus far before exiting.

Review and save your work:

1. Press **ENTER** or **RETURN** to place the cursor at the beginning of the session.

2. **OPTION-CLICK** (Mac) or **ALT-CLICK** (Windows) on the mute control of any muted track to unmute all of the tracks. Then re-enable the Mute control on the **Fire FX** track.

3. Press the **SPACEBAR** to play back the session and review your results.

4. Press the **SPACEBAR** a second time when finished.

5. Choose **FILE > SAVE** to save the session.

6. Choose **FILE > CLOSE SESSION** to close the session.

(i) Remember that you cannot close a Pro Tools session by closing its windows. You must choose CLOSE SESSION from the FILE menu.

Working with MIDI in Pro Tools

For this Lesson, we discuss how MIDI is commonly used in Pro Tools. This Lesson introduces some MIDI skills that any engineer might need when working with a MIDI musician in a studio environment.

Learning Targets

- Select appropriate virtual instruments and assign sounds

- Measure time in bars, beats, and ticks

- Understand how tick-based timing affects MIDI data

- Edit MIDI clips, notes, velocities, and continuous controller data

- Apply meter and tempo changes

TOPIC 10.1:
WORKING WITH VIRTUAL INSTRUMENTS

Now that you know how to get MIDI data onto tracks, we'll spend some time focusing on virtual instruments—how to choose the right one for the job and how to pick a sound for your tracks.

Discussion: Pro Tools Virtual Instrument Plug-ins

Like physical instruments, virtual instruments—VIs for short—come in all shapes and sizes. You have numerous VIs to choose from, with a dizzying array of creative tools. To get started, let's review some of the instruments that are included with Pro Tools Artist.

 All instruments discussed here are included with Pro Tools Artist; however, they are not automatically installed with Pro Tools. If any of these instruments are missing on your system, see the discussion on Installing Plug-Ins in Lesson 1 and review the steps outlined in Exercise 1.

Xpand!2

Xpand!2—created by the Advanced Instrument Research (AIR) group—is an example of a multi-timbral synthesizer. This plug-in has four parts, giving it the ability to create everything from layered leads and pads, to a respectable selection of drum kits.

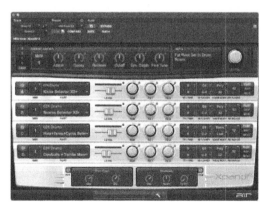

Figure 10.1 The Xpand!2 virtual instrument plug-in

Xpand!2 is a workhorse VI and is a great place to start when looking for a specific sound or instrument. One of the strengths of this instrument is the sheer number and variety of presets that it includes. You'll find presets for trumpets, violins, drum kits, choirs, pianos, bells, guitars, basses, xylophones, sitars, flutes, saxophones, trombones, timpani, synthesizers, and a whole lot more.

Boom

AIR's Boom virtual instrument is based on classic drum machines like the Roland TR-707 and TR-808. Drum patterns can be created using a 16th note pattern sequencer (on the left side of the plug-in window). Clicking on an "LED" will add a note on that step; successive clicks will cycle through velocity levels before removing the note.

Figure 10.2 The Boom drum machine virtual instrument

MIDI notes from C1 to D#2 trigger individual drum hits in Boom. MIDI notes from C3 to D#4 trigger each of the 16 drum patterns available through the pattern sequencer.

Mini Grand

AIR's Mini Grand is a great-sounding piano plug-in with just a few simple parameters. Although many other piano plug-ins exist on the market, Mini Grand can get you great sounds with minimal fuss!

Figure 10.3 The Mini Grand piano virtual instrument

DB-33

Another simple but effective plug-in instrument, AIR's DB-33 emulates a drawbar organ, paired with a rotating speaker. This VI is based on the Hammond B3, used in a wide range of styles, from rock to jazz.

Figure 10.4 The DB-33 drawbar organ virtual instrument

Vacuum

AIR's Vacuum emulates a vacuum tube synthesizer, a longtime favorite for all kinds of sounds. This instrument is especially useful for lead and bass sounds that can drive a mix.

Figure 10.5 The Vacuum synthesizer virtual instrument

Structure Free

Last on the list from AIR, Structure Free is a kind of MIDI instrument called a *sampler*. Simply put, a sampler uses short recordings (called "samples"), letting you play them from a MIDI keyboard. Samplers are especially well suited to recreating real instrument sounds, like drums, strings, or vocal phrases.

Figure 10.6 The Structure Free virtual instrument

SynthCell

Avid's SynthCell is a simple but flexible synthesizer plug-in. SynthCell features 32-note polyphony, two filters, two operators, a built-in arpeggiator, and integrated effects (reverb, delay, modulation, and distortion).

Figure 10.7 Avid's SynthCell virtual instrument

GrooveCell

Avid's GrooveCell emulates popular pad-based drum machines. This virtual instrument allows for sample layering (up to 3 layers per pad), has a built-in sequencer, and includes a host of other useful features. You can even drag clips directly from Pro Tools onto the pads to create drum kits from your own sounds!

Figure 10.8 Avid's GrooveCell virtual instrument

 Avid's latest virtual instrument, PlayCell, is a sample player with a large library of drums, pianos, guitars, basses, synths, orchestral instruments, and more. It includes a selectable list of musical scales to ensure you're never composing out of key and provides four macro controls to help you dial in the perfect sound.

Choosing Sounds

Once you've chosen an instrument to use, your next step is to pick the sound that you want. Most virtual instrument plug-ins include a number of presets that you can use for this purpose.

Presets are used by all types of plug-ins in Pro Tools. Presets are simply preconfigured settings for the plug-in.

 Sound presets for virtual instruments are often referred to as *patches*. This term finds its roots in the earliest days of synthesis, when different sounds were created by connecting (or patching) different electronic components together.

To select a preset for a virtual instrument:

1. If the plug-in window isn't open already, click the Insert button on the track. It will highlight, and the plug-in window will open.

2. Click the **LIBRARIAN** menu (which will initially display <factory default>). A menu of available sounds will appear, sometimes nested into submenus.

3. Choose the desired sound from the menu.

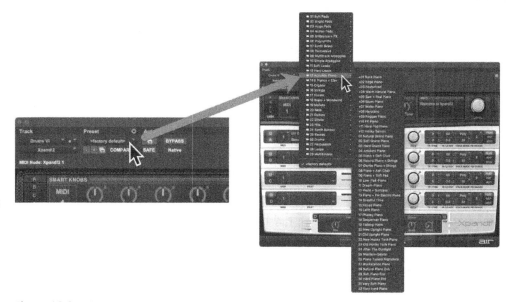

Figure 10.9 Selecting a sound using a preset from a plug-in's Librarian menu

Following are a few specific ways to work with some of the virtual instruments included with Pro Tools.

Choosing Parts in Xpand!2

You can change sounds within a preset by adding, removing, or changing sounds within any of Xpand!2's four layers (called *Parts*). Clicking the small triangle in the top right-hand corner of the part display will reveal a list of part presets that you can use. This lets you create custom layered sounds.

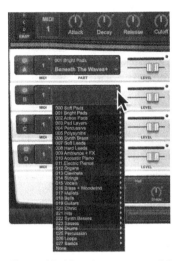

Figure 10.10 Selecting a sound for Part B in Xpand!2

 Each of Xpand!2's parts can be turned on or off at any time by clicking the Power button above the part letter. (When active, the Power button is colored green.)

Choosing a Drum Kit in Boom

To change the sound of the drums in the Boom virtual instrument, you can select a different drum kit. Just click the **DRUM KIT** menu button in the lower left-hand corner of the plug-in window. (This button will ordinarily display the currently used kit.)

From the pop-up menu, you can experiment with the 10 different kits provided with Boom. You can even change kits while Boom is playing, to pick out the best drum sound and style for your song.

Choosing a Piano in Mini Grand

The presets that come with the Mini Grand virtual instrument are especially useful, considering how central a good piano sound is to many compositions. These presets include everything from tuning to ambience, and of course, the kind of piano that is being used.

You can change the piano that is used by going to the **MODEL** knob and choosing from seven different fundamental sounds. If you find that a *Real* piano sound is getting lost in the mix, try changing to *Hard* and listen to the difference!

TOPIC 10.2:
TIME AND MIDI

Early in this course, you learned about samples and how they relate to digital audio. Audio files have a set number of samples per second. These samples play back at the same speed every time, so the audio characteristics don't change. For example, a one-minute audio file will always take one minute to play back.

Audio files are based on absolute time (hours, minutes, and seconds) and typically don't change their placement or duration based on tempo changes in a session.

Discussion: MIDI Data and Tempo

MIDI data is entirely different from audio. We typically want MIDI notes to change their speed, placement, and duration in response to the session tempo. In this section, we'll look at how MIDI makes this happen.

What is a Tick?

A tick is the smallest measurement of time used when working in Bars and Beats. Ticks are subdivisions of a quarter note. Pro Tools provides 960 ticks per quarter note. Ticks can designate musical measurements that are shorter than a quarter note. They can also indicate locations that are not exactly on a quarter note beat.

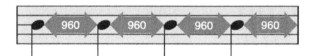

Figure 10.11 Pro Tools provides 960 subdivisions (ticks) between each beat in a measure.

Measuring in Ticks

Here's a scenario: Let's say that a musician plays a piece of music that consists of four quarter notes.

Figure 10.12 Four written quarter notes

Because humans may not play with absolute precision, a recorded MIDI performance will typically have some imperfections, as shown in Figure 10.13. In this illustration, you'll see that the second note is noticeably late—it is behind the beat at Bar 1, Beat 2 (shown as 1|2 on the Bars|Beats ruler). The fourth note of the performance is early, coming in slightly ahead of the beat at 1|4.

Figure 10.13 An imperfect performance recorded on a MIDI track

Ticks allow us to measure the imperfections in this performance. Here are the note locations, measured numerically in Bars, Beats, and Ticks:

■ The second note of the performance has a numeric location of Bar 1, Beat 2, Tick number 136. This is represented as 1|2|136 in the Main Counter when the note is selected. This number indicates that the note is *136 ticks behind* the beat.

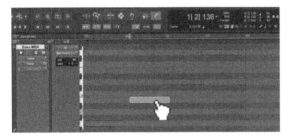

Figure 10.14 The second note in the performance selected

■ The fourth note of the performance is at Bar 1, Beat 3, Tick number 897. This is represented as 1|3|897 in the Main Counter when the note is selected. With 960 ticks in the beat, this tells us the note is *63 ticks ahead* of beat four (1|4|000).

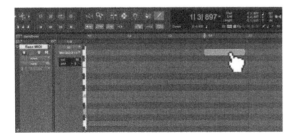

Figure 10.15 The fourth note in the performance selected

 The beginnings of notes aren't the only things measured in ticks; the ends of notes are also tick-based, which means that the starts, ends, and durations of the notes that you play can be designated down to 1/960th of a quarter note.

Track Timebases

Tracks in Pro Tools can be either *sample*-based or *tick*-based. MIDI and Instrument tracks are tick-based by default. This means that their contents are aligned to specific Bar|Beat|Tick locations. All other tracks are generally sample-based, meaning their contents are aligned to specific sample-number locations.

When you set the Main Counter to **BARS|BEATS**, you can view the passage of time in your session in bars, beats, and ticks. You'll see that the spacing of the grid lines changes as you change your session tempo: the higher the tempo, the faster the MIDI will play, and the closer the grid spacing will become.

Timebases and Tempo

Typically, you'll want your MIDI recordings to respond to tempo changes. Tick-based timing facilitates this. Because the clips, notes, and other data on MIDI and Instrument tracks are locked to Bar|Beat|Tick locations, they move in sync with the bars and beats when the tempo is changed.

A tick-based track is indicated by a green metronome icon in the lower left-hand corner of the track.

 A sample-based track is indicated by a small blue clock icon in the lower left-hand corner of the track.

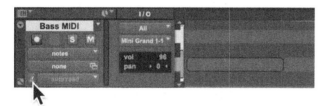

Figure 10.16 A track using tick-based timing, as indicated by the green metronome icon under the mouse cursor

You can change a track's timebase by clicking on the track's Timebase Selector and changing from **TICKS** to **SAMPLES** (or vice versa) in the menu that appears.

 When a track is set to use sample-based timing, clips, notes, and other events on the track will not respond to tempo changes.

 Audio tracks, Aux Input tracks, and Master Fader tracks are sample-based by default in Pro Tools Studio and Pro Tools Ultimate.

 You can change the default timebase for Audio tracks, Aux Inputs, and Master Faders by choosing Setup > Preferences, selecting the Editing tab, and enabling the New Tracks Default to Tick Timebase checkbox.

TOPIC 10.3:
EDITING MIDI

You've already learned how to use the basic Edit tools (Trim, Selector, and Grabber) with audio clips. These functions also apply to MIDI. But because MIDI is fundamentally different from audio, you have a few more editing operations to consider.

Discussion: MIDI Editing Operations

The first thing to consider when editing MIDI data is the track view. The Track View selector can be used to select different kinds of information to display on a given track. (Different track types will have different views available in this list.)

Depending on the track view you select for a MIDI or Instrument track, you will be able to make different kinds of adjustments using various Edit tools.

MIDI Track Views

MIDI and Instrument tracks have three primary track views that you can use to edit a performance: Clips view, Notes view, and Velocity view. You can change the current view by clicking on the **TRACK VIEW SELECTOR**, located just below the Record, Solo, and Mute buttons.

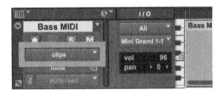

Figure 10.17 The Track View Selector on a MIDI track

Clips View

The default view of a MIDI or Instrument track is the Clips view. When you're in Clips view, you'll see your MIDI data in clip-sized blocks.

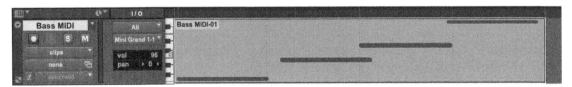

Figure 10.18 Clips view on a MIDI track

If you need to trim, select, or move a clip, this is the view you want. In this regard, editing is very similar to the work you've already done with Audio tracks.

Notes View

When you need to edit specific notes, you can work in Notes view. Changing to Notes view will give you access to each individual note, so that you can change it independently of other notes.

To switch to Notes view, click the **TRACK VIEW SELECTOR**. A list of options will display, with the currently active view checked. On a MIDI or Instrument track, you'll find **NOTES** just below **CLIPS** view in the menu.

In Notes view, you may see notes at the top or bottom of the track that are skinnier than the others—for example in the image shown below, the first and last of the four notes display as thin lines. This indicates that those notes are out of range of the current view.

Figure 10.19 Notes out of the visible range

You can scroll the viewing range by clicking the up or down arrow icons at the top or bottom of the Mini Keyboard on the left side of the track.

 MIDI vertical zooming will come in handy when working in Notes view. The MIDI vertical zoom button is in Zoom Controls area of the Edit window's toolbar, to the right of the Edit Mode buttons.

In Notes view, your Edit tools will take on different functions:

- The Trim tool can be used to adjust a note's length: move the cursor near the start or end of a note and drag to the desired point. As with trimming clips, the Trim operation will be subject to the current Edit mode. Choose **SLIP** mode for smooth dragging or **GRID** mode to snap edit points to the grid.

- The Selector tool lets you select a range of notes in Notes view; however, only notes whose start point is within the selection will be included. Selected notes can be further edited (copied, deleted, and so on).

- Double-clicking with the Selector tool in Notes view will select the area of the clip (or space between clips) where you are clicking. Triple-clicking will select all notes on the entire track.

- The Grabber tool lets you click on an individual note to select that note. You can also drag a note up or down to a new pitch location or forward or backward to a new time location. To select multiple notes with the Grabber, hold the **SHIFT** key while clicking.

 As with clips, holding the OPTION key (Mac) or ALT key (Windows) will create a copy as you drag, leaving the original note(s) unchanged.

Velocity View

MIDI velocity is a powerful parameter that can breathe life into your MIDI projects.

Velocity refers to the speed, or force, that a performer used to play a MIDI note. Notes that are played faster, with more velocity, typically result in an increased amplitude for the instrument. Velocity may also affect the timbre or character of the sound. Each instrument responds to velocity in different ways, but changes in velocity will generally result in changes in amplitude and tonal color.

 To get a MIDI composition to sound more lifelike while making it louder, raise the velocity before you reach for the volume fader. This will give you an amplitude and tonal change that will more naturally emulate what "real" instruments do.

To display MIDI velocity in Pro Tools:

1. Click the **TRACK VIEW SELECTOR** on a MIDI or Instrument track.

2. Select **VELOCITY** (just below Notes view in the menu).

In Velocity view, you'll see a vertical line with a diamond at the top at the beginning of each note. This line, called a velocity stalk, indicates the velocity value for that note: The taller the line, the higher the velocity.

As with Notes view, your Edit tools will take on different functions in this view:

■ The Selector tool will allow you to select multiple velocity stalks by clicking and dragging.

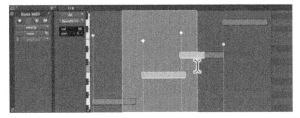

Figure 10.20 Selecting velocity stalks with the Selector tool

■ The Grabber tool will change to a finger icon when positioned near the top of a velocity stalk. Dragging up or down will change the velocity value for the associated note (or all selected notes).

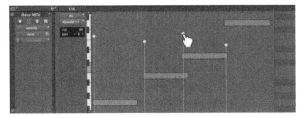

Figure 10.21 Changing velocity with the Grabber tool

Changing velocity for an unselected note will cause the note to become selected.

Editing MIDI with the Pencil Tool

Notes view is where the Pencil tool really shines! The tool changes function based on the position of your cursor, as follows:

- Placing the cursor over the middle of a note will make the Pencil tool behave like the Grabber tool, enabling you to select and move the note.

Figure 10.22 Using the Pencil tool to move a note

- Placing the cursor close to the beginning or end of a note will make the Pencil tool behave like the Trim tool, allowing you to adjust the note duration. (See Figure 10.23.)

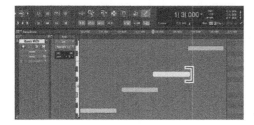

Figure 10.23 Using the Pencil tool to trim a note

- When positioned in an area where there is no note, the Pencil tool will allow you to create a new MIDI note by clicking on the track.

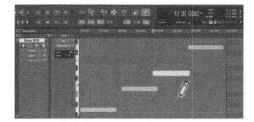

Figure 10.24 Using the Pencil tool to create a new MIDI note

■ Holding the **OPTION** key (Mac) or **ALT** key (Windows) will flip the Pencil tool over, to become an eraser. Clicking on a note while using the eraser will delete it.

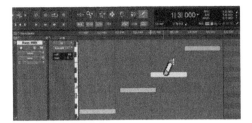

Figure 10.25 Using the Pencil tool to delete a MIDI notes

 You can also erase MIDI notes with the Pencil tool by double-clicking on them in Notes view.

In Velocity view, the Pencil tool can also be quite powerful: You can click and drag to "draw" velocity changes over multiple MIDI notes. Many musicians think of musical phrases as organic curves, with their own peaks and valleys—the Pencil tool makes it easy to draw those kinds of velocity changes.

Volume, Pan, and Continuous Controllers

Other views are available from the Track View selector—parameters like MIDI Volume, MIDI Pan, and MIDI Continuous Controllers. These parameters can change continuously over time. The data for these parameters is shown on a line graph, such as the **Pitch Bend** graph shown in Figure 10.26 below.

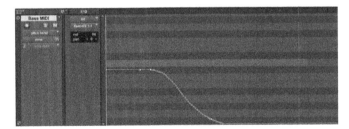

Figure 10.26 Pitch Bend continuous controller data

Here's how the Edit tools behave when working with MIDI continuous controller graphs:

■ The Pencil tool lets you draw the parameter line, according to Pencil tool mode you've chosen. Drawing with the Pencil tool creates a series of connected dots, called breakpoints.

■ The Selector tool lets you select a range of breakpoints, after which you can cut, copy, and paste.

■ The Trim tool can be used to increase or decrease the value of breakpoints by dragging up or down. After selecting a target range with the Selector tool, you can scale it up or down with the Trim tool.

■ The Grabber tool lets you work with single breakpoints:

   • Click where there are no existing breakpoints to create a new breakpoint.

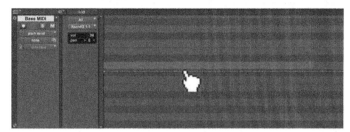

Figure 10.27 Creating a breakpoint with the Grabber tool

   • Click on an existing breakpoint to move it to a new location (left, right, up, or down).

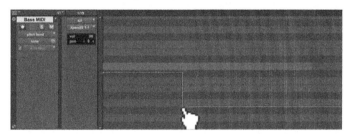

Figure 10.28 Moving a breakpoint with the Grabber tool

   • Hold **OPTION** (Mac) or **ALT** (Windows) while clicking on an existing breakpoint to delete it. (A small minus sign next to the finger icon indicates that the targeted breakpoint will be removed.)

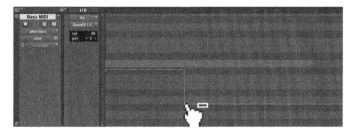

Figure 10.29 Deleting a breakpoint

TOPIC 10.4:
MORE WAYS TO WORK WITH MIDI

In this section, we take a quick look at how you might work more deeply with MIDI data. Here we explore advanced features for changing tempo and timing in a session, as well as advanced features for fine-tuning a MIDI performance.

Discussion: Working with the Graphic Tempo Editor

You learned how to set a basic tempo in Lesson 7. Earlier in this current lesson, you learned how tempo changes affect your tick-based tracks and rulers. Here, you'll learn another way to make changes, using the Graphic Tempo Editor.

To create graphic tempo changes:

1.   Click the triangle icon at the far left of the Tempo ruler to reveal the Graphic Tempo Editor. The tempo ruler will expand to show a tempo graph.

2.   Using the Pencil tool, draw tempo changes on the tempo graph. The Pencil tool allows you to create tempo curves, based on the currently active Pencil mode. Figure 10.30 shows a curve drawn with the **Free Hand** Pencil mode.

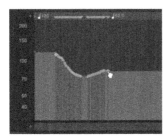

Figure 10.30 Drawing tempo changes with the Pencil tool

Insert Time and Cut Time

Another way to work with time is through the **TIME OPERATIONS** window. This window lets you insert time on the session timeline or cut time from the timeline, among other operations. To access the Insert Time or Cut Time operations, choose **EVENT > TIME OPERATIONS > INSERT TIME** or **EVENT > TIME OPERATIONS > CUT TIME**. The Time Operations window will open with the selected operation displayed.

The Insert Time operation (Figure 10.31) allows you to add a blank area anywhere in your timeline and shift elements in your mix later in your timeline. If you need to add a few bars between the first and second verse and shift tempo changes, clips, and other MIDI data later in time, Insert Time is your solution.

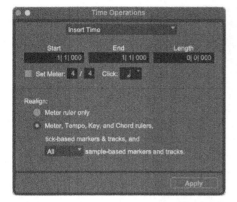

Figure 10.31 The Insert Time window

The opposite of Insert Time, the Cut Time operation allows you to remove any area of your timeline and shift subsequent material earlier in your timeline. Like Insert Time, this operation lets you including tempo changes and other MIDI data.

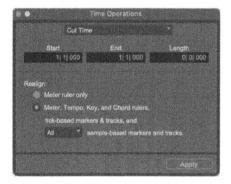

Figure 10.32 The Cut Time window

The Event Operations Window

Next we'll take a look at the Event Operations window and its operations. This window and its associated operations can be found under **EVENT > EVENT OPERATIONS**. (See Figure 10.33.) Most of the operations available here are traditional MIDI processes.

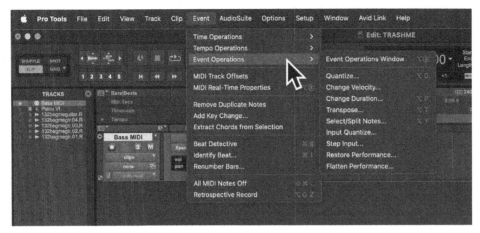

Figure 10.33 The Event > Event Operations menu

Included in the Event Operations window (and the Event Operations submenu) are the following operations:

- **Quantize:** This operation changes the timings of notes, aligning them to a selected grid value.

- **Change Velocity:** This operation changes the velocity of notes in different ways, including scaling them or randomizing their values.

- **Change Duration:** This operation changes the duration of notes, including removing any overlap of notes or changing the gaps between notes.

- **Transpose:** This operation shifts the pitch of notes up or down.

- **Select/Split Notes:** This operation selects notes based on different criterion and optionally lets you split them to new tracks. This operation is commonly used to split multiple drum notes of a MIDI drum performance to individual MIDI tracks (each track having only one drum part on it).

- **Input Quantize:** This operation changes the timing of MIDI notes during the record process.

- **Step Input:** This operation allows notes to be recorded from a MIDI controller one at a time, without having to record MIDI data in real time.

- **Restore Performance:** This operation reverts MIDI to the original performance, removing transformations made by quantizing, changing velocity, changing duration, or transposing notes.

- **Flatten Performance:** This operation creates a new restore point for a MIDI performance. Once an area is flattened, any later Restore Performance operation will go back to this state.

LESSON 10 CONCLUSION

In this Lesson, you learned advanced MIDI operations—from using virtual instruments to the effects of tempo on MIDI data and various ways to edit MIDI information. You also learned some advanced operations for working with tempo and time.

Discussion: Summary of Key Concepts

In this Lesson, you learned:

- How to choose the right Virtual Instrument for the job, and then how to choose the right sound preset (or "Patch") within that plug-in

- The difference between *ticks* and *samples*, and how tempo changes affect the timing of MIDI information

- How to edit different kinds of MIDI data, using various Edit tools (including the Pencil tool) and different track views in the Pro Tools Edit window

- How to work with tempo and time, as well as the basic functions included in the Event Operations window

Essential Keyboard Commands and Shortcuts

Below is a summary of modifier behaviors and shortcut operations that you should know from this Lesson.

- To flip the Pencil tool, turning it into an eraser, hold the **OPTION** key (Mac) or **ALT** key (Windows).

- To delete breakpoints with the Grabber tool, hold the **OPTION** key (Mac) or **ALT** key (Windows).

Activity: Lesson 10 Knowledge Check

This quiz will check your knowledge on material covered in Lesson 10.

1. Match the Virtual Instrument to its description.

Xpand!2	Electronic drum kit based on classic drum machines
Boom	Drawbar organ virtual instrument
Mini Grand	Four-part multi-timbral virtual instrument with a large library of presets
DB-33	Based on tube synthesizers
Vacuum	Great sounding but simple piano virtual instrument

2. How can you select different sounds, or "patches," in a virtual instrument?

    a. Click the TRACK VIEW SELECTOR under the Record, Solo, and Mute buttons.

    b. Click the LIBRARIAN menu in the plug-in window (where it displays <factory default>).

    c. Select the desired sound under the Edit menu.

    d. Click the Plug-In Automation Enable button in the plug-in window.

3. How many ticks are there in a quarter note in Pro Tools?

4. Which of the following is true of tick-based tracks in Pro Tools?

    a. Their contents are aligned to Bar|Beat locations.

    b. Their contents are aligned to Sample locations.

    c. Their contents are aligned to Min:Secs locations.

5. True or False. MIDI recordings typically respond to tempo changes in your session, speeding up when the session tempo increases and slowing down when the tempo decreases.

6.   What track view do you need to use on a MIDI or Instrument track to edit a MIDI note with the Grabber tool, moving it to a different pitch?

   a. Clips view

   b. Notes view

   c. Velocity view

   d. Pitch view

7.   Refer to the Image: The **Bass MIDI** track is shown in _____ view.

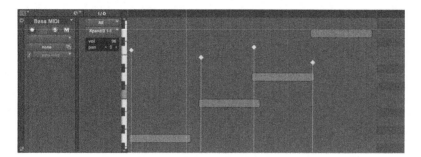

8.   True or False. The Selector tool functions as a Grabber when placed over the middle of a MIDI note and as a Trim tool when placed near the start or end of a MIDI note.

9.   What modifier can you hold while editing MIDI with the Pencil tool to flip the tool over to act as an eraser in order to delete MIDI notes?

10. Which of the following functions does the Grabber tool provide when editing breakpoints on a continuous controller graph?

   a. Lets you add new breakpoints by clicking on the graph with the Grabber tool

   b. Lets you select a range of breakpoints by clicking and dragging on the graph with the Selector tool

   c. Lets you invert existing breakpoints by clicking on them with the Scrubber tool

   d. Lets you remove breakpoints by **OPTION-CLICKING** (Mac) or **ALT-CLICKING** (Windows) with the Grabber tool

Adding MIDI and Virtual Instruments

In this exercise tutorial, you will import existing MIDI clips to supplement your MIDI recording. You will also configure additional virtual instruments to create a unique sound for your music tracks.

Exercise Details

■   **Required Media:** SynthBits.mid

■   **Exercise Duration:** 15 to 20 Minutes

Downloading the Media Files

To complete the exercises in this book, you will use files included in the **PT Academy Media Files** folder that you previously downloaded from the course learning module on ElementsED.com.

To re-download the media files, click on the **Access Files** link in the sidebar after logging in to your account. Consult your instructor or visit **nxpt.us/make-music** for more details.

Getting Started

You will start by opening the Pro Tools session you completed in Exercise 9. If that session is not available, you can use the provided Exercise10-Starter file in the **01. Starter Sessions** folder.

Open the session and save it as Exercise 10:

1.   Open the session file that you created in Exercise 9: Storage Drive/Folder > Exercises-XXX > Exercise09-XXX.ptx.

     Alternatively, you can use the Exercise10 Starter file: PT Academy Media Files > 01. Starter Sessions > Exercise10-Starter.ptx.

2.   Choose **FILE > SAVE AS** and name the session Exercise10-XXX, keeping the session inside the original folder. (Move the session into your Exercises-XXX folder if working from the starter file.)

Create New Instrument Tracks

In this part of the exercise, you will create two additional Instrument tracks and assign virtual instruments to the tracks. You will also configure the virtual instrument settings to create your unique sound.

Create two Instrument tracks:

1.   Press **COMMAND+SHIFT+N** (Mac) or **CTRL+SHIFT+N** (Windows) to open the New Tracks dialog box.

2.   Configure dialog box for two stereo Instrument tracks named **Synth Bits**.

Figure 10.34 New Tracks dialog box configured for two Instrument tracks

3.   Click **CREATE**. Two new Instrument track will be added to your session.

Assign virtual instruments to the new tracks:

1.   Press **COMMAND+=** (Mac) or **CTRL+=** (Windows) to display the Mix window.

2.   Click on **INSERT A** for the Synth Bits 1 track and choose **MULTICHANNEL PLUG-IN > INSTRUMENT > SYNTHCELL (STEREO)**. The SynthCell plug-in window will display.

3.   Close the plug-in window.

4.   Click on **INSERT A** for the Synth Bits 2 track and again choose **MULTICHANNEL PLUG-IN > INSTRUMENT > SYNTHCELL (STEREO)**. Close the plug-in window before continuing.

Import MIDI Clips

In this section, you will import MIDI clips from the SynthBits.mid file provided with the PT Academy Media Files. You will use these clips to add performances to the two Synth Bits tracks.

Import MIDI to the session:

1.   Press **COMMAND+=** (Mac) or **CTRL+=** (Windows) to switch to the Edit window.

2.   Choose **FILE > IMPORT MIDI** and navigate to PT Academy Media Files > 02. Exercise Media.

3.   Select the SynthBits.mid file and click **OPEN**. The MIDI Import Options dialog box will appear.

4.   In the dialog box, select **CLIP LIST** as the destination and click **OK**.

Figure 10.35 Selecting Clip List in the MIDI Import Options dialog box

Two new clips will be placed in the Clip List (SB1-01 and SB2-01).

Place MIDI clips on the Synth Bits tracks:

1. Using the **GRABBER** tool, select just the SB1-01 MIDI clip in the Clip List.

2. Drag the clip to the start of the Synth Bits 1 track.

3. Next, select the SB2-01 clip in the Clip List and drag it to the start of the Synth Bits 2 track.

4. Press **RETURN** (Mac) or **ENTER** (Windows) to go to the beginning of the session; then press spacebar to play back the session and hear the results.

Select Instrument Sounds

In this part of the exercise, you will select instrument sounds for each of the Synth Bits tracks.

Audition sounds for the Synth Bits tracks:

1. Press **COMMAND+=** (Mac) or **CTRL+=** (Windows) to switch back to the Mix window.

2. Click the plug-in button on Insert A of the Synth Bits 1 track to open the SynthCell plug-in.

Figure 10.36 Clicking the plug-in button to open SynthCell for the Synth Bits 1 track

3. Click on the button displaying <factory default> in the SynthCell plug-in window to open the **LIBRARIAN MENU** and select a preset.

Figure 10.37 Clicking the Librarian Menu in the SynthCell plug-in window

4. Select one of the preset options below. (Audition each by playing the session after making the assignment; then select your favorite option for the track.)

    • POLY SYNTH > 8BIT MARIO

    • LEADS > SMOOTHLEAD

    • LEADS > SQUIGGLELEAD

(i) Try soloing the track periodically as you listen to isolate the sound better. Also try changing the preset during playback to hear how the sound changes in the mix.

5. After selecting the preset of your choice, close the plug-in window. Be sure to unsolo the track before continuing.

6. Open the SynthCell plug-in on the **Synth Bits 2** track by clicking its plug-in button on Insert A.

7. Click on the **LIBRARIAN MENU** and select a preset for this track. Choose from the options below. (Audition each to select your favorite for the track.)

    • BASS > ACID WHISTLE

    • BASS > GROWL BASS

    • LEADS > LEADSAWSPREAD

8. Close the plug-in window when finished.

Finishing Up

To complete this exercise, you will need to save your work and close the session. You will be reusing this session in Exercise 11, so it is important to save the work you've done.

You can also listen to your progress thus far before exiting.

Review and save your work:

1. Press **ENTER** or **RETURN** to place the cursor at the beginning of the session.

2. Press the **SPACEBAR** to play back the session and review your results.

3. Press the **SPACEBAR** a second time when finished.

4. Choose **FILE > SAVE** to save the session.

5. Choose **FILE > CLOSE SESSION** to close the session.

(i) Remember that you cannot close a Pro Tools session by closing its windows. You must choose CLOSE SESSION from the FILE menu.

Taking Your Workflow to the Next Level

In this Lesson, we take a deeper look at workflow. The different steps you'll take during the course of production are fairly simple (you've learned many of these already), but you'll do certain things countless times during the course of your work. The trick is to execute the individual steps quickly and efficiently—the faster and easier you work, the more work you'll get done, and at a higher quality. That's what we mean when we talk about building your workflow skills.

This Lesson isn't so much a discussion of new editing concepts as it is an assortment of new ways to work, boosting your Pro Tools power.

Learning Targets

- Work on multiple tracks simultaneously

- Perform clip editing techniques

- Duplicate, repeat, separate, and consolidate clips

- Use the variations of the Trim tool—TCE Trim and Loop Trim

- Nudge clips

- Create and edit fade-ins, fade-outs, and crossfades

- Use the Tab key and Tab to Transient to navigate

TOPIC 11.1:
MANAGING MULTIPLE TRACKS

Working with individual tracks is one thing, but being able to deal with multiple tracks at once can be a huge time-saver!

Discussion: Selecting Multiple Tracks

You already know how to select an individual track. To review, here are some different ways:

- Click on the track name in the Edit window (at the head of the track).

- Click on the track name in the Mix window (at the bottom of the channel strip).

- Click on the track name in the Tracks List (in the left column of the Edit window or Mix window).

Here are some techniques you can use to select multiple tracks:

- To select a range of tracks, click on the first track name; then hold the **SHIFT** key while clicking on the last track name in the range.

- To individually select (or deselect) multiple tracks, hold the **COMMAND** key (Mac) or **CTRL** key (Windows) while clicking on the track name for any tracks that you want to select (or deselect).

- To select *all* tracks, hold the **OPTION** key (Mac) or **ALT** key (Windows) while clicking on any unselected track's name. All tracks will be selected. You can use the same process to deselect all tracks: Hold **OPTION** (Mac) or **ALT** (Windows) while clicking on any selected track.

 Using **Option** (Mac) or **Alt** (Windows) while selecting tracks in the Track List will select or deselect all tracks, shown and hidden. When used in the Edit or Mix window's Tracks area, this will select or deselect shown tracks only.

Changing Multiple Tracks

Often, you will want to change a setting on multiple tracks (for example, change an input or output). This can be done using modifier keys.

- To make a change to all shown tracks, hold the **OPTION** key (Mac) or **ALT** key (Windows) while making the change on any track. All tracks will be similarly changed. The **OPTION** or **ALT** key is known as the **DO TO ALL** modifier in Pro Tools.

■   To make a change to selected tracks only, hold **OPTION+SHIFT** (Mac) or **ALT+SHIFT** (Windows) while making the change on any selected track. All selected tracks will be similarly changed. The **OPTION/ALT+SHIFT** combination is known as the **DO TO SELECTED** modifier set in Pro Tools.

Making Selections on Multiple Tracks

Making Edit selections on multiple tracks can be a real time-saver, and you have a great deal of flexibility in the selections you make.

■   Making Edit selections on adjacent tracks with the Selector tool:

When using the Selector tool, if you click and drag horizontally, you'll make an Edit selection on a single track. However, you can easily make a selection on multiple tracks by clicking and dragging vertically over the tracks (and the area) that you want to select.

■   Making Edit selections on non-adjacent tracks with the Selector tool:

If you have a selected area on a track that you want to extend to another track, you can hold the **SHIFT** key and while clicking anywhere on the playlist of the additional target track.

Link Track and Edit Selection

The Link Track and Edit Selection function can make it easier to extend selections to different tracks. When this option is enabled, any Edit selection that you make on a track will automatically select that track; if you then select another track (or tracks), that selection will move accordingly.

To toggle Link Track and Edit Selection on/off, do one of the following:

■   From the **OPTIONS** menu, choose **LINK TRACK AND EDIT SELECTION**.

■   Click on the **LINK TRACK AND EDIT SELECTION** button in the Edit window toolbar. When enabled, the button will be colored blue.

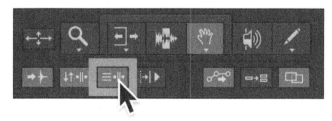

Figure 11.1 Enabling Link Track and Edit Selection

   The keyboard shortcut to toggle Link Track and Edit Selection on/off is SHIFT+T.

Here's how the Link Track and Edit Selection option works:

- When *disabled*, any Edit selection on a track is unrelated to the track selection(s). This means you can have a selection of material on one track while another track's nameplate is highlighted.

- When *enabled*, any track that has an Edit selection will also be selected (its name will be highlighted). Additionally, changing the track selection will affect the Edit selection as well: selecting a different track by clicking its nameplate will move the Edit selection to that track.

The ability to quickly and efficiently manage multiple tracks (and their Edit selections) is a skill that will help you in a number of situations, from recording, to editing, to mixing, and beyond!

TOPIC 11.2:
BASIC EDITING COMMANDS

In this section, we take a look at a variety of way to edit the media on your tracks. If you've ever typed an email or used any kind of text-based application, you'll understand how cut, copy, and paste works. Let's look at these processes and some related edit commands in Pro Tools.

Discussion: Common Editing Commands

Pro Tools includes common edit commands that you will find in almost any other application, from word processors to image editors. These commands work in Pro Tools very much like they do in other applications and typically use standard keyboard shortcuts that you may already be familiar with.

Cut, Copy, and Paste

When you use the **CUT** command on a selected area in Pro Tools (i.e., an Edit selection), the media will be removed from the playlist and stored in a data *clipboard* on your computer for later use. This is true for any empty areas, portions of clips, and entire clips within the Edit selection.

 The term *clipboard* is commonly used to describe a portion of the computer's RAM or internal memory used to store information on a temporary basis.

The **COPY** command works the same as Cut, but it does not remove the selected media from the playlist. Just like when you cut, the entire selection (including any empty area) will be added to the clipboard.

The **PASTE** command places the data from the clipboard onto the timeline at the edit insertion position. For example, if you copy media on a track from measure 3 to 4 (placing that data on the clipboard), and then move your Edit cursor to measure 7 and choose the Paste command, the copied material will be placed from measure 7 to 8 on the track.

 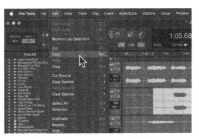 

Figure 11.2 The Cut, Copy, and Paste commands in the Edit menu (left to right)

The keyboard shortcuts for the Cut, Copy, and Paste operations use the COMMAND key (Mac) or the CTRL key (Windows) plus the X, C, and V keys, respectively.

Clear

You have the ability to clear an Edit selection (EDIT > CLEAR), removing the selected material from the track playlist without putting it onto the clipboard. This command has the same effect as pressing the BACKSPACE or DELETE key.

Undo/Redo

As you edit, from time to time you may make a mistake or do something that you wish you hadn't. You can undo or redo an action by accessing the associated commands from the Edit menu.

- To undo the last change you made, select EDIT > UNDO. The Undo menu item will display the most recent undoable operation.

- To reinstate an action that you've undone, select EDIT > REDO. Like the Undo command, the Redo menu item will display the most recent redo-able operation.

 The keyboard shortcuts for Undo and Redo are Command+Z (Mac) or Ctrl+Z (Windows) and Command+Shift+Z (Mac) or Ctrl+Shift+Z (Windows), respectively.

Duplicate and Repeat

At times, you'll want to repeat a clip or a selection, like a drum pattern that you want to use over many measures. You can OPTION-DRAG (Mac) or ALT-DRAG (Windows) a clip to create duplicate copies, but that can get tedious. And this operation cannot be used on a selection of just a part of a clip nor on a selection of more than one clip.

The DUPLICATE and REPEAT commands can get the job done more easily and flexibly. As Edit commands, these operations will work on *any* Edit selection, whether empty space, a partial clip, a full clip, multiple clips, or any combination.

Duplicate

The Duplicate command creates a copy of a clip or selection and places it immediately after the original.

To duplicate a selection:

1.   Select a clip or area to duplicate on a track.

2. Choose **EDIT > DUPLICATE**. A duplicate of the selected material will appear immediately after the end of the selection.

 The keyboard shortcut for the Duplicate command is COMMAND+D (Mac) or CTRL+D (Windows).

Repeat

The Repeat command lets you create multiple copies of a clip or selection in one quick process. This has the same effect as using the Duplicate command multiple times in succession.

To repeat a selection:

1. Select a clip or area to repeat on a track.

2. Choose **EDIT > REPEAT**. The Repeat dialog box will open.

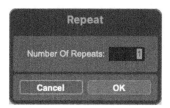

Figure 11.3 The Repeat dialog box

3. Enter the number of repetitions you want (excluding the original) and click **OK**. The selected material will be repeated the specified number of times and placed back-to-back on the track.

 The keyboard shortcut for the Repeat command is OPTION+R (Mac) or ALT+R (Windows).

TOPIC 11.3:
SEPARATING AND CONSOLIDATING

Other skills that will increase your efficiency include the ability to split clips and to merge clips—that's where the **SEPARATE**, **HEAL**, and **CONSOLIDATE** commands come into the picture.

Discussion: Separating and Combining Clips

Separating a clip involves breaking a single clip into two or more smaller clips. Combining clips involves joining two or more clips together into a single larger clip.

Pro Tools provides a few different ways to create clip separations and to combine clips together.

Basic Separate

Oftentimes, you will need to break a clip into two different parts. This could be necessary in order to affect the second half only, while performing an edit operation. Suppose, for example, that a line of dialog you have recorded needs a pause in the middle. You could separate the clip where you want to insert the pause and move the second half of the clip later on the track.

To break a clip into two separate clips:

1. Using the Selector tool, place the Edit cursor at the location where you want to make the separation.

2. From the **EDIT** menu, choose **SEPARATE CLIP > AT SELECTION**. The clip will be split into two smaller clips at the Edit cursor location.

Figure 11.4 Choosing the Separate Clip > At Selection command from the Edit menu

   The shortcut for the Separate Clip At Selection operation is **Command+E (Mac)** or **Ctrl+E (Windows)**.

If you make an Edit selection before using this command, the clip will be split into three smaller clips—one clip before the Edit selection, one clip where the Edit selection exists, and one clip after the Edit selection.

Separating on a Grid

A useful variation on the basic separation workflow creates separate clips at each grid line.

To separate a selection at grid lines:

1. Set your Grid value to the interval you want to use for the separations.

2. Select the area that you want to separate on the grid.

3. Select **EDIT > SEPARATE CLIP > ON GRID**. The **PRE-SEPARATE AMOUNT** dialog box will appear.

Figure 11.5 The Pre-Separate Amount dialog box

4. Optionally enter a value in the pre-separate amount to shift the separations earlier in time. For example, enter a pre-separate value of **3 mSec** to make separations 3 milliseconds before each grid line. To keep the separations precisely on each grid line, leave the value at **0**.

> (i) Use the pre-separate value to preserve the beginnings of sounds (attacks) that start before the grid line, such as for music with a rushed feel.

5. Click **OK** to complete the separation. The clip will be split into multiple pieces, corresponding to the current grid setting.

Separating on Transients

Another variation creates a new clip boundary at each detected transient within a selection.

A transient is a rapid increase in amplitude (loudness) found at the beginning of a percussive sound, such as where the hammer hits a piano string or where a drumstick hits the head of a drum. Different types of instruments have different kinds of transients, but they tend to be good visual cues when editing, indicating the beginnings of notes (or words, in the case of a vocal track).

To create separations at detected transients:

1. Select the area where you want to make transient separations.

2. Select **EDIT > SEPARATE > AT TRANSIENTS**. The **PRE-SEPARATE AMOUNT** dialog box will display.

3. Optionally enter a value above zero to add padding before the transient points. The greater the value, the farther ahead of each transient the separations will be.

4. Click **OK** to complete the separation. The clip will be split into multiple pieces, with separations at each detected transient.

Heal Separation

If you previously separated a clip, or deleted a portion in the middle of a clip, you may later find you need the original material back intact. That's what the Heal Separation command was designed for.

To rejoin clips that have a separation or deleted section:

1. Select across the area where you want to remove separations.

2. Select **EDIT > HEAL SEPARATION** or press **COMMAND+H** (Mac) or **CTRL+H** (Windows). Any separations within the selected area will be removed.

You can heal a separation only if the clips involved have not been moved in relation to each other. For example, if you split a clip and then move one of the resulting pieces, you wont be able to heal the separation.

Consolidating

As you progress in an editing session, you'll tend to accumulate more and more clips as you cut, copy, paste, and move clips on your tracks. At some point, the sheer number of clips on a track may become a nuisance. If you want to combine some clips into a new, single clip, you can consolidate the clips.

The Pro Tools Consolidate feature renders a selection into a single new clip. When applied to audio, this also creates a new audio file on disk.

To consolidate a selection as a new clip:

1. Select the area that you want to consolidate. This can be any combination of clips, partial clips, and blank space.

2. Select **EDIT > CONSOLIDATE CLIP**. The selected area will be combined into a single clip. Any spaces between clips will be rendered as silence.

The shortcut for the Consolidate Clip command is OPTION+SHIFT+3 (Mac) or ALT+SHIFT+3 (Windows).

TOPIC 11.4:
TRIM TOOL VARIATIONS AND CLIP LOOPING

You've learned previously how to use the Trim tool to remove the start or end of a clip. Here we'll take a look at advanced trim operations using two of the Trim tool's variations: TCE Trim and Loop Trim.

Discussion: Trim Tool Modes

The Trim tool in Pro Tools Artist provides three different modes of operation: the Standard Trim mode, TCE Trim mode, and Loop Trim mode. You can access the different modes by clicking and holding on the Trim tool button in the Edit Window Toolbar and selecting from the pop-up menu.

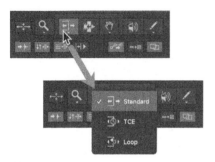

Figure 11.6 Accessing the Trim tool modes

The TCE Trim Tool

The first alternate mode is the Time Compression/Expansion (TCE) Trim tool. This variation of the Trim tool enables you to stretch (slow down) or shrink (speed up) an audio clip without changing its pitch.

To use TCE Trim:

1. Click and hold on the Trim tool button and select **TCE** from the pop-up menu. The icon will change to reflect the selected mode.

Figure 11.7 The active TCE Trim tool icon

   To toggle the Trim tool through its alternate modes, repeatedly press the **F6** key.

2.   Click on a clip boundary and drag left or right, just as if you were using the standard Trim tool.

When you release the mouse button, a new audio clip will be created with a different duration from the original clip, but with its pitch unchanged. This can be especially useful in Grid mode, for example, to slow down or speed up an imported loop to match the session tempo.

The Loop Trim Tool

The other trim tool variation is called the Loop Trim tool. This tool is used to create a clip loop. To activate the Loop Trim tool, click and hold on the Trim tool button and select **LOOP** from the pop-up menu. The icon for the Trim tool will change to reflect Loop Trim mode.

Figure 11.8 The active Loop Trim tool icon

The Benefit of Clip Loops

Clip loops take the Duplicate and Repeat commands a step further. Like those commands, the Clip > Loop command creates a repeating pattern. But in this case the result consists of a single clip rather than multiple independent clips. Clip loops can be trimmed, adding or removing loop iterations at any time.

Creating and Modifying Clip Loops

One simple way to create a clip loop is with the Loop Trim tool. With the Loop Trim tool active, the mouse cursor will display a trim bracket with a looping arrow when positioned at either end of a clip.

Figure 11.9 The Loop Trim tool icon

With this tool, you can create a clip loop by clicking and dragging outward on a clip boundary to extend the clip. You can also modify an existing clip loop by clicking and dragging in either direction. As you drag, the clip will be lengthened by adding loop iterations or shortened by removing loop iterations.

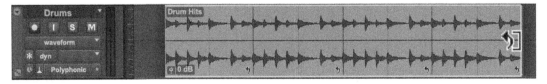

Figure 11.10 Creating a clip loop by adding loop iterations

TOPIC 11.5:
NUDGING

Moving clips in large increments is easy to do with the Grabber tool. But sometimes you need to move clips or selections with surgical precision. That's where the Nudge function comes in.

Discussion: Using the Nudge Function

To take advantage of nudging, you'll first need to set an appropriate Nudge value. This process is similar to setting the Grid value, as you learned in Lesson 6.

To set the Nudge value:

1.   Click on the down arrow to the right of the Nudge value display in the Edit window toolbar.

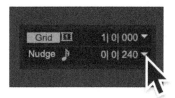

Figure 11.11 Clicking the Nudge Value selector

The Nudge Value pop-up menu will appear.

2.   In the lower section of the pop-up menu, select the *Time Scale* you want to use for nudging. Based on the Time Scale you choose, the options at the top of the list will change.

Figure 11.12 The Nudge Value pop-up menu

3.   After setting the Time Scale, reopen the menu and select the nudge increment from the top of the list.

Once you have selected an appropriate Nudge value, you can easily move your clips in Nudge increments.

To nudge clips:

1.   Using the **SELECTOR** or **GRABBER** tool, select the clip(s) you want to move.

2.   Do one of the following:

   •   Press the **PLUS [+]** key on the numeric keypad to move the selected clip(s) later in time (to the right) by the nudge amount.

   •   Press the **MINUS [−]** key on the numeric keypad to move the selected clip(s) earlier in time (to the left) by the nudge amount.

 Nudging uses the Plus and Minus keys on the numeric keypad only. This will not work using the plus and minus keys in the top row of the QWERTY keyboard.

 If you don't have a numeric keypad, you can nudge using the Edit Focus mode, as introduced in Lesson 6. With Edit Focus mode active, press the COMMA (,) key to nudge earlier or the PERIOD (.) key to nudge later.

TOPIC 11.6:
USING FADES

Fade-ins and fade-outs are used to gradually transition into or out of a clip. Additionally, you can create *crossfades* between clips to make a smooth transition from one clip to another. Although adding fades is an editing operation, it overlaps with the topic of mixing, since it involves changing the level of your audio content over time.

Discussion: Adding Fades to Clip Boundaries

Fades are essentially edits made at clip boundaries to gradually increase (fade in) or decease (fade out) the level of the audio as a clip starts or ends. Crossfades combine these two functions at the border between two clips, fading out the first clip while simultaneously fading in the second clip.

Creating a Fade-In or Fade-Out

Everybody has heard fade-ins used on a mix, such as when a song starts from silence and gets gradually louder until it reaches its running volume. A fade-out is just the opposite, with the sound getting progressively softer until it reaches silence.

In Pro Tools, you can create a fade-in or fade-out for any individual audio clip on a track.

To create a fade-in or fade-out:

1. Using the Selector tool, select the area of a clip that you want to have fade in or fade out.

    For a fade-in, make a selection that begins at or before the clip start point and extends into the clip; for a fade-out, make a selection that begins within the clip and extends up to or beyond the clip end point.

    > (i) For the Fade operation to be available, your selection must touch or cross a clip boundary. Fade-ins will be created starting at the clip start point and fade-outs will be created ending at the clip end point, regardless of where your selection starts or ends, respectively.

2. Choose **EDIT > FADES > CREATE** or press **COMMAND+F** (Mac) or **CTRL+F** (Windows).

    The Fades dialog box will open. (See Figure 11.13.) The curves shown in the Fades dialog box will be different depending on whether you're creating a fade-in or fade-out, but the controls are the same.

Figure 11.13 The Fade In dialog box

3. Use the section of the dialog box labeled **In Shape** (fade in) or **Out Shape** (fade out) to control the contour of your fade.

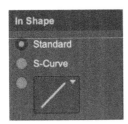

Figure 11.14 The In Shape section of the Fade In dialog box

- Click on the **STANDARD** option to select a basic linear or logarithmic shape for the new fade. (The shape changes depending on what you select in the **Slope** section.)

- Click on the **S-CURVE** option to select an S-shaped curve for the new fade.

- Click on the **PRESET CURVE** option to select a standard fade curve from a menu.

4. Click the **OK** button at the bottom right of the dialog box to apply the fade. The Fades dialog box will close.

After creating a fade-in, you'll see the fade shape applied at the start of the clip. Similarly, after creating a fade-out, you'll see the fade shape applied at the end of the clip. (See Figure 11.15.)

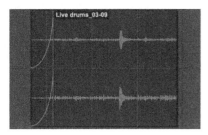 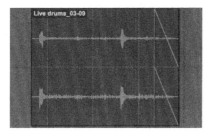

Figure 11.15 A fade-in (left) and a fade-out (right) applied to an audio clip

Creating a Crossfade

A *crossfade* is a simultaneous fading out of one sound while another sound fades in, creating a smooth transition from one sound to the other. You can create a crossfade between any two overlapping clips.

To create a crossfade:

1. Select across the border between two clips. Note that the clips must overlap, meaning they must be subset clips with underlying audio available on either side of the current border.

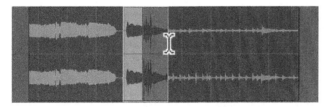

Figure 11.16 Selecting an area for a crossfade

2. Choose **EDIT > FADES > CREATE** or press **COMMAND+F** (Mac) or **CTRL+F** (Windows). The Crossfade dialog box will display.

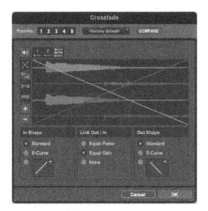

Figure 11.17 The Crossfade dialog box

3. Select the In Shape curve and Out Shape curve for the crossfade as you would for fade-ins and fade-outs.

4. Use the Link Out/In section to change the gain at the center point of the crossfade:

    - **EQUAL GAIN:** Select this option to place the midpoint of the fade curves at half amplitude. When crossfading very similar audio, this will typically create a smooth transition from clip to clip.

    - **EQUAL POWER:** Select this option to compensate for the volume drop that sometimes occurs when significantly different waveforms are combined. This boosts the midpoint of the fade curves.

    - **NONE:** Select this option to change the fades independently. This lets you adjust the shape, beginning, and ending of the curves using the small black handles that appear on either end of each fade curve.

5. Click the **OK** button in the Fades dialog box to apply the crossfade.

If there's not enough overlapping audio in both clips when you apply a crossfade, a notification will appear. Here you can choose either to skip the crossfade or to let Pro Tools adjust the fade boundaries as needed.

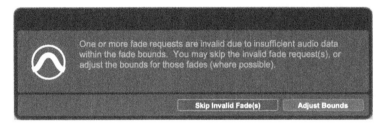

Figure 11.18 The Invalid Fades notification

Creating Fades with Edit Focus Mode Shortcuts

You can apply fade-ins, fade-outs, and crossfades using Edit Focus mode shortcuts.

To create a fade-in or fade-out with Edit Focus mode:

1. Using the Selector tool, place your Edit cursor within a clip, either where you want a fade-in to end or where you want a fade-out to start.

2. Press the **D** key to create a fade-in from the start of the clip to the cursor location, or press the **G** key to create a fade-out from the cursor location to the end of the clip.

To create a crossfade with Edit Focus mode:

1. Using the Selector tool, select an area of two overlapping clips where you want to add a crossfade.

2. Press the **F** key.

Editing Fades

To change the shape of a fade that you previously applied, you can simply double-click on the fade graphic with the Grabber tool. The Fade dialog box will reopen, allowing you to make changes as needed.

Some other ways you can edit an existing fade include the following:

- Use the **GRABBER** tool to adjust the placement of the fade by clicking and dragging. For fade-ins and fade-outs, this will also trim the start or end of the clip, respectively.

- Use the **TRIM** tool to adjust the duration of a fade by clicking on either end of the fade and dragging, just as you would do with an audio clip.

Deleting Fades

Deleting a fade you don't want is also easy. There are a number of ways you can do it:

- Select the fade that you want to delete and press the **DELETE** or **BACKSPACE** key. The fade will be removed, and the original (non-faded audio) will remain.

- Right-click a fade (or a selection that has fades in it). From the pop-up menu, choose **DELETE FADES**. Any selected fades will be removed.

- Select a fade (or make a selection that includes multiple fades) and choose **EDIT > FADES > DELETE**.

TOPIC 11.7:
USING THE TAB KEY

The Tab key provides a great way to navigate your session. The Tab functionality can also be used to create selections.

Discussion: Navigating and Selecting with the Tab Key

The Tab key can operate in one of two different modes: basic tabbing and tabbing with Tab to Transients. Here we will explore both options.

Basic Tabbing

We'll look at basic tab behavior first. The general idea is that the Tab key will allow us to navigate from one clip to the next on a track without reaching for the mouse. For this, the **TAB TO TRANSIENTS** function should be disabled.

To navigate through clip boundaries:

1. Disable the **TAB TO TRANSIENTS** button in the Edit Window toolbar (below and left of the Zoomer tool). The button will display in gray when disabled.

Figure 11.19 The Tab to Transients button in the toolbar

 To toggle the Tab to Transients feature on and off from the keyboard, press
OPTION+COMMAND+TAB (Mac) or CTRL+ALT+TAB (Windows).

2. With the Edit cursor on a track containing several clips, press the **TAB** key. The Edit cursor will move forward to the next clip boundary. If the Edit cursor was before a clip, it will move forward to the start of that clip; if the Edit cursor was at the start of a clip or within a clip, it will move forward to the end of the clip.

 Modifier keys will affect tab behavior. Holding the OPTION key (Mac) or CTRL key
(Windows) will reverse the behavior and tab backward through clip boundaries.
Holding the SHIFT key will make or extend a selection while tabbing.

Tab to Transients

With the **TAB TO TRANSIENTS** function enabled, the Tab key will continue to advance through to clip boundaries, but it will also stop at each transient with a clip. The first step is to enable Tab to Transients.

To enable Tab to Transients, do one of the following:

- Click the **TAB TO TRANSIENTS** button in the Edit Window toolbar so that it becomes highlighted in blue. This indicates that Tab to Transients is active.

- Choose **OPTIONS > TAB TO TRANSIENT**. When active, there will be a checkmark next to the **TAB TO TRANSIENT** menu item. Selecting this function from the **OPTIONS** menu will toggle its state.

To navigate though transients with Tab to Transients enabled:

1. With the Edit cursor on the target track, press the **TAB** key. The Edit cursor will move forward to the next clip boundary, if starting from outside of a clip, or to the next transient within the current clip, if starting from within a clip. If no transient is detected within the current clip, the cursor will advance to the end of the clip.

2. Press the **TAB** key again to advance the cursor to the next detected transient or the next clip boundary. As you tab, the Edit cursor will jump from transient to transient. This is a fantastic way to locate drum hits and other transient-based audio.

Modifier keys function similarly when using Tab to Transients: The OPTION key (Mac) or CTRL key (Windows) will reverse the tab direction; the SHIFT key will make a selection while tabbing.

The TAB key is also useful for navigating MIDI and Instrument tracks, allowing you to navigate between clip boundaries. With Tab to Transients active, the TAB key will navigate from note to note within each MIDI clip.

LESSON 11 CONCLUSION

This lesson focused on workflow techniques to make your work in Pro Tools more efficient. It covered track management techniques, editing techniques, and navigation techniques that you will use regularly as you edit and arrange the media in your sessions.

Discussion: Summary of Key Concepts

In this lesson, you learned:

- How to work on multiple tracks simultaneously

- How to apply basic editing techniques (Cut, Copy, Paste, Clear, and Undo), and when to use each

- How to duplicate and repeat selections

- Different ways to separate and combine clips

- How to use the variations of the Trim tool—TCE Trim and Loop Trim

- How to nudge clips by a selected increment

- How to create and edit fade-ins, fade-outs, and crossfades

- How to use the **TAB** key to navigate in your session

- How the **TAB TO TRANSIENT** function changes the Tab key behavior

Essential Keyboard Commands and Shortcuts

Below is a summary of modifier behaviors and shortcut operations that you should know from this Lesson.

- To cut a selection, press **COMMAND+X** (Mac) or **CTRL+X** (Windows).

- To copy a selection, press **COMMAND+C** (Mac) or **CTRL+C** (Windows).

- To paste a selection, press **COMMAND+V** (Mac) or **CTRL+V** (Windows).

- To undo an edit, press **COMMAND+Z** (Mac) or **CTRL+Z** (Windows).

- To redo an edit, press **COMMAND+SHIFT+Z** (Mac) or **CTRL+SHIFT+Z** (Windows).

- To duplicate a selection, press **COMMAND+D** (Mac) or **CTRL+D** (Windows).

- To repeat a selection, press **OPTION+R** (Mac) or **ALT+R** (Windows).

- To heal a separation, press **COMMAND+H** (Mac) or **CTRL+H** (Windows).

- To consolidate a clip, press **OPTION+SHIFT+3** (Mac) or **ALT+SHIFT+3** (Windows).

- To nudge a selection, press plus [**+**] or minus [**–**] on the numeric keypad or press period or comma in Edit Focus mode.

- To select a range of tracks, click on the first track name; then hold **SHIFT** while clicking on the last track name.

- To select or deselect individual non-contiguous tracks, hold **COMMAND** (Mac) or **CTRL** (Windows) while clicking on each track name.

- To select all tracks, hold **OPTION** (Mac) or **ALT** (Windows) while clicking on the name of any unselected track.

- To make a routing change on all tracks, hold **OPTION** (Mac) or **ALT** (Windows) while making the change on any track.

- To make a routing change on all selected tracks, hold **OPTION+SHIFT** (Mac) or **ALT+SHIFT** (Windows) while making the change on any selected track.

- To extend an Edit selection to another track, hold **SHIFT** while clicking on the playlist of the target track with the **SELECTOR** tool.

- To create a fade-in, fade-out, or crossfade, press **COMMAND+F** (Mac) or **CTRL+F** (Windows).

- To move the Edit cursor forward to the next clip boundary or next transient (with Tab to Transients active), press the **TAB** key.

- To move the Edit cursor backward to the previous clip boundary or transient, hold **OPTION** (Mac) or **CTRL** (Windows) while pressing the Tab key.

- To make a selection while tabbing, hold the **SHIFT** key.

Activity: Lesson 11 Knowledge Check

This quiz will check your knowledge on material covered in Lesson 11, Taking Your Workflow to the Next Level.

1. Match the action to the modifier used.

    Make a change to all tracks   Shift

    Select/deselect non-contiguous tracks   Option+Shift (Mac) or Alt+Shift (Windows)

    Select a range of tracks   Command (Mac) or Ctrl (Windows)

    Make a change to all selected tracks   Option (Mac) or Alt (Windows)

2. Match the action with the default shortcut.

    Cut   Command+V (Mac) or Ctrl+V (Windows)

    Copy   Command+Z (Mac) or Ctrl+Z (Windows)

    Paste   Command+X (Mac) or Ctrl+X (Windows)

    Undo   Command+C (Mac) or Ctrl+C (Windows)

    Redo   Shift+Command+Z (Mac) or Shift+Ctrl+Z (Windows)

3. True or False? The **EDIT > DUPLICATE** command can be used repeatedly to create multiple copies of a clip.

4. What command lets you break a selected clip into multiple smaller clips at each grid line?

    a. Trim Clip > Start To Insertion

    b. Match Grid

    c. Separate Clip > On Grid

    d. Clip > Ungroup

5. The Consolidate command can be used to do which of the following?

    a. Rejoin clips that have a deleted section, restoring the original audio

    b. Combine multiple clips together into a single clip

    c. Break a clip into multiple separate clips

    d. Move all clips used on a track or in the session to a new location

6. What are the three modes of the Trim tool in Pro Tools Artist?

7. True or False? In order to nudge a clip, your computer's keyboard must have a numeric keypad.

8. Match the action to the default shortcut.

Create a fade-in or fade-out on a selected area	The G key
Create a fade-in from the clip start to the Edit cursor	Command+F (Mac) or Ctrl+F (Windows)
Create a fade-out from the Edit cursor to the clip end	The D key

9. How can you move the Edit cursor to the start or end of a clip without using the mouse?

    a. Press the **TAB** key

    b. Press the **F** key

    c. Press **COMMAND+=** (Mac) or **CTRL+=** (Windows)

    d. Press **SHIFT+RETURN** (Mac) or **SHIFT+ENTER** (Windows)

10. What is the purpose of the Tab to Transients feature in Pro Tools?

    a. Enables a metronome click based on the transients on a track

    b. Enables you to navigate through a clip, moving the Edit cursor to successive transients

    c. Enables you to add a transient to a track at the Edit cursor location by pressing the **TAB** key

    d. Enables you to add a space on a track at every transient location

Exercise 11

Editing the Session

In this exercise, you will configure options to help navigate the session you've been building. You will then identify key locations in the session and create changes or edits at these points.

Exercise Details

- **Required Media:** none

- **Exercise Duration:** 15 to 20 Minutes

Downloading the Media Files

To complete the exercises in this book, you will use files included in the **PT Academy Media Files** folder that you previously downloaded from the course learning module on ElementsED.com.

To re-download the media files, click on the **Access Files** link in the sidebar after logging in to your account. Consult your instructor or visit **nxpt.us/make-music** for more details.

Getting Started

You will start by opening the Pro Tools session you completed in Exercise 10. If that session is not available, you can use the provided **Exercise11-Starter** file in the **01. Starter Sessions** folder.

Open the session and save it as Exercise 11:

1. Open the session file that you created in Exercise 10: Storage Drive/Folder > Exercises-XXX > Exercise10-XXX.ptx. The session will open with the Mix window displayed.

    Alternatively, you can use the Exercise11 Starter file: PT Academy Media Files > 01. Starter Sessions > Exercise11-Starter.ptx.

2. Choose **FILE > SAVE AS** and name the session **Exercise11-XXX**, keeping the session inside the original folder. (Move the session into your **Exercises-XXX** folder if working from the sample file.)

Configure the Session for Editing

In this part of the exercise, you will configure various settings in the Pro Tools Edit window and rearrange the order of tracks in the session. You will also verify the Preferences setting for the Scrubber tool behavior.

Configure the session:

1. Press **COMMAND+=** (Mac) or **CTRL+=** (Windows) to toggle to the Edit window.

2. Enable the following options, as needed, by clicking the associated buttons in the Edit window toolbar (buttons should be lit blue, as shown in Figure 11.20):

   • Tab to Transients

   • Link Timeline and Edit Selection

   • Link Track and Edit Selection

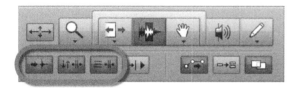

Figure 11.20 Buttons enabled in the Edit window toolbar

3. Click and drag on the nameplates to arrange the track order as follows, from top to bottom:

   • VO

   • Drums

   • Hi Hat

   • Guitar

   • Synth Bits 1

   • Synth Bits 2

   • Beat Wave

   • Beach FX

   • Fire FX

   • Click 1

   • Master 1

Set the Scrubber tool behavior:

1. Choose **SETUP > PREFERENCES** to open the Preferences dialog box.

2. Select the **OPERATION** tab.

3. Enable **EDIT INSERTION FOLLOWS SCRUB/SHUTTLE** at the top left of the page.

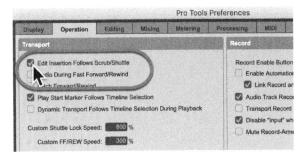

Figure 11.21 Enabling the Scrubber tool setting in Preferences

4. Click **OK** to accept the change and close the dialog box.

Navigate Audio and Edit Clips

In this part of the exercise, you will use the Tab to Transient function to locate the start of the voiceover on the VO track. Then you will trim the start of the clip to remove any background noise that might be present. Next you will use the Scrubber tool to locate the position for the fire sound effect, and then place the sound effect at that location.

Navigate to the voiceover start location:

1. Select the VO track by clicking on the track nameplate so that it becomes highlighted. The Edit cursor will appear on the track.

2. Press **RETURN** (Mac) or **ENTER** (Windows), if needed, to return the cursor to the start of the track.

3. Tab to the first major transient on the track to locate the start of the voiceover. This should be 2 to 3 seconds into the track. (If your recording includes a lot of background noise, you may have to tab several times to get to the start of the spoken script.)

4. If needed, press the **SPACEBAR** to audition the track and verify the location. (Solo the VO track, if necessary.) Press the **SPACEBAR** a second time to end the audition and make adjustments as needed.

5. Once you've verified the location, choose **EDIT > TRIM CLIP > START TO INSERTION** to remove the portion of the clip before the Edit cursor.

Navigate to the location for the Fire FX clip:

1. Activate the Scrubber tool.

Figure 11.22 Activating the Scrubber tool in the Edit window

2. Click and drag with the Scrubber across the VO track around Bar 6 or 7. Listen for the words "so you don't get baked by the sun."

3. Scrub back and forth to locate the start of the word "baked" and release the mouse at that position. The edit cursor will be placed at the released location.

4. Activate the **GRABBER** tool (hand icon); then hold **CONTROL** (Mac) or **START** (Windows) and click on the clip on the Fire FX track. The start of the clip will snap to your Edit cursor location.

(i)   The Control key on Mac (Start key on Windows) activates Snap to Head behavior in Pro Tools, allowing you to quickly align the head of a clip to the Edit cursor.

5. Unmute the Fire FX track so that the fire sound becomes audible in the mix.

Shorten the Music Tracks

In this section, you will remove a portion of the music tracks to fit within the 30-second radio ad. In order to remove the target area on the Beat Wave track, you'll have to first split the sustained note in that area.

Separate MIDI on the Beat Wave track:

1. Click on the **GRID** button on the left side of the Edit window toolbar to activate Grid mode, if not already selected. The Grid button will light blue when active.

2. Activate the **SELECTOR** tool in the Edit window toolbar.

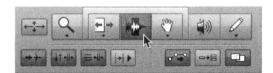

Figure 11.23 Enabling the Selector tool in the Edit window toolbar

3. Place the cursor at Bar 15 on the Beat Wave track by clicking near the associated grid line. In Grid mode, the cursor will snap to the closest grid location. (See Figure 11.24 below.)

4.   Press the **MINUS** key (-) to toggle the **Beat Wave** track from **CLIPS** view to **NOTES** view.

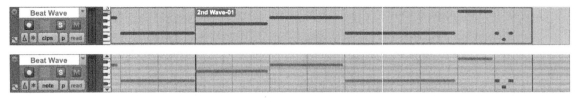

Figure 11.24 The Beat Wave track in Clips view (top) and in Notes view (bottom)

5.   Select **EDIT > SEPARATE NOTES > AT SELECTION**. The MIDI note under the Edit cursor will be cut in two, as shown below.

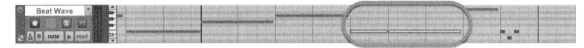

Figure 11.25 Separated MIDI note at Bar 15 on the Beat Wave track

6.   Press the **MINUS** key again and return the track to **CLIPS** view.

Select the audio and MIDI data to remove:

1.   Make a selection on the **Beat Wave** track from Bar 15 to Bar 17 (15|1|000 to 17|1|000).

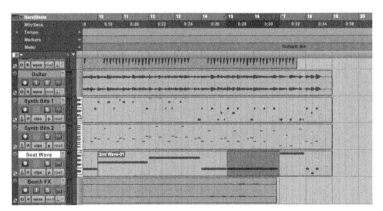

Figure 11.26 Two-bar selection on the Beat Wave track, starting at Bar 15

2.   Extend the selection across all the music tracks (above) by holding **SHIFT** while clicking on the nameplate of the Drums track.

Remove the selected media:

1.   Put the session into **SHUFFLE** mode by clicking on the Shuffle button in the toolbar. The Shuffle button will light red when active.

2. Press the **DELETE** or **BACKSPACE** key. The selected audio and MIDI material will be removed, and the remaining material on the tracks will slide over to close up the gap.

3. Return the session to **GRID** mode when finished.

4. Next, double-click on the **ZOOMER** tool icon to zoom out and view the entire session.

5. Activate the **SELECTOR** tool when finished. Your tracks should look similar to the image below.

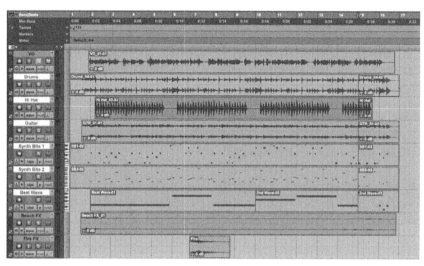

Figure 11.27 Tracks in the Edit window after editing

Finishing Up

To wrap up this exercise, you can listen to the work you've completed up to this point. You will be reusing this session in the next exercise, so it is important to save the work you've done before closing the session.

Review and save your work:

1. Clear any solos you might have in the session, such as on the **VO** track.

2. Press **ENTER** (Windows) or **RETURN** (Mac) followed by the **SPACEBAR** to begin playback from the session start and hear the results of your edits.

3. After listening through the session, press the **SPACEBAR** a second time to stop playback.

4. When finished, save and close the session.

> ⓘ Remember that you cannot close a Pro Tools session by closing its windows. You must choose **CLOSE SESSION** from the **FILE** menu.

The Basics of Audio Mixing

The mixing process represents the culmination of all your composition, recording, and editing. Mixing processes, techniques, and goals are debated vigorously among professionals; there are few rights and wrongs. Mixing is also *nuanced*; the tiniest tweak can significantly change a mix.

At its core, mixing combines individual elements (such as vocal tracks, bass tracks, sound effects tracks, and so on) into a final product that can be enjoyed by the audience. Care must be taken to make sure that all elements work well collectively, creating a harmonious whole.

Despite its rigorous demands, mixing is also a heck of a lot of fun. It is one area of production where your artistic vision can really shine. Even though mixing techniques and approaches may vary, its fundamental rules are consistent and simple enough to get started quickly.

Learning Targets

- Understand mixing concepts, including "in the box" and "out of the box" mixing
- Discern the difference between *mixing* and *mastering*
- Learn about the signal flow for Audio, Aux Input, and Instrument tracks
- Set up and create a "static" mix
- Use track meters and set mixing levels
- Create and control submixes
- Use Master Fader tracks effectively in a mix

TOPIC 12.1:
WHAT IS MIXING?

Multitrack recording became popular in the 1960s, and with that technology came the need to blend individual recorded tracks. In the early days, the same person who recorded the music would do the mixing as well. As mixing tools and effects evolved over the years, mixing as a specific profession became more common. By the 1980s, mix engineers like Dave Pensado, Chris Lord-Alge, and Bob Clearmountain started making names for themselves due to their iconic mixes.

But what constitutes a "good" mix? There's no single answer—mixing is a topic that involves no small amount of subjectivity, and whether a mix is good or bad is ultimately a matter of personal preference.

Discussion: The Components of a Complete Mix

At its most basic level, mixing combines different simultaneous audio elements (sounds played at the same time) into a cohesive whole. Here are a few ways to achieve that cohesion:

- **Manage the *levels* of different tracks.** Each track should be appropriately loud in relation to one another. This involves making choices about which sounds should be most prominent. For example, in a typical movie, the single most important element is the dialog. If other sounds obscure what's being said, the mixer needs to lower those sounds, raise the dialog, or a bit of both.

- **Ensure that sounds can be heard clearly.** This applies even to sounds that are relatively quiet in the mix. Improving clarity can involve changing the *timbre* of the sound. For example, in a song that has kick drum and bass guitar, the low frequencies of the two instruments can cause them to obscure each other. Through tonal shaping tools like equalization (EQ), mixers carve out frequencies in one or both of the tracks, allowing them to coexist in a way where both musical parts can be clearly heard.

- **Add a sense of space to the mix.** Mixers will commonly add ambient effects like reverb and delay for this purpose. Careful use of ambient effects can create the impression of depth in a mix.

- **Imprint a characteristic style to the mix.** Iconic, trademark sounds can be added as part of the mixing process. For example, reggae music typically has exaggerated reverb and delay, and the liberal use of those effects is completely appropriate for this style. However, the same treatment would be inappropriate for a string quartet playing a Bach chorale! Mix engineers must understand the stylistic requirements of the work, and their mix choices should support the artists' vision.

Mixing In the Box versus Out of the Box

Before the digital audio revolution, the mixing process involved large mixing consoles (analog mixing boards) combined with numerous hardware devices that could be patched into an audio signal path. Effects units (typically mounted in racks) were used to add processing, like EQ, reverb, and delay.

The advent of DAWs changed that. Today, the power of hundreds of hardware devices is available right from your computer. The mixing power of DAWs like Pro Tools has allowed for professional work to be done entirely within the computer at a fraction of the cost of building a studio. Mixing entirely on the computer is what is known as mixing *in the box*.

Although mixing in the box has become commonplace, you will still find mixers who prefer to complete at least some aspect of the mixing process using external gear. Known as *out of the box* mixing, this involves taking audio from Pro Tools and routing it out of the computer for processing. This could entail routing the audio through an external effects unit and back into Pro Tools. It could also involve routing Pro Tools' outputs into an analog mixing console where the final mixing and summing is done.

 For the purposes of this course, we focus on in-the-box mixing. The concepts you learn here are applicable to a wide range of mixing scenarios, and many will apply equally to out-of-the-box mixing.

Mixing versus Mastering

While you're mixing a song, a few things define the process. Ideally, you should mix in a room that provides a good sonic space. This lets you clearly hear all of the details of the sound. Professional mixing rooms, built with sound treatment, are specifically designed to present your mix with sonic accuracy.

Many mixes (particularly music projects) require an additional final stage called *mastering*. People often think of mastering and mixing as being related phases of production, and they are, up to a point. Once a final mixdown (or *bounce*) is created—typically as a stereo file—it is sent to a mastering engineer. The goal of mastering is to "polish" the mix and make it sound as good as possible for consumer delivery. This involves using tools and techniques that you normally would not use during the mixing process.

The Art of Mastering

If you master your own mixes, this is a chance to shift your focus. While *mixing* a multi-track session, you focus on fine details; during the *mastering* phase, you must take a step back and consider the entire sonic landscape. Because many details can't be changed in mastering, like tempo and individual track levels, attention is often drawn to aspects of the overall track that weren't noticed before.

Another important function of mastering is to ensure that a song sounds good in a wide a variety of listening environments. Your song won't sound the same over cheap headphones as it does when played through professional studio monitor speakers. It is the job of the mastering engineer to make the most of the final mix, so that it can be fully enjoyed on many different playback devices.

Although some producers also master their own mixes, many professionals will opt to use a dedicated mastering engineer. This is someone who has devoted their professional life to mastering mixes. Mastering engineers will often be able to bring things out of a track that a producer can't. The mastering process allows for a second set of ears to listen objectively, bringing a deep understanding of genre to the mix.

A thorough discussion of mastering is beyond the scope of this course, but many mixing topics we cover can also be applied when mastering a final mix. If you are going to master your own tracks, here are a few tips:

- **Take some time off.** Give yourself a few days—or better yet, a few weeks—between completing the mix and beginning to master the project. You'll be surprised at what you'll hear after some time away from the session, including details you didn't notice while you were in the thick of mixing.

- **Listen and study.** Professional mastering engineers usually bring a deep understanding of different musical styles and the sonic aspects that define them. If you plan to master your own mix, it's important to listen critically to other music in the same style. While taking time away from your mix prior to mastering, immerse yourself in critical listening of similar songs to help prepare your ears.

- **Compare.** As you work, switch periodically between the mastered version of your song and your original mix. Are the changes you're making improving the song or not? In Pro Tools, you can have one track containing the unmastered final mix, and a second track containing your in-progress master. You can use the original track as a reference track, keeping it muted as you work. Every so often, unmute/solo it to compare your mastering work to what you did as a mix engineer.

- **Make small moves.** When a mastering engineer gets a mix, they are getting what the mixing engineer considers to be the final product. Any changes made to this mix should be very nuanced. Mastering is a subtle and profound part of the production process.

- **Don't be fooled by loudness.** Louder isn't necessarily better. During mastering, certain dynamic effects are used. These tend to raise the overall amplitude of the mix. It can be easy to perceive these changes as improvements just because they make things louder. It's important to guard against this. Compare the peak levels of the mastered track to the levels on the unmastered reference track to make sure that they are as similar. That way, you can make an unbiased comparison between the two. You might want your track to be louder, but you also want to make it sound better.

- **Compare different playback devices.** Listen to your mastered track on headphones, in the car, and on your TV. The more environments you can hear your work in, the better you'll understand how the mix translates to different listening environments. The goal is to make your masters sound as good as possible in a wide range of listening conditions.

More about Mastering: A Deep Dive

Bob Katz is one of the world's most sought-after mastering engineers. His technical and artistic expertise is matched only by his generosity in sharing what he knows. His website, Digital Domain (www.digido.com) is a great place to learn more about the mastering engineer's world. It is also a great source of information on a wide range of audio and music production topics.

TOPIC 12.2:
SIGNAL FLOW, SIGNAL FLOW, SIGNAL FLOW

To quote an old joke, "What are the three most important things in mixing? Signal flow, signal flow, and signal flow." It's funny, but true: When you begin mixing, you're fundamentally working with *signal flow*. The more complex your mix gets, the more complex signal routing can be. But even the most complex mixes can be reduced to a few simple elements applied in a specific order.

Discussion: Audio Processing Stages

Signal flow in Pro Tools is straightforward and consistent. Each track has up to seven processing stages that determine how the audio signal is affected between the track's input and its output. In this discussion, we'll focus on Audio and Aux Input tracks, although the concepts apply to other track types as well.

Stage 1: Input

On an Audio or Aux Input track, the input can be from an audio interface or an internal bus path. In the case of an Audio track, the input can also come from the audio clips on the track. When an Audio track is playing back clips that are already on the track, the track does not require any input routing.

 An interface input is a signal coming from outside of Pro Tools (like a connected microphone), while a bus input is a signal routed from another track or other internal source from within Pro Tools.

Figure 12.1 The Input Path selector on an Audio track

Stage 2: Inserts

Inserts are most commonly used for effects. Inserts are patch points that are placed in-line with the signal flow of the track, between the input and the output stages. If a plug-in effect is placed on an insert, the entire signal of the track is routed through that effect before passing on to the next stage in the track's signal flow. Inserts are processed in series, from top to bottom.

Pro Tools provides up to 10 insert positions on every Audio and Aux Input track. (See Figure 12.2.)

Figure 12.2 Insert positions on an Audio track, with EQ and dynamics plug-ins applied to the top two inserts

Stage 3: Pre-Fader Sends

A send is a copy of the signal from one or more tracks that can be routed to a different destination for parallel processing. Sends in Pro Tools can be either pre-fader or post-fader.

A pre-fader send makes a copy of the signal before it hits the track's volume fader. This means that the send level is not affected by any changes made to the source track's output volume.

The destination of a send can be an interface output (for routing outside of Pro Tools) or an internal bus (for routing to a different track within Pro Tools).

Pre-fader sends are indicated by a blue Send Selector button to the left of the send's output path name.

Figure 12.3 Send positions on an Audio track, with a pre-fader send applied at the top send position

Stage 4: Volume Fader

The track's volume fader is where you control the output amplitude of the track. This stage is used to boost or cut the signal going to the track's output.

Remember that the volume fader controls the output of the track only, meaning that it has no effect on the track's input levels. When routing audio into a track, you may need to adjust the level of the source signal to prevent clipping.

Figure 12.4 The volume fader on a track

Stage 5: Post-Fader Sends

This kind of send makes a copy of the track's signal after it has been altered by the track's volume fader. As with a pre-fader send, the destination can be an interface output or a bus.

A post-fader send is indicated by a grey Send Selector button to the left of the send's output path name.

Sends in Pro Tools are post-fader by default; they can be switched to pre-fader mode using the PRE button in the send window (discussed in Lesson 14).

Figure 12.5 A post-fader send applied at the top send position

Stage 6: Pan

The next processing stage is where panning is applied. Pan controls on a track set the balance of the signal between the left and right outputs. Pan controls let you create a stereo mix from your mono or stereo tracks. Using panning, you can create unique placements for individual sounds within the stereo field.

Figure 12.6 The pan knob on a mono Audio track

Stage 7: Output

The final stage is the track output. This is used to route the signal out of the track to an interface output or an internal bus path. In a basic mix, track outputs are typically used to route the track's signal through an audio interface, which in turn connects to monitor speakers or headphones for playback.

Figure 12.7 The Output Path selector on an Audio track

The Pro Tools Mixer Strip

The layout of a channel in the Mix window doesn't exactly follow the signal flow from top to bottom. Let's take a look at the layout of an Audio track in the Mix window.

1. The **I/O** view in the middle of the Mix window is where you select the **INPUT** (stage 1) and the **OUTPUT** (stage 7). The Input selector is above the Output selector in this section.

2. The Inserts section at the top of the Mix window provides 10 insert slots, in two banks of 5: **INSERTS A-E** and **INSERTS F-J**. These two views can be individually shown or hidden.

3. The Sends section is below the Inserts section in the Mix window. This section provides 10 send slots, in two banks of 5: **SENDS A-E** and **SENDS F-J**. This is where you apply both pre-fader and post-fader sends.

4.   The **VOLUME FADER** in the bottom half of the mixer strip allows you to adjust the output volume of a track. When you create a track, the Volume Fader is set to 0 dB, commonly called unity. You can boost the level of a track by up to 12 dB, or reduce it to silence at minus infinity ($-\infty$).

5.   Although it represents the last stage before the track output, the **PAN** control is located above the Volume fader in the mixer strip. This control allows you to balance the post-fader signal between the left and right speakers.

The signal flow of an Aux Input track is identical to that of an Audio track, with the exception that Aux Inputs cannot use clips on the track as their input source (they cannot contain clips). These same signal flow stages are used for audio routing through an Instrument track. The only primary track types that are significantly different are MIDI tracks (which have no audio signal flow) and Master Fader tracks, which are discussed later in this lesson.

TOPIC 12.3:
CREATING A "STATIC" MIX (ROUGH MIX)

In this section, we take a look at basic mixer settings to create a static mix. In a simple project, this may be all you need to complete the mix for your project. More commonly, the static mix may represent the rough mix stage of your project, where you get basic levels and balance set before you start fine-tuning the details.

Discussion: Setting Up a Static Mix

A static mix is the simplest kind of mix. In this scenario, your mixer settings (such as volume faders and pan knobs) don't change over time. The static mix may not always be your final mix, but it's a great place to start. Creating a good-sounding static mix provides a strong foundation for your finished product.

Configuring Track Settings

Here are the first steps to creating a static mix:

1. Confirm that the *output* of each track is set correctly, so that you can hear each one. If you're in doubt about a given track, it's a good idea to solo that track to make sure it's audible.

2. When a track is playing back its content, the input setting will not impact that track. However, if you use effects returns or submixes (which you'll learn about later), you'll need to make sure that their inputs are set correctly.

3. Optionally disable automation on your tracks by setting them to **OFF** mode. You can do this using the Automation Mode selector at the head of the track in the Edit window.

 Hold OPTION (Mac) or ALT (Windows) while selecting OFF mode for any track to set all tracks to Off mode.

Setting Levels

It is important to adjust the volume when you're working on your static mix so that the relative levels of the different tracks sound good. Adjusting a track's volume fader works pretty much like you would expect—just click and drag up to increase the volume level or drag down to decrease it.

Here are some tips when adjusting levels:

■ Adjust faders by **2 to 3 dB** at a time to make small but noticible changes to track levels.

■ Adjust faders by **6 to 9 dB** at a time to make large, dramatic changes to track levels.

- Rough in the levels across all tracks to get started so that the parts start to fit together and each track is audible in the mix.

- While you listen and make other mixing changes, fine-tune the track levels periodically. This will be an iterative process.

Here are a couple modifier behaviors that may be useful as you set levels:

- To move faders in very small increments (0.1 dB steps), hold **COMMAND** (Mac) or **CTRL** (Windows), while dragging up or down.

> (i) The COMMAND modifier on Mac or CTRL on Windows provides fine control for mixer settings and other Pro Tools parameters.

- To quickly reset a volume fader to unity on a track, hold **OPTION** (Mac) or **ALT** (Windows) while clicking on the fader. The fader will jump back to 0 dB.

> (i) The OPTION modifier on Mac or ALT on Windows provides a reset behavior in Pro Tools, setting controls back to their default or nominal values.

Setting Pan

Along with volume, positioning various elements of your mix with panning is an important part of a static mix or rough mix. When you listen to a musical group perform, the players do not all occupy the exact same location. Rather they have individual positions in relation to you, the listener. That's essentially what we want to do when we *pan*: to create a sonic landscape with different elements placed in different locations. This not only creates a sense of realism, it also allows each element to be heard as clearly as possible.

Here are some guidelines when it comes to panning:

- Lead vocals, bass guitar, kick drums, and snare drums are commonly panned dead center.

- In audio for video, dialog is typically panned dead center (even if the speaker is not in the center of the screen). However, off-screen dialog is often panned to whichever side the off-screen speaker is.

- Drum kits are panned either from the drummer's perspective or the audience's perspective. In the drummer's perspective, the hi-hat would be placed to the left and the toms would span from left-to-right. In audience perspective, the hi-hat is panned to the right and the toms are panned right-to-left.

- Other instruments are panned off-center, giving more sonic space to the lead vocal, kick, snare, and bass. There are few established traditions when it comes to these instruments, so experiment!

- Watch the left and right meters on the Master Fader and try to keep them in the same range. If your left side's meter is significantly louder than your right side's meter, your mix will sound lopsided.

Revisit your volume settings after making panning changes. A track's level—both actual and perceived—can change based upon its position.

Approaches to Creating a Static Mix

They say that rules are made to be broken, and that is certainly true of mixing. Some of the most famous mixes in the world have been made using unconventional techniques. That being said, some traditions have evolved over time precisely because they work in most cases.

Try to avoid going into a mixing session without having a clear idea of what your final product will sound like. Picture in your mind how you want your mix to sound and keep that vision throughout the entire process. A common mistake is to simply start moving faders and pan knobs without a clear goal, hoping that something good will emerge. More often than not, this approach only leads to confusion and frustration.

Here are a few common approaches when creating a static mix:

■ **Make the Most of Each Track:** One approach is to listen to only one family of instrument—drums, for example—and make sure it sounds as good as possible before moving on to other elements. When using this method, be aware that if every element of the mix sounds full by itself, they'll all compete when combined, and the mix may suffer.

■ **Work Up From the Bottom:** This approach starts by introducing elements from the bottom up, making sure that the drums and the bass sound good together, before adding other elements. This can work well for some styles of music, particularly for styles that depend on a strong beat.

■ **Work From the Most Important Part:** With this approach, you identify the most important part of the song and then make sure it sounds exactly the way that you want. Then slowly bring in other elements, making sure that they don't overshadow the part you've deemed the most important.

■ **Create a Landscape:** One great way to solidify a concept for your final mix is to draw it out. Figure 12.8 shows a sample chart that you can use for this purpose. This chart represents an overhead view of your mix. Concentric circles indicate perceived distance from the listener. Simply write the names of the different sonic elements in the position and distance that you envision them. Taking the time to think through the sonic landscape and to sketch it out can be a very useful exercise!

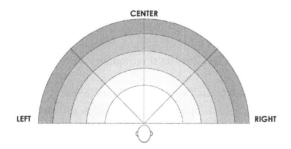

Figure 12.8 Panning chart

TOPIC 12.4:
CONTROLLING LEVELS

When you're mixing, you should always let your ears be the final judge of the results. However, meters can give you important visual feedback. There are a number of things to watch for in your meters. In this section, we discuss some details about what your meters tell you and how they function.

Discussion: Metering in Pro Tools

Every track in Pro Tools includes a level meter in both the Edit window and the Mix window. Edit window meters are relatively small, especially at reduced track sizes. For that reason, the meters in the Mix window provide a better reference, since they are larger and more detailed.

Mix by Numbers

You will notice that the meters in the Mix window have a value of 0 (zero) at the top of their scale. The numbers below this point get steadily larger as you work your way down the meter. This may seem odd, but there is a reason for the backward numbering process.

The numbering you see on meters is related to a concept that we mentioned in Lesson 1: digital audio signals are measured in decibels relative to full scale, known as dBFS. The value 0 dBFS represents the loudest signal that can be recorded at a given bit depth. All signals below this point have decibel values below full-scale audio. So the number 10 on the meter represents 10 dB below full scale, or -10 dBFS.

Avoid Clipping

When it comes to audio, especially digital audio, louder is not always better. One absolute rule of mixing digital audio is that you must avoid clipping at your outputs. But what exactly *is* clipping?

In digital audio, loudness values are stored using a string of ones and zeros. A 16-bit audio file uses sixteen ones and zeros per sample; a 24-bit file uses twenty-four ones and zeros. When all 16 or 24 of these digits are ones, you've hit the loudest signal you can accurately represent: full-scale audio. Recording or playing anything louder than this will cause clipping.

Clipping is indicated by a yellow or red light that appears at the top of a track's meter. The red clip light tells you that clipping is occurring at the input or output of your audio interface, which will result in digital distortion. In this case, you should reduce the input or output levels to preserve quality.

A yellow clip indicator is a warning that the signal on that track exceeds the 0 dBFS limit of your audio interface. However, this will not clip the Pro Tools mixer, which operates at a higher resolution. As long as you attenuate the signal before the final output stage (at the Master Fader), yellow clips wont hurt your mix.

This all boils down to one simple principle while mixing: watch the meter on your Master Fader. If a red clip indicator appears, adjust your levels until it goes away. Since clip indicators are persistent, you will have to clear them after you make an adjustment to see if you've solved the problem. To clear a clip, click on the clip indicator light at the top of the meter.

Select a Metering Option: Pre-Fader versus Post-Fader

Pro Tools offers two different ways for you to view your meters: *pre-fader* or *post-fader*. Pro Tools uses pre-fader metering by default, but changing to post-fader metering is easily done.

To change metering modes:

1. Click on the **OPTIONS** menu.

2. Select **PRE-FADER METERING** to toggle its state (from checked to unchecked or vice versa).

Here's how your levels will display in each mode:

- **Pre-Fader Metering:** In pre-fader metering mode, the meters of your tracks will reflect signal levels after the insert stage, but before the volume fader. Changing the gain of a plug-in will affect the meter levels, but changing the volume fader will not. This mode of metering (Pro Tools' default) is useful in showing if your signal is clipping as a result of effects on your inserts.

- **Post-Fader Metering:** When Pre-Fader Metering is disabled, your meters will show the level of your tracks after any adjustments on the volume fader. In this case, any level changes that you make with a fader will be reflected in the metering on that track. The advantage of this metering choice is that it gives a clear visual indication of the relative output levels of your tracks.

TOPIC 12.5:
USING SUBMIXES

In a large mix, trying to adjust the relative levels of related tracks can be a challenge. One solution is to use submixes. In this section, we'll take a look at using submixes (sometimes called subgroups) as a way to simplify the mix for a large session.

Discussion: Submixing Techniques

In a complex mix, you will often need to balance the levels between sets of tracks. After creating the perfect blend of lead and background vocal tracks, for example, you might find that the vocals as a group need to be louder in the mix. Adjusting each track up by a few dB and trying to maintain their relative levels in the process is time consuming and tedious. By submixing the tracks, you can control levels for the entire group.

What is a Submix?

Simply put, a submix takes the outputs of a set of source tracks and routes them to the input of a destination track (usually a stereo Aux Input or Routing Folder track). The audio from the source tracks plays through the destination track. You can adjust the level for the group using the destination track's volume fader. As an added benefit, you can add processing to the group using an insert on the destination track.

Creating Submixes

Creating a submix is easy, as long as you think of the process in terms of signal flow. Here we'll outline the steps for submixing to an Aux Input track.

 Submixing using Routing Folder tracks is described in the Pro Tools 110 course in the Avid Learning Series.

To submix a set of tracks to an Aux Input:

1. Create a stereo Aux Input track to serve as the submix destination and give the track a suitable name.

Figure 12.9 Creating an Aux Input for a vocal submix

2. Assign an unused bus to the input of the submix track. (See Figure 12.10.)

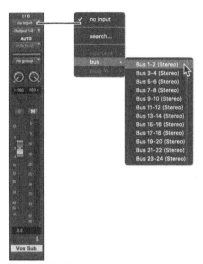

Figure 12.10 Assigning Bus 1-2 as the input to the Aux Input track

3. Select the source tracks that you want to submix by clicking on the nameplate of the first track and then Shift-clicking on the nameplate of the last track.

Figure 12.11 Vocal tracks selected in the Mix window

4. Hold **OPTION+SHIFT** (Mac) or **ALT+SHIFT** (Windows) while clicking the output of one of the source tracks and selecting the same bus assigned to the input of the submix track. The outputs of all selected tracks will be assigned simultaneously.

 Option+Shift (Mac) or Alt+Shift (Windows) is the Do-To-Selected modifier set.

The Aux Input track's fader will now control the overall volume of the submixed tracks. The metering on the submix track will show the combined level of all the member tracks.

The Effect of Solo Safe Mode

Ordinarily when you solo a track, all other tracks in the session are muted. To prevent this from affecting Aux Input tracks that you use for submixing, these tracks use a feature called solo safe mode.

Without this, soloing a member track within a submix would effectively silence the submix (by muting it), and you would hear nothing. Solo safe mode prevents the Aux Input track from muting when any other track in the session is soloed.

In current versions of Pro Tools, Aux Input tracks are in solo safe mode by default. This is indicated by a dimmed Solo button on the track.

To toggle solo safe mode on or off, hold the **COMMAND** key (Mac) or **CTRL** key (Windows), while clicking on the target track's Solo button.

TOPIC 12.6:
USING MASTER FADERS

As you have learned earlier in this book, Master Fader tracks become important when mixing. Although a Master Fader looks similar to an Audio or Aux input track, its function is substantially different from those and other track types that we have been exploring to this point.

Activity: Managing Output Levels

- Open the Activity 12.6.ptx session. The session will open showing multiple tracks displayed in the Mix window.

- Press the spacebar to begin playback.

  Note that a red clip indicator appears at the top of the Master Fader track (far right) as soon as the drums come in. This warns you that the outputs are overloading, causing digital distortion.

- Stop playback and clear the clip indicator by clicking on it.

- Reduce the Master Fader by approximately 2.5 dB and begin playback again. The output levels will be reduced, but the session will still clip as more instruments come in.

- Repeat the process, making small adjustments until you can play back the entire session without clipping.

Discuss what you've experienced. How far did you have to reduce the fader to avoid clipping? What visual indications are available to guide you in this process? How else might you prevent clipping in this session without using the Master Fader?

Discussion: The Function of a Master Fader

The Master Fader track typically controls the output level of your entire session. The metering on this track represents the sum total of the signals from all of your tracks.

What is a Master Fader?

Although a Master Fader track is commonly used to control the output of a session that is playing out to your audio interface, it can also be used to control the output of any bus in the session. This is typically only necessary in complex mixing scenarios, but it illustrates what a Master Fader actually is: a handle to adjust the signal level of a combined (mixed) set of tracks.

With this simple but powerful track, you can control the entire level of any summed signal your session.

One of the most striking differences between a Master Fader track and other track types is that the Master Fader doesn't have an input in the I/O section. This underscores the function of a Master Fader—it controls the amplitude of signal going out of a session, like a faucet's handle controls the amount of water coming out of the spout.

Master Fader Signal Flow

As with everything related to mixing, understanding the signal flow behind Master Fader tracks will help you use them more effectively.

The signal flow of a Master Fader track has fewer stages than an Audio track, and the processing at those stages works somewhat differently.

Stage 1: Volume (Fader)

This is where you control the output volume of the bus path selected for the Master Fader. This is the *first* stage in signal flow—a significant difference between Master Faders and other kinds of tracks.

Stage 2: Inserts

Like other tracks, one hundred percent of the signal passes through each insert on a Master Fader, and the plug-ins used on inserts are processed in series. Unlike other tracks, all the inserts on a Master Fader are *post-fader*, meaning that the changes that you make to the Volume Fader will change the signal level going to the inserts, potentially altering the tone of the final output.

Stage 3: Output

After these stages, the signal continues out through the associated interface output or bus.

What's Not Included

You'll note that in addition to the differences in signal flow between Master Faders and other kinds of tracks, many processing stages found on other tracks are completely absent on Master Faders.

Here's what you won't find:

- Send selectors
- Input path selector
- Pan knobs
- TrackInput button
- Record Enable button
- Solo button
- Mute button

Setting Up a Master Fader Track

The first order of business is to create a Master Fader track. Next, you'll need to select the output or bus for the track. This will determine what signal it is controlling.

To set up a Master Fader track:

1. Using any of the techniques you've learned, add a stereo Master Fader track after the last track in your session.

2. Click on the track's **OUTPUT PATH** selector and select your session's main outputs (typically the audio interface outputs connected to your stereo speakers).

> (i) A Master Fader's output can be set in either the Mix or Edit windows. This track type also cannot hold clips—in this regard, it's similar to an Aux Input track.

Using a Master Fader Track

Master Fader tracks have two defining characteristics: They provide metering for the session's total output, and their inserts are *post-fader*. This makes the Master Fader ideal for managing levels for your final mix.

- **Control the Total Output of Your Mix:** The most common use of a Master Fader is to control the level of your entire session. Having a single Master Fader assigned to the output for your main monitor speakers is an easy way to take control of the total output of your mix.

- **Apply Post-Fader Inserts:** A Master Fader track can be used to get the final levels for your mix just right. You can optimize output levels using certain plug-ins (such as a Limiter or Maximizer, discussed in the next lesson). You'll want such plug-ins to be the last thing in your signal flow. Putting them on a Master Fader track ensures that processing is applied in the final stage of the mix.

LESSON 12 CONCLUSION

This Lesson provided an important first step into the big wide world of mixing. The concepts you've explored here will serve you well throughout your mixing career!

Discussion: Summary of Key Concepts

In this Lesson, you learned:

- How mixing is used to blend together different sonic elements into a cohesive whole

- The difference between mixing "in the box" versus "out of the box"

- The distinction between mixing and mastering

- Approaches you can take to mastering your mix

- The signal flow of Audio, Aux Input, and Instrument tracks

- How to set up and create a static mix

- The importance of setting mix levels

- Different ways of viewing your track meters

- How to control a large mix with submixing

- How to use Master Faders in your mix

Essential Keyboard Commands and Shortcuts

Below is a summary of modifier behaviors and shortcut operations that you should know from this Lesson.

- To apply a change to all tracks in the session, hold the **OPTION** key (Mac) or the **ALT** key (Windows) while making the change on any one track.

- To apply a change to all selected tracks in the session, hold **OPTION+SHIFT** (Mac) or **ALT+SHIFT** (Windows) while making the change on any one selected track.

- To reset the volume level to unity on a track, hold the **OPTION** key (Mac) or **ALT** key (Windows) while clicking on the track's Volume Fader.

- To adjust a Volume Fader in fine resolution (0.1 dB steps), hold **COMMAND** (Mac) or **CTRL** (Windows) while moving the fader.

Activity: Lesson 12 Knowledge Check

This quiz will check your knowledge on material covered in Lesson 12, The Basics of Audio Mixing.

1.   Fill in the blank. Mixing entirely within a DAW like Pro Tools is referred to as mixing _____.

2.   True or False? Inserts on an Audio track are post-fader (affected by the track's volume fader setting).

3.   Match the following terms to the appropriate description.

Input	Processed in series
Insert	Can be from an audio interface or an internal bus path
Send	Set the left/right balance of the track
Pan	Processed in parallel

4.   Which modifier key can you use to quickly set a volume fader to unity (0) by clicking on it?

5.   In audio for video, where is dialog typically panned: left, right, or center?

6.   True or False? Meters on an Audio track are always post-insert.

7.   True or False? Sends on an Audio track are always post-fader.

8.   Which modifier key can be used to toggle solo-safe on/off for a track by clicking on the Solo button?

9.   True or False? Inserts on a Master Fader track function exactly the same as inserts on Audio tracks.

10. Which of the following controls can be found on a Master Fader track? (Select all that apply.)

   a. Input selector

   b. Insert selectors

   c. Send selectors

   d. Output selector

Creating a Basic Mix

In this exercise, you will set levels and panning for the music tracks in your radio ad session. You will also organize the session with a submix for the music tracks. Then you will set an initial balance for the mix by adjusting the levels on the VO, FX, and music submix tracks.

Exercise Details

- **Required Media:** None

- **Exercise Duration:** 15 Minutes

Downloading the Media Files

To complete the exercises in this book, you will use files included in the **PT Academy Media Files** folder that you previously downloaded from the course learning module on ElementsED.com.

To re-download the media files, click on the **Access Files** link in the sidebar after logging in to your account. Consult your instructor or visit <u>nxpt.us/make-music</u> for more details.

Getting Started

You will start by opening the Pro Tools session you completed in Exercise 11. If that session is not available, you can use the provided Exercise12-Starter file in the 01. Starter Sessions folder.

Open the session and save it as Exercise 12:

1. Open the session file that you created in Exercise 11: Storage Drive/Folder > Exercises-XXX > Exercise11-XXX.ptx.

    Alternatively, you can use the Exercise12 Starter file: PT Academy Media Files > 01. Starter Sessions > Exercise12-Starter.ptx.

2. Choose **FILE > SAVE AS** and name the session Exercise12-XXX, keeping the session inside the original folder. (Move the session into your Exercises-XXX folder if working from the starter file.)

Play the Session and Set Levels

In this part of the exercise, you will select the entire duration and play it back in Loop Playback mode so that you can make adjustments to the levels on each track.

Set levels for your music mix:

1. Using the Selector tool, triple-click anywhere on the audio playlist for the **Drums** track. The entire track contents will become selected.

2. Select **OPTIONS > LOOP PLAYBACK** to enable loop playback mode. A looping arrow will appear on the Play button.

Figure 12.12 Loop Playback mode active

3. Press **COMMAND+=** (Mac) or **CTRL+=** (Windows) to activate the Mix window.

4. Mute the **VO** track along with the **Beach FX** and **Fire FX** tracks so that you can focus on mixing just the music tracks.

5. Begin playback and adjust the levels of each of the music tracks to achieve a clear, balanced music bed. All parts should be audible without being overbearing.

   Following are some suggestions for balancing the levels (feel free to experiment):

   - The **Synth Bits** tracks may be too loud in the mix compared to other elements. Try lowering the faders on both of the **Synth Bits** tracks anywhere from 3 to 7 dB. Adjust as needed, depending on the sounds you selected for each track.

   - The Xpand!2 synthesizer part is a bit too prominent and tends to overpower the guitar and drum tracks. Try lowering the fader on the **Beat Wave** track by 3 to 6 dB.

   - The guitar part may get a bit buried in the mix. Try raising the Guitar fader by 1 or 2 dB.

   - As you work, solo individual tracks from time to time to remind yourself what each track sounds like. Unsolo the track and make sure that it is not too loud compared to other tracks.

   - Also try muting each track from time to time. You should notice something missing from the mix when the track is muted. Adjust levels as needed to hear each track's contribution when unmuted.

6. Stop playback when finished and save your work in progress.

Set Pan Positions

In this part of the exercise you will use the pan controls on each track to position each instrument in the stereo mix.

Adjust track placement:

1. Start playback.

2. Adjust the panning for various tracks to create a balanced mix, with some instruments offset to the left and others offset to the right. Try to give certain sounds a unique position within the stereo field.

   Following are some suggestions for panning the tracks (feel free to experiment):

   - Pan the **Hi Hat** track to the left, for a drummer's perspective. Try a setting between 35 and 60.

   - Offset the **Guitar** track to the right. Try setting the left pan knob between 25 and 40.

   - Offset the **Synth Bits1** track to the left, opposite of the **Guitar** track. Set the right pan knob to the same value that you used for the left pan on the **Guitar** track to balance the two tracks.

   - Narrow the width on the **Beat Wave** track. Try setting both the left and right pan knobs to a value between 35 and 50.

3. Stop playback when finished and save your work in progress.

Submix the Music Tracks and Balance the Mix

In this part of the exercise, you will create a submix for your music tracks. Then you will use the submix fader to set the levels relative to the **VO** track and **FX** tracks.

Submix the music tracks:

1. Select the **Drums** track by clicking on its nameplate.

2. Shift-click on the **Beat Wave** track to extend the track selection to all of the music tracks.

3. Hold **OPTION+SHIFT** (Mac) or **ALT+SHIFT** (Windows) while completing this step: click the Output Path selector on any selected track and choose **BUS > BUS 1-2**.

ⓘ   The Output Path selector is the bottom selector in the I/O section.

All of the music tracks should now be routed to Bus 1-2. (See Figure 12.13.)

Figure 12.13 Output routing for the music tracks

4. Choose **TRACK > NEW** to open the New Tracks dialog box.

5. Configure the dialog box for a stereo Aux Input track named **Music Sub**.

Figure 12.14 Creating a music submix destination

6. Click Create to add the track to your session.

7. Click on the Input Path selector for the **Music Sub** track and select **BUS > BUS 1-2** to set it as the submix destination.

8. Play back a portion of the session to verify that you can hear the music through the **Music Sub** track. You should see metering on this track when the music begins.

Balance the Mix:

1. Unmute the **VO** track and begin playback.

2. Lower the fader on the **Music Sub** track until you can hear the voiceover track clearly. The amount of attenuation you'll need depends on the amplitude of the voiceover you recorded, but you will likely need to bring the music down by around 10 to 15 dB.

3. Unmute the **Beach FX** and **Fire FX** tracks.

4. Use the faders on each of these tracks to adjust their levels relative to the music and voiceover. Again your needs will vary, but here are a few suggestions:

   - Make sure that the **Beach FX** track can be heard clearly to establish the beach ambience. You may need to increase the level of this track by **1** to **2 dB** or more to keep it audible throughout the mix, but be careful not to obscure the dialog.

   - Make sure the **Fire FX** track is not too loud. Sound effects should generally add a subtle enhancement without drawing attention to themselves. You may need to reduce the level on this track by somewhere between **4** and **7.5 dB** or so.

5. Stop playback when finished.

Finishing Up

To complete this exercise tutorial, you will need to save your work and close the session. You will be reusing this session in Exercise 13, so it is important to save the work you've done.

You may also want to take another listen to your mix and make additional level changes before exiting.

Review and save your work:

1. Press **ENTER** or **RETURN** to place the cursor at the beginning of the session.

2. Press the **SPACEBAR** to play back the session and review your results. Adjust individual tracks or submix levels as needed.

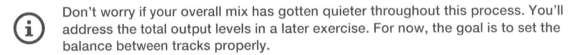 Don't worry if your overall mix has gotten quieter throughout this process. You'll address the total output levels in a later exercise. For now, the goal is to set the balance between tracks properly.

3. Press the **SPACEBAR** a second time when finished.

4. Choose **FILE > SAVE** to save the session.

5. Choose **FILE > CLOSE SESSION** to close the session.

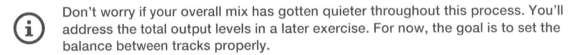 Remember that you cannot close a Pro Tools session by closing its windows. You must choose CLOSE SESSION from the FILE menu.

Lesson 13

Using Inserts for Effects Processing

Mixing largely involves adjusting volume and pan controls, as you saw in the previous lesson. However, these changes don't affect the tone or character of your tracks. To do that, you'll need to start using effects.

When considering effects, it's common to divide them into different types. One approach is to divide them into families like gain-based processing (effects that change the amplitude of a sound) and time-based processing (effects that operate in the time domain). Another is to separate them into types like filters, spectral effects, and more—and many effects defy categorization entirely.

In this Lesson, we look at effects processors like EQ and dynamics that you that you can apply directly to individual tracks. We also discuss common parameters for these types of processors.

Learning Targets

- Understand inserts and how they are used in Pro Tools

- Work with plug-ins on inserts

- Use parameters in a plug-in window, including presets

- Select between multichannel and multi-mono plug-ins

- Make effective use of EQ parameters and EQ plug-ins

- Apply and manipulate Dynamic processors

TOPIC 13.1:
INSERTS

In Lesson 12, you learned about basic signal flow for Audio tracks, Aux Input tracks, Instrument tracks, and Master Fader tracks. In this section, we dig deeper into the inserts stage and how to use inserts in Pro Tools.

Discussion: Processing Audio with Inserts

The term *insert* has its origin in the early days of analog mixing desks. Inserts were used by audio engineers to add external hardware processing devices into the signal chain on a mixer channel. Insert points could vary. Some mixing boards had them after the built-in microphone preamps; others, after the built-in EQ.

Using inserts, an engineer could introduce a new processor into a channel. For example, if a mixing desk didn't have an onboard compressor, you could add one using an insert. Patch cables would connect an external compressor to a mixer channel's insert. Inserts weren't required, and if a particular effect wasn't needed, it simply wouldn't be patched in.

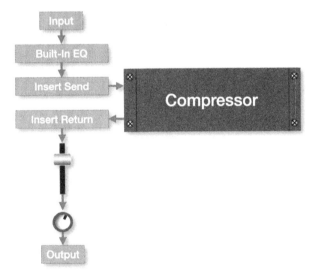

Figure 13.1 A channel signal flow structure

With the advent of DAWs, inserts have been virtualized to a large degree. But the fundamental logic behind them is quite the same as in the early days of analog mixing desks.

Using Inserts in Pro Tools

Inserts can be used in Pro Tools to add both external effects and internal plug-ins to your mix. Below are some basic guidelines for using plug-ins on inserts.

Instantiating a Plug-In

As you have learned, Pro Tools has ten (10) insert positions. These are available for Audio, Aux Input, Instrument, and Master Fader tracks. Placing a plug-in on an insert position is known as *instantiating* the plug-in on the track. (This is a fancy way of saying you're putting an *instance* of the plug-in on the track.)

To instantiate a plug-in on a mono Audio track:

1. Display the **INSERTS A-E** or **INSERTS F-J** view, as needed, by selecting **VIEW > EDIT WINDOW VIEWS** or **VIEW > MIX WINDOW VIEWS** and selecting the appropriate option from the submenu.

2. Click on any insert position where you want to add a plug-in.

Figure 13.2 Clicking on Insert A

The Insert Selector menu will appear.

3. Move your cursor over the **PLUG-IN** menu item. A submenu of plug-in categories will appear.

Figure 13.3 Plug-in submenu for Insert A

4. Select the desired effect category (such as **EQ**). A second submenu will appear, showing all the specific plug-ins of that type. (See Figure 13.4.)

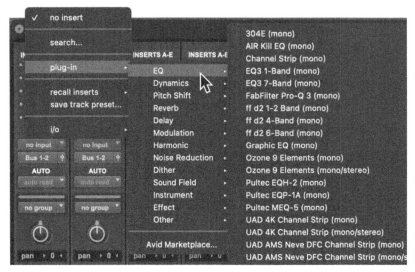

Figure 13.4 Plug-ins available in the EQ category

5. Select the desired plug-in. The plug-in will be added to the insert position, and the associated plug-in window will open.

6. Set the plug-in parameters as desired.

7. When finished, you can close the plug-in window by clicking the red close button in the top left corner (Mac) or top right corner (Windows).

Moving and Copying Inserts

As you learned in Lesson 12, inserts are processed in series, from Insert A through Insert J (top to bottom). The order of your inserts can have a profound effect on the result that you hear. You can easily rearrange the plug-ins on your inserts or make copies of them on other tracks at any time.

To move a plug-in:

■ Click and drag an Insert Assignment from its original position to a new insert position. As you drag, a yellow outline will indicate the targeted position.

 You can use this method to reorder plug-ins on a track or to move plug-ins to a different track.

To copy a plug-in:

- Hold the **OPTION** key (Mac) or **ALT** key (Windows) while dragging a plug-in assignment. A copy will be instantiated in the new location, leaving the original plug-in assignment unchanged.

In addition to moving and copying plug-ins, you can also bypass or deactivate plug-ins on inserts.

Managing Plug-Ins

After instantiation plug-ins on your tracks, you will need to make changes from time to time. This could involve modifying parameters in the plug-in windows, auditioning tracks with and without their plug-ins, moving plug-ins to new locations, and more.

Viewing Plug-In Windows

To reopen an insert's plug-in window after it has been closed, simply click on the **INSERT ASSIGNMENT** button for the plug-in. While an insert's window is open, the Insert Assignment displays in light grey. When the window is closed, it displays in dark grey.

If you click on a second Insert Assignment, the plug-in window for that insert will replace the previous one, by default. If you want to open multiple plug-in windows simultaneously, you can do one of the following:

- Click the **TARGET BUTTON** of the first plug-in window(s) to deselect it before opening the second plug-in window. The Target Button will change from red to grey. (See Figure 13.5.)

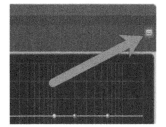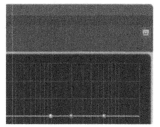

Figure 13.5 A plug-in window with an active target button (left) and an inactive target button (right)

- Hold the **SHIFT** key as you click the Insert Assignment button for the second plug-in.

Using either of the above methods, the second plug-in will appear in a new window, without affecting the previously displayed plug-in window.

Bypassing Plug-ins

A bypassed plug-in will allow signal to pass through it unchanged. For example, if you have an EQ plug-in on a track, but you want to temporarily hear the unprocessed original sound, you can bypass the EQ.

To bypass a plug-in, do one of the following:

■ In the plug-in window, click the **BYPASS** button located in the upper right-hand area. When engaged, the bypass button will be orange, as shown in Figure 13.6.

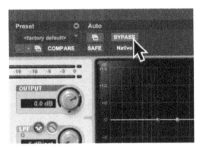

Figure 13.6 Clicking the Bypass button in an EQ plug-in

■ Right-click the **INSERT ASSIGNMENT** button and select **BYPASS** from the pop-up menu. The Insert Assignment button will change to a darker color, indicating that the plug-in is bypassed.

■ **COMMAND-CLICK** (Mac) or **CTRL-CLICK** (Windows) on the **INSERT ASSIGNMENT** button for the plug-in. The Insert Assignment will change to a darker color, indicating that the plug-in is bypassed.

Deactivating Plug-Ins

Bypassed inserts remain active, meaning that they continue to use the computer's processing power. By contrast, if you make an insert *inactive*, the insert will stop processing audio and will no longer use any computer resources. You can activate and deactivate plug-ins at any time.

To toggle a plug-in from active to inactive, do one of the following:

■ Right-click the **INSERT ASSIGNMENT** button for the plug-in and choose **MAKE INACTIVE** from the pop-up menu.

■ Hold **COMMAND+CONTROL** (Mac) or **CTRL+START** (Windows) while clicking the **INSERT ASSIGNMENT** button for the plug-in.

When inactive, the Insert Assignment button will appear greyed out with the name of the plug-in displayed in italic text.

Removing Plug-Ins

If you need to remove an insert, do the following:

1. Click the **INSERT SELECTOR** for the plug-in that you want to remove. This is the small dot to the left of the plug-in name. The Insert selector menu will appear.

2. At the top of the menu, choose **NO INSERT**. The insert will be removed.

Inserts on Master Faders

Previously, we discussed how signal flow on a Master Fader track is different from other tracks in Pro Tools. One significant difference is that on Audio tracks and others, inserts are *pre-fader*, while on a Master Fader they are *post-fader*. This has a direct bearing on how you use plug-in effects.

Later in this lesson, we discuss dynamic effects, which can add punch and power to your mix and help you manage levels:

- **Dynamic effects on Audio/Aux/Instrument tracks:** Since inserts on these tracks are pre-fader, the input signal is processed by any dynamic plug-ins before it goes to the volume fader. This means you can change the output level without affecting the processing being applied.

- **Dynamic effects on Master Fader tracks:** Since insets on Master Faders are post-fader, the fader is the first step in the signal flow, followed by the inserts. This means the fader levels *will* affect the processing being applied on that track's inserts. This can dramatically change the character and function of a dynamics plug-in.

TOPIC 13.2:
PLUG-IN EFFECTS

A *plug-in* is a bit of computer code that adds functionality to a host program. When a plug-in is added within the host program, it can add features and possibilities that the host application on its own doesn't provide. Many applications use plug-ins, from word processors and web browsers, to every DAW on the market. In the DAW world, plug-ins initially replaced hardware effects and instruments. They have since become more complex and loaded with exotic features.

Discussion: Working with Plug-Ins

In this section, we discuss how to work with plug-ins in Pro Tools. Here, we focus particularly on the controls within the plug-in window that are the same from one plug-in to the next. In later sections, we dig into unique controls for specific types of plug-ins.

Plug-In Formats

Different types of plug-ins are supported by different DAWs. The three major audio plug-in formats are VST, AU, and AAX.

- **VST (Virtual Studio Technology):** Introduced by *Steinberg*, this format is widely supported by many DAWs, including *Cubase*, *Studio One*, and *Ableton Live*. This format is particularly popular with freeware developers and is a common format for virtual instruments (a variant called VSTi).

- **AU (Audio Units):** AU plug-ins were designed for use with Apple's *Logic Pro* DAW, but the format is supported by other DAWs as well. AU plug-ins are available on the Mac operating system only.

- **AAX (Avid Audio eXtension):** The AAX plug-in format was designed for use in Pro Tools and other Avid products. This format operates on both Mac and Windows systems and is the only plug-in format supported and available within Pro Tools.

Getting Around the Plug-in Window

Plug-in windows can vary based on their parameters and features. However, some important controls are common to all plug-in windows:

- The **TRACK SELECTOR** shows the track that the plug-in is associated with. To quickly jump to another track, click the **TRACK SELECTOR** and choose another track from the displayed list to instantly open the plug-in window at the same insert position on that track. (See Figure 13.7.)

Figure 13.7 The Track Selector

■ The **INSERT POSITION SELECTOR** is a small, lettered button to the right of the Track Selector that displays the position of the insert on the track. To jump to a different insert position, click this button and choose a position (a through j) from the displayed list.

Figure 13.8 The Insert Position Selector

■ The **PLUG-IN SELECTOR** (immediately below the Track Selector and Insert Selector) shows the name of the plug-in used at the selected insert position. To assign a different plug-in, click this selector and navigate to the desired a plug-in from the displayed menu.

Figure 13.9 The Plug-In Selector

■ The **LIBRARIAN** menu lets you select a preset for the plug-in. (See Figure 13.10.) Most plug-ins provide a selection of preconfigured settings (presets) that will display in a pop-up menu here.

Figure 13.10 The Librarian menu

(i) You can also change a plug-in's preset without opening the plug-in window: Just right-click on the corresponding Insert Assignment button and choose a preset from the User Presets submenu.

■ The **PREVIOUS** and **NEXT** buttons are small **minus** (–) and **plus** (+) buttons below the Librarian menu. These buttons apply the previous or next preset available in the Librarian menu. Click these buttons while playing the track to browse presets and see what sounds best.

Figure 13.11 The Previous Setting (–) and Next Setting (+) buttons

■ The **COMPARE** button is situated to the right of the Previous and Next buttons. After you've made changes to a preset, this button will turn blue. Clicking it will toggle between the changes you've made and the original preset, allowing you to hear the settings back-to-back.

Figure 13.12 The Compare button in an EQ plug-in

■ The **BYPASS** button is situated on the right side of the plug-in window. As discussed previously, this button lets you bypass the plug-in so that its processing does not affect the audio signal on the track.

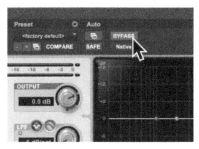

Figure 13.13 The Bypass button in an EQ plug-in

Plug-Ins on Stereo Tracks

The steps to instantiate a plug-in on a stereo track are similar to those on a mono track, as covered earlier. However, on a stereo track, you have an additional option to consider: multichannel versus multi-mono.

■ A **multichannel plug-in** is a plug-in that processes multiple audio streams within a single plug-in window. Any changes you make in the plug-in window will be applied to both the left and right channels of the track.

■ A **multi-mono plug-in** typically works the same as a multichannel plug-in, applying your changes to both channels of the track. However, multi-mono plug-ins offer the unique ability to process each channel independently, if needed.

For the purposes of this course, we will be using only multichannel plug-ins.

To instantiate a plug-in on a stereo track:

1. Click the **INSERT SELECTOR** for the target insert position. The Insert Selector menu will appear.

2. Select either **MULTICHANNEL PLUG-IN** or **MULTI-MONO PLUG-IN** from the Insert Selector menu.

(i) For simplicity as you work through this course, select MULTICHANNEL PLUG-IN if given the choice.

3. Proceed through the submenus to select the desired plug-in, as you would for a mono track.

TOPIC 13.3:
USING EQ

One of the most important mixing effects in the mixer's bag of tricks is equalization (EQ). An EQ processor gives you direct control over parameters like bass (low frequencies), mid-range (mid frequencies), and treble (high frequencies).

Discussion: Applying EQ to Tracks

An EQ processor lets you adjust the relative amplitude of frequency ranges within an audio stream. If a vocal performance sounds too nasal, just identify the offending high frequency and reduce it without affecting other frequencies within the sound. If you want to add more low frequency power to a kick drum, you can boost the low frequencies without touching the highs.

EQ Types

EQ processors are available in two basic types that are commonly used in audio production: the graphic EQ and the parametric EQ. Although they have similar functions (boosting or cutting frequencies), the way they achieve the task is fundamentally different.

Graphic EQ

A graphic equalizer divides the frequency range into a series of bands, with the number and width of the bands varying depending on the model of the EQ. You can raise or lower the level of an individual frequency band using its associated slider.

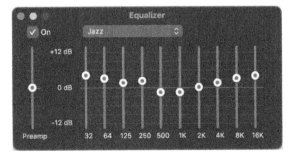

Figure 13.14 A graphic equalizer plug-in

Graphic EQs are quite easy to use and provide a good view of the adjustments you're making to a sound. However, the EQ bands are fixed, and sometimes this won't provide enough flexibility.

Parametric EQ

A parametric equalizer typically has fewer knobs and sliders than a graphic EQ, but it gives you more control. Parametric EQs feature a number of bands, each of which lets you adjust the frequency, amplitude, and bandwidth (or "Q") for that band.

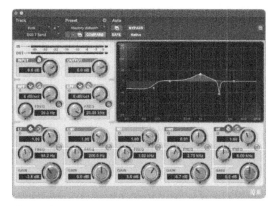

Figure 13.15 A parametric EQ plug-in

Although it might not be as intuitive as a graphic EQ, you'll have more precise control of the sound using a parametric EQ. The included parameters let you zero in on the exact frequencies that you want to change.

Using EQ

In Pro Tools, you'll use EQ to shape the tone of individual tracks, allowing them to better fit together, and allowing the parts that need to stand out to do so without simply relying on volume and pan.

EQ processors can be used in many ways, and mixing is often a process of making educated guesses and experimenting. That said, there are some traditional roles that equalization can play, as outlined below.

Tonal Control

When you record a sound into a DAW like Pro Tools, EQ will enable you to cut the frequencies of the sound that you don't like and boost the frequencies you do like. Let's say you record a vocalist and the recorded part has too much low frequency content as a result of proximity effect (discussed in Lesson 7). To address this you can reduce the lows a bit. If you also notice a nasal quality you don't care for somewhere in the higher frequencies, a parametric EQ will let you zero in on the offending frequency range and reduce it to the point where the sound is more pleasing.

Special Effects

You can create different special effects with EQ. A common approach for background vocals is to reduce the low end and pan them away off-center; this can give them an airy quality (especially when combined with reverberation, which you'll learn more about in Lesson 14). If you want a track to sound like it's coming through a phone, you can cut both the low frequencies and high frequencies, so that you only have the mid frequencies, imitating the frequency output range of a hand-held device.

Mix Cohesion

Try as you might, volume and pan settings alone will not be enough to let all the different elements of your mix be heard clearly. Often, the problem stems from competing frequencies between multiple tracks. That's where EQ comes in handy, allowing you to sculpt the tonal qualities of a track, so that it fits within the mix.

Here's a classic example: both kick drum and bass are low-frequency instruments. After bringing out the best in each track, and they may sound fantastic when you solo them. However, when you put them together, the two tracks become muddy and indistinct. At this point, you can reduce the prominent frequency range of each of the two instruments in the opposite track to allow them each their own space. This sort of carving out space in the frequency spectrum is not limited to kick and drum tracks; you'll do this in all kinds of tracks and submixes as well.

Additive EQ versus Subtractive EQ

EQs can be used to boost or cut individual frequency ranges (bands) on your tracks. Knowing whether to boost or cut is important. There are two different approaches to EQ: Additive and Subtractive.

- **Additive EQ** is an approach where the desirable frequencies are boosted. If a specific frequency band captures the best character of a sound, find that frequency and raise the level of that band. Although this is an intuitive way to work, it can lead to excessive gain, causing a track to clip.

- With **subtractive EQ,** instead of boosting the desired frequencies, you cut the unwanted ones. This is a popular approach these days for two reasons: First, if you have a loud signal, cutting frequencies won't cause it to clip. Also, cutting unnecessary frequencies tends to reduce unwanted noise. (Noise may be barely audible on one track, but it quickly accumulates when you add noisy tracks together.)

You don't have to commit yourself to one approach or another. In professional workflows, even mixers who prefer subtractive EQ will boost frequencies when it's needed.

EQ Parameters

Avid's EQ3 7-Band equalizer is a fitting example of a parametric EQ. Understanding the key parameters of this plug-in will allow you to understand virtually every EQ processor.

Input and Output Meters and Controls

In the upper left-hand corner of the plug-in window, you'll see input and output level meters. These will help you view the incoming and outgoing signal. To the far right of these meters are clip indicators – if they turn red, your signal is too loud and might be distorted. Below the meters are two knobs that you can use to adjust these levels.

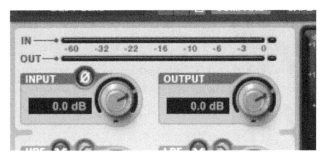

Figure 13.16 Input and output meters and controls in the plug-in window

Frequency Bands and Settings

Different EQ plug-ins have different numbers of bands. The EQ3 7-Band plug-in has seven bands:

- High Pass Filter (HPF)

- Low Pass Filter (LPF)

- Low Frequency (LF)

- Low Mid Frequency (LMF)

- Mid Frequency (MF)

- High Mid Frequency (HMF)

- High Frequency (HF)

There's a good bit of similarity in the controls of the different bands. We'll use the Mid Frequency band as an example to discuss a few of the most important parameters.

- Each band can be enabled or disabled with the Band Enable (**IN**) button. This button lets you compare the sound with or without a particular band's changes.

Figure 13.17 The Band Enable button

- The Frequency control (**FREQ**) allows you to choose the center frequency of the band. Any changes you make to the frequency are reflected in the associated node in the frequency graph.

- The **GAIN** control lets you cut or boost frequencies. In the EQ3 7-Band plug-in, you can boost or cut a frequency by up to 18 dB.

- The **Q** control lets you adjust how wide a band is. This control takes some getting used to: Setting the knob to the 12 o'clock position (at a value of **10**) gives you the narrowest bandwidth. Turning the knob counterclockwise from this position broadens the bandwidth, to a minimum value of **0.10**.

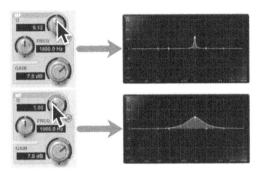

Figure 13.18 The effect of the Q control (high Q: top; lower Q: bottom)

High Pass and Low Pass Filters

A common first step of subtractive EQ is to cut out low and high frequencies that aren't needed. This is where the High Pass Filter (HPF) and Low Pass Filter (LPF) will help. The HPF cuts the low frequencies out of a signal, allowing the higher frequencies to pass through; the LPF does the opposite, cutting high frequencies and letting the lower frequencies pass through.

- By default, these two bands are not enabled. To use them, first click the **IN** button.

- Use the **FREQ** parameter to set the center frequency at which the filter will apply the cut.

- Use the **Q** parameter to determine how aggressive the cut is. The higher the value, the steeper the slope of the filter.

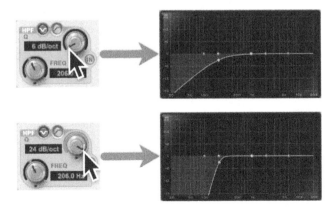

Figure 13.19 The effect of the Q setting on the HPF (low setting: top; high setting: bottom)

TOPIC 13.4:
USING DYNAMIC EFFECTS

Dynamic effects are processors that change the dynamic range of a signal in some way. In this lesson, we'll focus on the basic controls and uses of these powerful mixing tools.

Discussion: Controlling the Dynamics of a Track

Four primary dynamic effects are commonly used on individual tracks: Compressors, Limiters, Expanders, and Gates. The functions and controls of these processors are similar, although they serve different purposes.

Compressors and Limiters

Compression/limiting can be enormously powerful for the mixing engineer, but it can easily cause problems if not used with care. In this section, we talk about what a compressor/limiter does, the primary parameters involved, and how to apply this effect in mixing.

What is a Compressor?

The goal of a compressor is to reduce the dynamic range of a track (the difference between the track's loudest and softest parts). It does this by attenuating the track's peaks.

Compressors are used in a variety of ways in mixing:

- To manage the levels of a track, so that the levels are more consistent.

- To add punch to drums and other instruments that have a strong initial attack.

- To enhance an entire mix, making it louder overall and more "radio-ready."

Basic Compressor Parameters

Avid's *Dyn3 Compressor/Limiter* is a great example of a compressor. Its basic parameters illustrate how a compressor works.

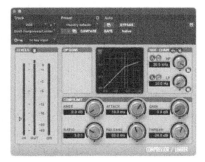

Figure 13.20 The Avid Dyn3 Compressor/Limiter plug-in

In the center of the Dyn3 Compressor/Limiter plug-in window, you'll see a graph with a broken diagonal line. This graph provides visual feedback about the plug-in's operation. Here's how it works:

- The bottom (x) axis corresponds to the incoming signal — the sound coming in from the track.

- The left side (y) axis corresponds to the outgoing signal — the sound going out of the compressor.

- The diagonal white line and vertical orange line indicate where and how compression is being applied.

- During playback, a small square appears, indicating the current level of the signal.

Figure 13.21 shows an example at two different signal levels.

- The graph on the left shows a signal coming into the compressor at a level of –40 dB and going out of the compressor unchanged at –40 dB.

- This graph on the right shows a signal coming into the compressor at –10 dB and going out of the compressor at –20 dB. Here, the outgoing sound level is reduced, as indicated by the red square icon.

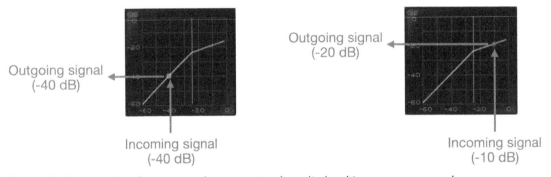

Figure 13.21 Examples of incoming and outgoing signals, as displayed in a compressor graph

The Threshold Control

The primary control for a compressor is the Threshold. This is the decibel (dB) level at which the signal will begin to be attenuated (made quieter).

The Threshold (**THRESH**) value is indicated by a vertical orange line. All the levels below the threshold (left of the line) remain unaffected. Whenever the incoming signal exceeds the threshold, the outgoing signal is reduced, or attenuated.

The Ratio Control

The **RATIO** setting determines the amount of attenuation that gets applied. The lowest ratio setting is 1.0:1; at this setting (a one-to-one ratio), no attenuation is applied. As you increase the Ratio, the amount of attenuation will increase. For example, at a ratio of 2.0:1 (two-to-one), any signal that exceeds the threshold will have its increase cut in half. A signal that exceeds the threshold by 2 dB at the input will result in a 1 dB increase at the output.

As the ratio value gets higher, the line to the right of the threshold will become flatter, and amplitudes that cross the threshold will be reduced by a higher percentage.

The Gain Control

Since the compressor works by making the loudest parts of a signal quieter, the end result would naturally be a quieter track. Typically, the opposite is the goal: making the track louder without clipping. That's where something called "Makeup Gain" comes in.

The **GAIN** knob (Figure 13.22) allows you to compensate for the decrease in volume you get from the compressor's gain reduction. This has the effect of raising the compressed dynamic range to a higher level.

Figure 13.22 The Gain control in the Dyn3 Compressor/Limiter plug-in

Level Meters

On the left side of the plug-in window you'll find the level meters. From left to right, the meters are:

- **Input Meter (IN):** This shows the level coming into the plug-in. An orange triangle on this meter indicates the Threshold setting. (You can also drag this icon to change the Threshold setting).

- **Output Meter (OUT):** This shows the level going out of the plug-in, including any makeup gain that has been applied.

- **Gain Reduction Meter (GR):** This meter shows the amount of gain reduction (attenuation) being applied to the signal when it exceeds the threshold. This is represented by a downward-moving orange indicator.

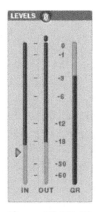

Figure 13.23 The meters in the Dyn3 Compressor/Limiter plug-in

Compressors versus Limiters

The basic difference between a compressor and a limiter is how they treat audio above the threshold. A limiter will cap the output level at the threshold value. This is effectively achieved using the Ratio control.

As you increase the Ratio setting, the output levels will move closer and closer to the threshold level. Eventually, the ratio will become a ceiling, beyond which the levels will not pass. For example, if you set your ratio to 100.0:1 and the threshold to –20 dB, the output level will be capped at –20 dB.

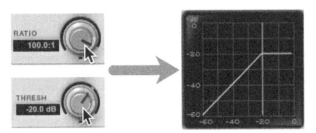

Figure 13.24 Setting the Dyn3 Compressor/Limiter to cap the audio output level

Expanders and Gates

As its name suggests, an *expander* does the opposite of what a compressor does. Instead of reducing the difference between loud and quiet sounds, an expander increases that difference. However, expanders operate much the same as compressors. What you've learned about compressors will help you to quickly understand how to use an expander.

Avid's Dyn3 Expander/Gate is a notable example of an expander.

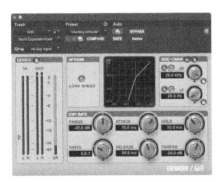

Figure 13.25 The Avid Dyn3 Expander/Gate plug-in

Expanders can be used in a variety of ways in mixing:

- To decrease ambient noise

- To reduce "bleed" from a microphone that picks up sound from other instruments (like a snare drum microphone that picks up a kick drum)

- To emphasize attacks by de-emphasizing the decay of a sound

- To shorten reverb by reducing the amplitude of the reverb tail

Basic Expander Parameters

The expander plug-in window looks like its compressor counterpart, and in many ways, it operates similarly.

- The **THRESHOLD** and **RATIO** parameters operate as on a compressor, but in reverse: When an incoming signal drops below the threshold level, it is attenuated downward according to the ratio settings. When the ratio is set to its lowest setting (1.0:1) there will be no attenuation; as the level is increased, the amount of attenuation will increase accordingly.

- The **LEVEL METERS** on the Dyn3 Expander/Gate plug-in are identical to those of the Dyn3 Compressor/Limiter. The only significant difference is how the GR meter behaves, since the gain reduction increases as the incoming signal gets quieter.

Expanders versus Gates

Just as a compressor with an extreme ratio becomes a limiter, an expander with an extreme ratio becomes a gate. The maximum ratio setting (100.0:1) will not allow any sound below the threshold to be heard. Gates are less common in mixing than expanders, but some situations (and styles of music) call for them. An example would be 80s-style drums, in which the gated snare drum was an iconic sound.

LESSON 13 CONCLUSION

When it comes to creating a final mix, volume and pan controls will only take you so far—at some point you'll want to add effects to sculpt the sound of your tracks. In this Lesson you learned about applying effects to tracks using inserts.

Discussion: Summary of Key Concepts

In this Lesson, you learned:

- What inserts are and how they are used in Pro Tools

- How to work with plug-ins on inserts:

  - Managing multiple plug-in windows

  - Moving plug-ins

  - Copying plug-ins

  - Bypassing plug-ins

  - Deactivating plug-ins

  - Removing plug-ins

- How inserts are used on Master Fader tracks

- How to use the plug-in window, including how to apply presets

- The difference between multichannel and multi-mono plug-ins

- How EQ is used in mixing and the different parameters in Pro Tools' EQ plug-ins

- How dynamic effects (compressors, expanders, limiters, and gates) are used in mixing

- The key parameters for dynamic effects

Essential Keyboard Commands and Shortcuts

Below is a summary of modifier behaviors and shortcut operations that you should know from this Lesson.

■   To open a new plug-in window without closing existing plug-in windows, hold **SHIFT** while clicking the plug-in insert selector.

■   To make a duplicate copy of a plug-in, hold **OPTION** (Mac) or **ALT** (Windows) while dragging the Insert Assignment button to a new location.

■   To bypass a plug-in, hold **COMMAND** (Mac) or **CTRL** (Windows) while clicking the Insert Assignment for the plug-in.

■   To deactivate a plug-in, hold **COMMAND+CONTROL** (Mac) or **CTRL+START** (Windows) while clicking the Insert Assignment for the plug-in.

Activity: Lesson 13 Knowledge Check

This quiz will check your knowledge on material covered in Lesson 13, Using Effects Processing.

1. How many inserts are available on an Audio track?

2. Which modifier would you hold while dragging an Insert Assignment button to make a duplicate copy of the insert on another track?

3. True or False? An inactive plug-in will not consume any CPU resources.

4. For each of the following track types, indicate whether inserts are pre-fader, post-fader, or configurable as either pre- or post-fader. (Circle the correct response.)

Audio tracks	Pre-fader — Post-fader — Configurable
Instrument tracks	Pre-fader — Post-fader — Configurable
Aux Input tracks	Pre-fader — Post-fader — Configurable
Master Fader tracks	Pre-fader — Post-fader — Configurable

5. When instantiating a plug-in on a stereo track, what two plug-in format options are available? (Select two.)

   a. Non-sequential

   b. Multi-mono

   c. Interspaced

   d. Multichannel

6. What are two common types of EQ processors? (Select two.)

   a. Macrosonic EQ

   b. Simple-Sonic EQ

   c. Parametric EQ

   d. Graphic EQ

7.   What is the LPF function in the EQ3 7-Band plug-in?

   a. Light Phase Frequency

   b. Last Part First

   c. Low Pass Filter

   d. Listen Pre-Fader

8.   True or False? The goal of a compressor is to reduce the dynamic range of a track.

9.   All of the following are standard Compressor parameters *except*: (Select one.)

   a. Threshold

   b. Ratio

   c. Q

   d. Gain

10. What does the GR meter in the Dyn3 Compressor/Limiter plug-in show?

   a. The level coming into the plug-in

   b. The level going out of the plug-in

   c. The amount of attenuation being applied to the signal

   d. The granularity of the signal passing through the plug-in

Adding Insert Processing

In this exercise, you will add EQ processing to the voiceover in your radio ad session. You will also add dynamics processing with a compressor.

Exercise Details

- **Required Media:** None

- **Exercise Duration:** 10 Minutes

Downloading the Media Files

To complete the exercises in this book, you will use files included in the **PT Academy Media Files** folder that you previously downloaded from the course learning module on ElementsED.com.

To re-download the media files, click on the **Access Files** link in the sidebar after logging in to your account. Consult your instructor or visit **nxpt.us/make-music** for more details.

Getting Started

You will start by opening the Pro Tools session you completed in Exercise 12. If that session is not available, you can use the provided **Exercise13-Starter** file in the **01. Starter Sessions** folder.

Open the session and save it as Exercise 13:

1. Open the session file that you created in Exercise 12: Storage Drive/Folder > Exercises-XXX > Exercise12-XXX.ptx.

   Alternatively, you can use the Exercise13 Starter file: PT Academy Media Files > 01. Starter Sessions > Exercise13-Starter.ptx.

2. Choose **FILE > SAVE AS** and name the session Exercise13-XXX, keeping the session inside the original folder. (Move the session into your **Exercises-XXX** folder if working from the starter file.)

Adding Plug-In Processing

In this part of the exercise, you will insert an EQ plug-in on the VO track and use it to boost and cut selective frequencies. Then you will add a Compressor plug-in to reduce the dynamic range and increase the overall amplitude.

Add an EQ plug-in:

1. Press **COMMAND+=** (Mac) or **CTRL+=** (Windows) as needed to switch to the Mix window.

2. Click on **INSERT SELECTOR A** toward the top of the VO track (under the Inserts A-E label).

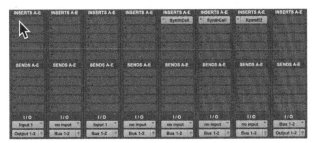

Figure 13.26 Clicking Insert A on the VO track

3. From the resulting menu, choose **PLUG-IN > EQ > EQ3 7-BAND (MONO)**. The plug-in window will display.

4. Click the **LIBRARIAN** menu (where it initially shows <Factory Default>) and select a preset from the **VOCALS** category.

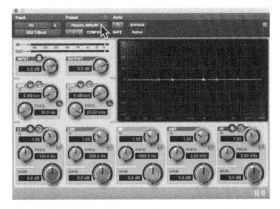

Figure 13.27 Clicking the Librarian menu for the EQ3 7-band plug-in

5. Begin playback and toggle the **BYPASS** button on/off to discern the difference the preset is making.

6. Audition a few other presets in the **VOCALS** category and select your favorite.

7. Increase the Gain on the Mid Frequency (MF) band or High Mid Frequency (HMF) band to 4.5 dB or more.

8. Adjust the frequency (Freq) and bandwidth (Q) controls to maximize clarity for the track.

9. Make other adjustments as desired.

10. Stop playback and close the plug-in window when finished.

Add a Compressor plug-in:

1. Click on INSERT SELECTOR B on the VO track (underneath the EQ plug-in you added).

2. Choose PLUG-IN > DYNAMICS > DYN3 COMPRESSOR/LIMITER (MONO). The plug-in window will display with default settings.

3. Verify that the Ratio control is set to 3.0:1. Make adjustments as needed.

4. Begin playback and adjust the Threshold (Thresh) control until you see the peak indicator on the Gain Reduction (GR) meter hitting around -6 dB.

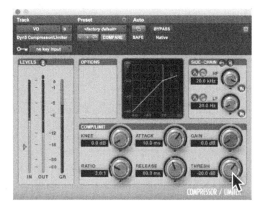

Figure 13.28 Adjusting the Threshold control on the Dyn3 Compressor/Limiter plug-in

5. Increase the Gain control to around 5.5 dB to compensate for the gain reduction.

6. Stop playback and close the plug-in window when you're finished.

Finishing Up

To complete this exercise, you will need to save your work and close the session. You will be reusing this session in Exercise 14, so it is important to save the work you've done.

You should also listen to your mix and make any required adjustments before exiting.

Review and fine-tune your work:

1. Press **ENTER** or **RETURN** to place the cursor at the beginning of the session.

2. Press the **SPACEBAR** to play back the session and review your changes.

3. Adjust the levels on the Music Sub, Beach FX, and Fire FX tracks as needed to rebalance the mix and compensate for the changes you've made to the VO track.

4. Press the **SPACEBAR** a second time when finished.

5. Choose **FILE > SAVE** to save the session.

6. Choose **FILE > CLOSE SESSION** to close the session.

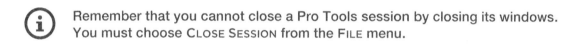 Remember that you cannot close a Pro Tools session by closing its windows. You must choose CLOSE SESSION from the FILE menu.

Lesson 14

Other Effects Processing Options

Although effects are commonly applied directly to a track using an insert, this is not always the most effective approach. Certain types of effects lend themselves to being shared across multiple tracks in a session. This is particularly true of reverbs and delay processors.

In this Lesson, we examine how to set up shared effects that help add a sense of ambience to a mix. We also explore various parameters that are commonly found in reverb and delay processors. At the end of the Lesson, we take a look at a file-based processing option known as AudioSuite.

Learning Targets

- Set up send-and-return processing for effects

- Add ambience with reverb and delay

- Recognize common parameters in reverb and delay processors

- Work with AudioSuite plug-ins

TOPIC 14.1:
USING EFFECTS SENDS

Gain-based effects like an EQ and Dynamics plug-ins are placed on track inserts and affect 100 percent of the signal on that track. For other effects, like reverb and delay, you will want to blend the original "dry" signal with the processed "wet" signal. To get this done, you can use sends.

Discussion: Adding Parallel Processing with Sends

Sends are used to take a split of a signal from one or more tracks and route it to a separate destination for parallel processing. In this section, we explore how and why that is done.

Sends and Returns

The term "send-and-return" comes from mixing on an analog desk or mixing board. Here, you would use controls on each channel (usually knobs) to route a copy of the signal out to an external processor, such as a reverb unit.

After being processed by the reverb unit, the affected signal would be returned to the mixing board through a separate "return" channel. This signal would then be blended back in with the original source channels.

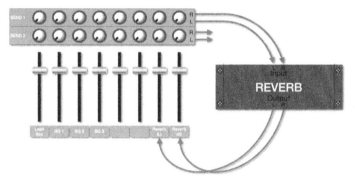

Figure 14.1 Using a send and return to add reverb to a mix on an analog board

Here's what you can do with a setup like this in Pro Tools:

- Adjust the send controls on an individual track to add more or less of that track's signal to the effect. If you want more reverb on the lead vocal, you can turn up the send on that one track.

- Use the fader on the return track to control how much of the effect gets added to your mix. Adjusting the fader on the reverb return would increase or decrease the overall reverb in the mix.

Send-and-return routing is traditionally used for effects like reverb and delay. Both of these fall into the category called time-based effects. Using this approach lets you preserve the original tracks (the "dry" signal) and blend them with a parallel return track (the "wet" signal).

Why Use Send-and-Return Routing?

In a DAW like Pro Tools, you can certainly put reverb or delay plug-ins directly on a track, like we do for EQs and Dynamic effects. Although there is nothing wrong with this from a technical point of view, you will find that send-and-return routing offers several advantages in most situations. Remember that multiple tracks can be sent to the return track to use a single, shared effect.

Some advantages of using this process for blended effects include the following:

- **Mixer-Level Access:** Having reverbs and other blended effects on their own tracks simplifies your job as a mixer. You can use the fader on the reverb track to set the level of the effect throughout the mix.

- **Mix Agility:** When you want to make a change to the effects settings, you need only change the one plug-in. If instead of using a shared reverb you had put individual reverbs on each track, you'd have to adjust all of them individually each time you needed to make a change to the reverb settings.

- **Processing Efficiency:** In a send-and-return setup, your computer runs a single plug-in for a shared effect. If you instead put a copy of that plug-in on each track, you multiply the demand on the host computer. This proliferation of plug-ins can start to tax your computer's CPU.

- **Realism:** Routing signals from multiple tracks to an ambient effect like reverb mimics the way sound in the real world behaves. Signals combine and interact within a single reverb effect in the same way that sound from multiple performers in a room combine. This can produce a more realistic result.

Creating Effect Sends

Now that we've covered the purpose of using sends, let's dive in to how to use them. The setup in Pro Tools is a bit different from what you would see on an analog mixing board. It may also be different from what you've experienced in other DAWs. But if you understand the concept, you'll find the process fairly logical.

Viewing Sends

Pro Tools provides 10 send positions for every Audio track. To use a send, you'll need to display the associated send position in the Mix or Edit window.

To review, here are a few ways that you can show sends, if needed:

- Go to the **VIEW** menu and choose **EDIT WINDOW VIEWS** or **MIX WINDOW VIEWS**. From there, select **SENDS A-E** or **SENDS F-J**.

- In the Edit window, click the **EDIT WINDOW VIEW SELECTOR** (small white icon at the left, above the tracks—see Figure 14.2). Select **SENDS A-E** or **SENDS F-J**.

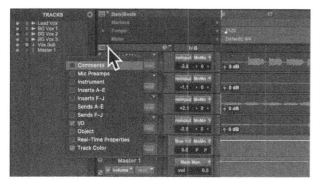

Figure 14.2 The Edit Window View selector

■   In the Mix window, click the **MIX WINDOW VIEW SELECTOR** (small white icon in the bottom left corner). Select **SENDS A-E** or **SENDS F-J**.

Creating Sends and Returns in Pro Tools

After creating a send from one or more tracks, the signal must be returned to the mixer in order to hear the result. In Pro Tools, we use an Aux Input track for this purpose. When mixing in the box, you will use the return track to add the effects processing.

Here's an example of how this could be done to add reverb to some vocal tracks:

1.   Click on an available send position on one of the vocal tracks. A pop-up menu will appear.

Figure 14.3 The send menu on the Lead Vox track

2. Select **Bus** from the menu and choose an available mono or stereo bus from the submenu. Here, we'll select a stereo option (**Bus 1-2**), since the signal will be sent to a stereo track.

Figure 14.4 Selecting Bus 1-2 for the send

 Any busses already in use by the session will display in bold orange text. Select one of the unused options when creating a new send.

3. In the Send window that displays, optionally raise the fader to set the send level. (Alternatively, you can return to this window later to set the level.)

Hold OPTION (Mac) or ALT (Windows) to set the Send fader to 0 dB (unity gain).

4. Repeat this process on the other vocal tracks, assigning the same bus you used for the first track.

5. When finished, close any Send window that may be displayed.

6. Next, create a stereo Aux Input track to function as the return and give it an appropriate name (we'll name it **Verb** in this example).

7. On the new Aux Input track, use any insert position to add your desired reverb plug-in. Here we've added the **AIR REVERB** plug-in on Insert A. (See Figure 14.5.)

Figure 14.5 Reverb plug-in added to the return track

8. Set the plug-in parameters as desired, or select an appropriate preset from the Librarian menu. Ensure that the **MIX** parameter is set to 100% **Wet**.

> See the discussion on Basic Reverb Parameters in Topic 14.2 below for a detailed discussion of the available parameters.

9. Click the **AUDIO INPUT PATH SELECTOR** on the Aux Input track (top selector in the I/O view) and select the same stereo bus you used for the sends from the source tracks.

10. Verify that the Aux Input track is solo safe-enabled, so that it doesn't mute when another track is soloed. The Solo button will have a dimmed appearance when solo safe is active.

> In current versions of Pro Tools, Aux Input tracks are solo safe-enabled by default.

> To toggle solo safe mode on/off for a track, hold COMMAND (Mac) or CTRL (Windows) while clicking on the track's SOLO button.

Figure 14.6 Routing to sends from the vocal tracks and to the Verb Aux Input track as a return

Adjusting Send Parameters

When you create a send on a track in Pro Tools, a Send window will display. You can close this window using the close button in the top left corner (Mac) or top right corner (Windows). To reopen a Send window at a later time, you can click on the associated Send Assignment button.

Figure 14.7 An open Send window

When you open a new Send window, it replaces the previous Send window by default; however, you can open multiple Send windows by holding **SHIFT** while clicking on subsequent Send Assignment buttons.

Send Volume

You can set the send level for the track using the fader in the Send window, as described above.

Send Pan

At the top of the Send window, you'll find the Send Pan control (stereo sends only). This control lets you position the signal that is sent to the effect on the return track. Panning the send can be is useful if you want the reverb or delay for a track to be off-center, for example.

 Above the pan control on the right is a button labeled FMP, for Follow Main Pan. When active, this function will cause the track to mirror the panning of the source track. This is useful to ensure that effects follow the track position.

Pre-Fader Mode

Sends are switchable between pre-fader and post-fader mode. When a new send is created, it is post-fader by default.

Centered above the pan knob in the Send window, you'll see a button labeled **PRE**. When this button is highlighted in blue, the send is pre-fader; when it is gray (not highlighted), the send is post-fader. Clicking on the button will toggle its state. For sends to effects, you will typically want to leave the **PRE** button off.

Figure 14.8 The PRE button in a Send window (shown inactive)

Working with Sends

Sends and inserts share some common behaviors:

- You can move a send from one track to another (or to another position within a track) by clicking and dragging. As you drag the send, a yellow box will indicate the target destination.

- You can duplicate a send by holding **OPTION** (Mac) or **ALT** (Windows) while dragging the send to another track.

- You can remove a send by clicking the **SEND SELECTOR** and choosing **NO SEND** from the pop-up menu.

TOPIC 14.2:
ADDING AMBIENCE TO YOUR MIX

Sends provide a good way to add ambient effects like *reverb* and *delay* to your mix. You can use such plug-ins on effect return tracks (Aux Inputs) and you can send signals to them from any number of source tracks.

To get started with ambient effects, you'll need to be familiar with reverb and delay plug-ins. In this section, we explore both types of processors and focus on the key parameters of each.

Discussion: Configuring Reverb Plug-Ins

Reverberation (or reverb for short) is the persistence of sound after the source signal stops. Reverb is the result of sound reflecting off of the walls and other surfaces of a room or space. The character of reverberation is what gives a sound its unique space and distance. A person speaking directly in front of you in a small room will sound different from that same person speaking from a distance in a large cathedral.

How Reverb Is Used in a Mix

Here are a few traditional uses for reverb in a mix:

- **Mix Cohesion:** Audio is often recorded in acoustically "dead" studios—rooms specifically designed to minimize reverberation. Adding a reverb to a mix can place all the instruments into a single cohesive space, adding a sense of realism to the mix.

- **Physical Space Re-Creation:** A good dialog mixer for a movie or TV program will devote attention to choosing the right reverb—one that matches the physical space of an actor on the screen—so that the recorded material sonically matches the visual environment.

- **Ambient Effects:** Many styles of music (and audio for games, TV, and cinema) utilize reverb to create ambience that can't be found in the natural world.

Reverb Types

Reverbs come in several types. Here are a few types of reverb that you should be aware of.

- **Plate:** This kind of reverb originated from vibrating metal plates. Plate reverbs don't sound especially real, but they're dense and have a shimmer in the high end that works nicely for musical instruments.

- **Spring:** This kind of reverb originated from vibrating springs. Like plate reverbs, spring reverbs are a bit bright, which is perfect for some instruments (commonly used on guitars, for example).

- **Convolution:** This kind of reverb is used to replicate the sound of real spaces. The effect is created by recording an initial sound in a space and calculating an *impulse response* from the results. The reverb processor then applies this impulse response to other audio playing through the reverb, effectively making this audio sound like it is coming from the same space.

- **Hall:** This kind of reverb emulates a concert hall, with a very big, lush space.

- **Chamber:** This kind of reverb also emulates a big space, but not quite as huge as a hall. Chambers are lush, but have a bit more clarity than halls.

- **Room:** This type of reverb is smaller than halls or chambers and will feel more like a natural space for most applications. If you want to give your mix a sense of having walls, this is a good option.

Basic Reverb Parameters

The Avid **D-Verb** plug-in is included with Pro Tools and is an example of a multipurpose reverb plug-in. The parameters in D-Verb are representative of those typically found on reverb processors.

Figure 14.9 The Avid D-Verb plug-in

At the top of the plug-in window are buttons for choosing the reverb type and size:

- **HALL:** Large and diffuse concert hall

- **CHURCH:** Large and diffuse church space

- **PLATE:** Plate reverb emulation

- **ROOM 1:** Medium-sized room

- **ROOM 2:** Smaller and brighter room

- **AMBIENT:** Sparse, airy reverb

- **NON-LINEAR:** Builds up gradually and ends abruptly; good for special effects and an aggressive sound

Each algorithm can be set to **SMALL**, **MEDIUM**, or **LARGE** options. Changing these settings will change the perceived size of the space.

Decay

The time that it takes for the reflections from a reverb to die out is called **DECAY**.

Figure 14.10 The Decay parameter in D-Verb

This parameter on a reverb lets you change how long it takes for the energy of the incoming signal to decrease to silence. Use this to fine-tune the sound of the selected reverb to suit your needs.

 At its maximum setting, the Decay parameter will create an infinite reverb that never stops ringing out. This can be useful for different kinds of surreal effects.

Pre-Delay

The **PRE-DELAY** parameter is the time between the initial sound and the first reflections from the reverb. This represents the time the sound needs to travel, hit a surface, and reflect back to the listener.

Figure 14.11 The Pre-Delay parameter in D-Verb

A larger pre-delay value will increase the time it takes for the incoming signal to start to reverberate, simulating a larger space and a closer listening position.

Mix

The **MIX** parameter is used to set the wet/dry balance for the signal coming out of the plug-in. When used on a return track, the reverb's Mix parameter should be set to 100% wet, since the source tracks in the mix will provide the dry signal.

Figure 14.12 The Mix parameter in D-Verb

Discussion: Configuring Delay Plug-Ins

A delay plug-in does what its name implies—it delays the incoming sound. When used in a send-and-return setup, the source tracks will not be delayed, while the return track is delayed. This results in an echo effect, which is what delay processing is all about.

How Delay Is Used in a Mix

Delays are used in a variety of ways in mixing. Here are a few examples:

- **Thickening:** A short delay can add body to an individual track or group of tracks.

- **Stereo Widening/Positioning:** A small amount of delay on only one side (left or right) can increase the perceived width of a track or create a perception of panning.

- **Ambient and Rhythmic Effects:** Delays are less diffuse than reverb and can be more distinctly heard. This makes them useful in reinforcing the rhythmic feel or groove of a song.

 At times, delay should be used directly on the source track (for example, to widen the stereo image of the track). The discussion below focuses on send-and-return routing, for simplicity.

Basic Delay Parameters

Avid's **Mod Delay III** plug-in is a good example of a delay. The parameters in Mod Delay III are representative of common controls in a delay processor.

Figure 14.13 The Avid Mod Delay III plug-in

Delay Time

The Delay Time parameter is quite simple—it's the amount of time (in milliseconds) that the incoming signal is delayed before leaving the processor.

Figure 14.14 The Delay Time parameter in the Mod Delay III plug-in (mono: left; stereo: right)

On a stereo track, this plug-in will have two independent controls, providing the option to set a different delay time on the left and right sides.

Feedback

The **FEEDBACK** (or **FBK**) control sets the level at which the plug-in's output is routed back to its input. By default, the Mod Delay III plug-in's feedback is **0%**—no feedback whatsoever. This provides a single delay of the incoming sound, or a single echo.

Increasing the FBK parameter to **50%** causes fifty percent of the delayed signal to be routed back into the plug-in. This quieter signal is then delayed again, causing a second, quieter echo. Then fifty percent of that signal is fed back into the input of the delay again, creating an even quieter third echo. This continues until the level of the fed-back signal is inaudible.

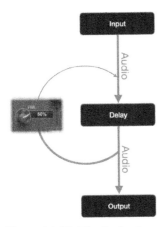

Figure 14.15 The feedback process in a Delay plug-in

Smaller Feedback settings will give you fewer delay repetitions that die out quickly. Larger settings will create more audible repetitions. Setting Feedback to **100%** will create an infinite delay.

 Setting the FBK parameter to a negative percentage will invert the phase of the fed-back signal. This can create a more intense, "flanged" sound when used with shorter delay time settings.

The Mix Parameter

As with reverb processors, The **MIX** parameter on a delay is used to set the wet/dry balance for the signal. When using delay on a return track, be sure to set the Mix parameter to 100% wet. Remember that the source tracks in the mix will provide the dry signal in this case.

Figure 14.16 The Mix parameter in the Mod Delay III plug-in

 In cases where you put a delay (or reverb) plug-in directly on the source track, you can use the Mix parameter to set the desired dry/wet balance.

Discussion: Using Presets for Reverb and Delay

In our discussions of EQ, compressors, and limiters, we focused on individual parameters more than on the presets that each plug-in comes with. That was because each audio track is unique, and presets probably won't be a perfect fit in most cases.

 You *can* use presets as an effective way to select a starting point for EQ and dynamics processing. They may get you 80 or 90 percent to where you want to be, making it easier to fine-tune the settings.

Reverbs and delays are a bit different. They often fill the role of replicating a physical space in your mix. With reverbs and delays, you will likely find the included presets to be quite useful. You still may need to fine-tune the effect, but often, selecting a preset may be all you need.

TOPIC 14.3:
ANOTHER WAY TO WORK: AUDIOSUITE

The plug-in effects we've seen so far change the sound of a track in *real time*—the signal coming into a track is processed at an insert while the audio is playing back. As such, the sound can change as you modify the effect's parameters. But there is an alternative.

Discussion: Applying Non-Real-Time Effects

Pro Tools provides another way of applying effects, called AudioSuite processing. AudioSuite plug-ins provide *file-based* processing. They work directly on selections and write their effects into audio files. This type of processing is not done during real-time playback and is often called non-real-time processing.

To use an AudioSuite plug-in, do the following:

1. Select the clip or area that you want to process.

2. Click the **AUDIOSUITE** menu. A list of plug-in categories will display.

3. Choose the desired plug-in category to display the submenu of plug-ins for that category.

4. Select the desired plug-in. The AudioSuite plug-in window for that processor will display.

5. Adjust the parameters in the plug-in window as desired.

6. Optionally use the **PREVIEW** button (speaker icon) at the bottom left to audition your settings before applying them; then make adjustments as needed.

Figure 14.17 The Preview button (speaker icon) in an AudioSuite plug-in

(i) Some AudioSuite plug-ins do not include a Preview button.

7. Click the **RENDER** button in the bottom right corner of the window to apply the effect.

When you apply an AudioSuite plug-in to a selection, the selection is generally replaced by a new clip. The name of this new clip will include a suffix reflecting the AudioSuite process that was applied. For example, a selection within a clip named **Tuba Stem** will create a clip named **Tuba Stem-Norm_01** when processed with the **NORMALIZE** AudioSuite plug-in.

Getting Around the AudioSuite Plug-in Window

Although each AudioSuite plug-in has unique parameters, they all share some common elements.

In the upper-left corner of the AudioSuite window, you'll find the **PLUG-IN SELECTOR**. This displays the name of the current plug-in, such as Normalize, and lets you to change effects without closing the window.

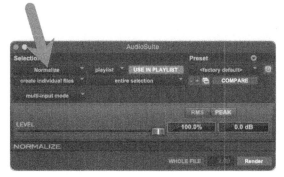

Figure 14.18 The Plug-In Selector in an AudioSuite plug-in window

The **SELECTION REFERENCE** menu lets you determine what selection will be processed.

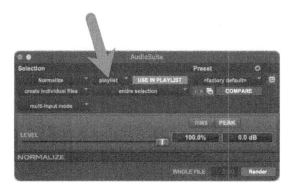

Figure 14.19 The Selection Reference menu in an AudioSuite plug-in window

The options in this menu are:

- **Playlist:** The plug-in will process the selected audio on your track(s).

- **Clip List:** The plug-in will process any audio clip(s) selected in the Clips List. This can be useful if you have multiple instances of the same clip in your session.

The **USE IN PLAYLIST** button determines whether the processed clip will be placed on a track or not. When the button is highlighted in blue, the processed clip will appear on the track. When it is grey (off), the new clip will appear in the Clips List only.

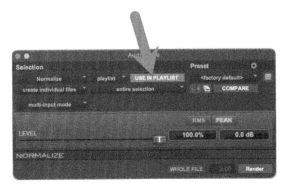

Figure 14.20 The Use In Playlist button

 A common mistake that Pro Tools users make is to apply AudioSuite processing with the USE IN PLAYLIST button off. In this case, it may appear that the plug-in is doing nothing, since no change is made on the track.

The **PROCESSING OUTPUT MODE** selector lets you choose how processing will be applied.

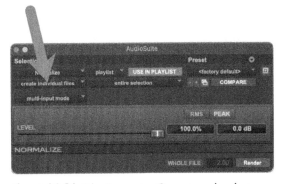

Figure 14.21 The Processing Output mode selector

This selector provides up to three different processing options:

- **Overwrite Files:** With this option chosen, the selected audio will be processed destructively. This means that the original file will be rewritten on disk and permanently changed.

- **Create Individual Files:** This mode is nondestructive and will create new audio files for each selected clip. If multiple clips are selected, multiple new files will be created.

- **Create Continuous File:** This mode is also nondestructive. In this case, a single new audio file will be created, regardless of how many clips are selected.

(i)   The OVERWRITE FILES option is not available in some AudioSuite plug-ins.

The **PROCESSING INPUT MODE** selector determines how selected clips will be analyzed when processing.

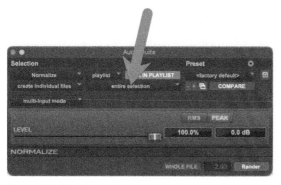

Figure 14.22 The Processing Input Mode selector

This selector provides two options:

- **Clip by Clip:** With this option, each selected clip will be individually analyzed and processed.

- **Entire Selection:** With this option, all selected clips will be analyzed prior to being processed.

The choice between **CLIP BY CLIP** processing and **ENTIRE SELECTION** processing can make a difference for certain types of plug-ins. When applied to multiple selected clips, plug-ins like **AUDIOSUITE > OTHER > REVERSE** can be used to either affect one clip at a time or to affect all of the selected clips as a group.

LESSON 14 CONCLUSION

Effects processing can do a lot to change the character of a mix. In this Lesson, you learned how to add effects to a session using send-and-return configurations. You learned the applications and basic controls for reverb and delay processing. You also learned about file-based processing with AudioSuite.

Discussion: Summary of Key Concepts

In this Lesson, you learned:

- What a send-and-return configuration is

- How to add sends to a bus from the tracks in your session

- How to configure various send parameters (send volume, send pan, etc.)

- How to create a return track for effects processing

- How reverb and delay effects can be used to add ambience to a mix

- How AudioSuite plug-ins differ from real-time effects

- How to navigate an AudioSuite plug-in window

Essential Keyboard Commands and Shortcuts

Below is a summary of modifier behaviors and shortcut operations that you should know from this Lesson.

- To enable/disable Solo Safe mode for a track, hold **COMMAND** (Mac) or **CTRL** (Windows) while clicking on the track's Solo button.

- To open a new send window without closing existing send windows, hold **SHIFT** while clicking the send selector.

- To set a send level to unity, hold **OPTION** (Mac) or **ALT** (Windows) while clicking the send fader.

- To make a duplicate copy of a send, hold **OPTION** (Mac) or **ALT** (Windows) while dragging the send button to another track.

Activity: Lesson 14 Knowledge Check

This quiz will check your knowledge on material covered in Lesson 14, Using Effects Processing.

1.   How many sends are available on an Audio track?

2.   Which modifier would you hold while clicking on a send fader to set it to unity gain?

3.   In a send-and-return configuration, what should the **AUDIO INPUT PATH** on the return Aux Input track be set to?

    a. Input 1-2

    b. Bus 1-2

    c. A reverb or delay plug-in

    d. The same bus used for the sends from the source tracks

4.   True or False? The send in the image below is configured as a pre-fader send.

5.   How can you set a send level to unity gain?

    a. Click on the PRE button in the send window so it is highlighted in blue

    b. Click on the FMP button in the send window so it is highlighted in amber

    c. Option-click on the Send Fader

    d. Option-click on the track's Solo button

6.   How is reverb used in a mix? (Select all that apply.)

   a. For cohesion, to place all the instruments into a single space in the mix

   b. For dynamics control, to reduce the dynamic range and help prevent clipping

   c. To re-create a physical space of an actor on the screen to match the visual environment

   d. To add ambient effects that can't be found in the natural world

7.   What parameter can you use in a reverb processor to control the time that it takes for the sound reflections to die out?

   a. Threshold

   b. Make-Up Gain

   c. Frequency

   d. Decay

8.   How should you typically set the **Mix** parameter (wet/dry balance) for a reverb or delay plug-in on a return track, in a send-and-return configuration?

   a. 100 percent dry

   b. 50 percent dry/50 percent wet

   c. 100 percent wet

   d. Anywhere between dry and wet, as long as you avoid extremes

9.   What is the Feedback control used for in a delay processor?

   a. Sets the amount of time that the incoming signal is delayed before leaving the processor

   b. Causes the delayed sound to start ringing at a high pitch

   c. Sets the level at which the plug-in's output is routed back to its input

   d. Sets the balance between the original dry signal and the delayed wet signal

10. True or False? AudioSuite processing in Pro Tools is applied to tracks in real time.

Adding Effects Processing

In this exercise, you will add reverb and delay to your radio ad session. These processors will be used to create a sense of space in the mix and to add emphasis to the voiceover track.

Exercise Details

- **Required Media:** None

- **Exercise Duration:** 10 Minutes

Downloading the Media Files

To complete the exercises in this book, you will use files included in the **PT Academy Media Files** folder that you previously downloaded from the course learning module on ElementsED.com.

To re-download the media files, click on the **Access Files** link in the sidebar after logging in to your account. Consult your instructor or visit **nxpt.us/make-music** for more details.

Getting Started

You will start by opening the Pro Tools session you completed in Exercise 13. If that session is not available, you can use the provided **Exercise14-Starter** file in the **01. Starter Sessions** folder.

Open the session and save it as Exercise 14:

1. Open the session file that you created in Exercise 13: **Storage Drive/Folder > Exercises-XXX > Exercise13-XXX.ptx.**

    Alternatively, you can use the Exercise14 Starter file: **PT Academy Media Files > 01. Starter Sessions > Exercise14-Starter.ptx.**

2. Choose **FILE > SAVE AS** and name the session **Exercise14-XXX**, keeping the session inside the original folder. (Move the session into your **Exercises-XXX** folder if working from the starter file.)

Adding Reverb

In this part of the exercise, you will create sends from the Drums and Guitar tracks to an available bus. Then you will create an Aux Input track to serve as a reverb return and route the bus into the track's input. Lastly, you will insert a reverb plug-in on the track and select an appropriate preset.

Assign sends on the Drums and Guitar tracks:

1. Click on SEND SELECTOR A on the Drums track (under the Sends A-E label) and select BUS > BUS 3-4 (STEREO). The Send window will open.

     Bus 1-2 is already used in this session (for the Music Sub), as indicated by the gold color displayed in the Send Selector menu.

2. Raise the Send fader for the Drums track to around -10.5 dB.

3. Close the Send window when finished.

4. Repeat the above process to assign a send on the Guitar track.

5. Raise the Send fader for the Guitar track to around -7.5 dB and close the window when finished.

Create a reverb return:

1. Select the Fire FX track by clicking on its nameplate in the Edit window.

2. Choose TRACK > NEW and create a new stereo Aux Input track named Reverb. The new track will appear to the right of the Fire FX track in the Mix window.

3. Click on the AUDIO INPUT PATH SELECTOR for the Reverb track (the top selector under the I/O label) and select BUS > BUS 3-4 (STEREO). (See Figure 14.23.)

Figure 14.23 Audio Input Path selector on the Reverb track

4. Click on **INSERT SELECTOR A** for the Reverb track (under the Inserts A-E label) and choose **MULTICHANNEL PLUG-IN > REVERB > AIR REVERB (STEREO)**. The plug-in window will open.

5. Select the **08 DRUM ROOM** preset using the **LIBRARIAN** menu (displaying <factory default>).

6. Close the plug-in window when you're finished.

Creating a Delay Effect

Next, you will create an Aux Input track to function as a delay return. Then you will insert a delay plug-in on the track and create sends from the VO track and the Fire FX track to the delay effect.

Create a delay return:

1. With the Reverb track selected, choose **TRACK > NEW** and create a new stereo Aux Input track named Delay. The new track will appear after the Reverb track.

2. Click on the **AUDIO INPUT PATH SELECTOR** for the Delay track and select **BUS > BUS 5-6 (STEREO)**.

3. Click on **INSERT SELECTOR A** for the Delay track and choose **MULTICHANNEL PLUG-IN > DELAY > AIR DYNAMIC DELAY (STEREO)**. The plug-in window will open.

4. Select the **05 TWO AGAINST THREE** preset using the **LIBRARIAN** menu.

5. Lower the **FEEDBACK** parameter to 40% and increase the **MIX** parameter to 100%.

Figure 14.24 The AIR Dynamic Delay plug-in configured for the session

6. Close the plug-in window when you're finished.

Assign sends on the VO and Fire FX tracks:

1. Click **SEND SELECTOR A** on the Fire FX track and select **BUS > BUS 5-6 (STEREO)**. The Send window will open.

2. **OPTION-CLICK** (Mac) or **ALT-CLICK** (Windows) on the Send fader to set it to 0.0 dB.

3. Close the Send window when finished.

4. Repeat the above process to assign a send on the VO track.

5. Raise the Send fader for the VO track to around -7.0 dB. Leave the send window open when finished.

Finishing Up

To complete this exercise tutorial, you should listen to your work and save your session. You will be reusing this session in Exercise 8, so it is important to save the work you've done.

Review and save your work:

1. Press **ENTER** or **RETURN** to place the cursor at the beginning of the session.

2. Press the **SPACEBAR** to play back the session and review your results. Stop playback when finished.

3. Choose **FILE > SAVE** to save the session.

4. Choose **FILE > CLOSE SESSION** to close the session.

(i) Remember that you cannot close a Pro Tools session by closing its windows. You must choose CLOSE SESSION from the FILE menu.

Automation and Mixdown

The rough mixes you've been working with up to now have been static—meaning none of the controls (volume, pan, and so on) are changing over time during playback. The limitation of static mixes is that the settings you need for one section of your session might not be the right settings for other sections. This can be addressed with mix automation, as discussed here.

This final lesson will also deal with the mixdown process, allowing you to render your Pro Tools session to a format compatible with media players in the outside world.

Learning Targets

- Understand and use mix automation

- View mix automation in a Pro Tools session

- Create mix automation using the Pencil, Trim, and Grabber tools

- Use automation modes to write and play back mix automation

- Understand different methods of creating a mixdown

- Bounce a session using the Bounce Mix dialog box

- Back up and archive a session

TOPIC 15.1:
INTRODUCTION TO MIX AUTOMATION

Mix automation lets you create dynamic changes to aspects of your mix (such as volume, panning, or effects) over time and have those automated changes stored within your session. Once changes have been written as automation, they can be played back and added to, giving you the ability to program multiple simultaneous parameter changes throughout your session.

Activity: Playing Tracks with Automation

■   Open the Activity 15.1.ptx session. The session will open showing several tracks in both the Edit window (top) and in the Mix window (bottom). The Edit window shows each track with its Volume automation graph displayed over the track waveforms.

■   Press the spacebar to begin playback. The volume faders in the Mix window will move up and down automatically, following the Volume graphs shown in the Edit window.

■   Stop playback and use the **PENCIL** tool to redraw the graph on one or more tracks.

■   Begin playback again. The fader movements will follow the shape of the new graphs.

■   Using the **SELECTOR** tool, click at different locations in the Edit window. What happens?

Discuss what you've experienced. What is the relationship between the automation graph and the fader on each track? When do the volume faders move on a track? During playback only? How do you think an automation graph might look for pan controls?

Discussion: Working with Automation

Automation can either be *written* to tracks during playback or created while the transport is stopped, using various *editing* techniques. When you play a session, any existing automation can be played back (read) or ignored, depending on your settings. Let's start by considering how existing automation can be displayed.

Viewing Automation in Pro Tools

Though you'll do much of your mixing work in the Mix window, viewing automation is something you'll do in the Edit window. The Edit window not only shows you a visual representation of the automation on a track, but it also lets you edit the automation easily.

Volume Automation View

In Lesson 10, you learned how to change the track view on MIDI and Instrument tracks from **CLIPS** view to **NOTES** view or **VELOCITY** view. You can use the same process to view Volume automation for a track.

To display Volume automation on a track:

1. Display the Edit window.

2. Click the **TRACK VIEW SELECTOR** for the target track and select **VOLUME** from the pop-up menu. A line called the automation graph will display superimposed on the audio waveform.

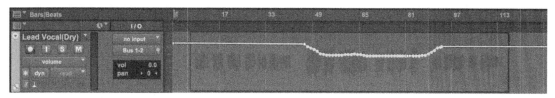

Figure 15.1 The Lead Vocal (Dry) track's volume automation graph showing existing automation changes

Automation Lanes

One limitation of changing your track view is that while viewing an automation playlist, you won't be able to edit the audio on the track. As an alternative, you can view automation using an automation lane, leaving the track in **WAVEFORM** view.

To display an automation lane:

1. Click on the **SHOW/HIDE AUTOMATION LANES** button (square icon on the bottom left) to expand the automation lanes beneath the track. The Volume lane will display by default for an Audio track.

2. Optionally click on the **ADD LANE** button, indicated by a **PLUS (+)** icon, to display a second lane (such as mute or pan).

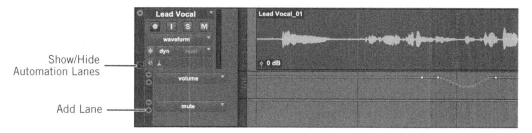

Figure 15.2 Volume and Mute automation lanes shown beneath a track

> (i) On MIDI and Instrument tracks, you can also use automation lanes to view Velocity values and Continuous Controller (CC) data.

TOPIC 15.2:
CREATING, EDITING, AND PLAYING AUTOMATION

All automation graphs begin as a straight line (meaning that the mix parameter does not move or change). One easy way to get started with automation is to use editing tools (like the Grabber and Pencil) to modify the automation graph for the parameter you wish to automate. Alternatively, you can write automation in real time using one of the automation modes provided in Pro Tools.

Discussion: Using Edit Tools for Automation

When a parameter has been automated, its automation graph will show a number of small dots. These dots are called automation breakpoints. Breakpoints define the shape of an automation graph, providing points where the graph can change direction. The Edit tools can be used to add, delete, or modify breakpoints.

Automation and the Grabber Tool

The Grabber tool provides a simple way to work with breakpoints. Using the Grabber, you can easily create, modify, and delete automation breakpoints:

- To create an automation breakpoint, click anywhere on a displayed automation graph. A new breakpoint will be added at the clicked location or at the nearest Grid increment (in Grid mode).

(i) You'll generally want to work in Slip mode when adding breakpoints with the Grabber tool, in order to position the breakpoints precisely.

- To modify placement of an existing automation breakpoint, click and drag on the breakpoint. You can drag breakpoints up or down and earlier or later, to the desired location.

- To delete an existing automation breakpoint, hold **OPTION** (Mac) or **ALT** (Windows) while clicking on the breakpoint.

Automation and the Pencil Tool

The Pencil tool allows you to draw automation using a variety of different shapes.

1.   To select a shape, click and hold on the **PENCIL** button in the Edit window toolbar. A pop-up menu will appear displaying available Pencil tool modes. (See Figure 15.3.) For this first example, we'll select the default Free Hand shape.

Figure 15.3 Available drawing shapes for different Pencil tool modes

2. Position the Pencil tool over the automation graph where you want to draw in automation changes.

3. Click and drag with the mouse. The Free Hand Pencil tool will draw over any existing automation, using the shape you trace out.

Other Pencil tool modes are also useful for certain kinds of automation. For example, to create a smooth ramp up or down, you can switch to the Line mode of the Pencil tool. With this tool, you can drag from a point where you want a volume ramp to start to a point where you want the ramp to end: Pro Tools will create a straight line between the two points.

When working with pan automation, you may wish to sweep back and forth from left to right. In this case, you can use the Pencil tool in Triangle mode. Let's walk through that process:

1. Click and hold the **Pencil** tool button and select the **Triangle** shape.

2. Set the Grid value to a small value (such as **1/8 notes**) for quick panning or a large value (such as **1/2 notes**) for slower panning. (The *Triangle, Square,* or *Random* Pencil tool modes use the Grid value as their modulation frequency.) In this example, we'll use a **1 Bar** Grid value.

3. Click on the **Track View selector** at for the track and select **Pan** to display the pan graph.

4. Click and drag with the Pencil tool to begin writing new automation: drag horizontally and vertically to define the automation range and depth. In the case of pan automation, a larger triangle wave will translate into more extreme panning from left to right.

5. Release the mouse button to commit the automation.

(i) To align the apex of the triangle wave with the grid lines, draw the automation in Grid mode. This will keep the panning extremes aligned to the beat (1/4 note grid) or measure (1 Bar grid).

Discussion: Using Automation Modes

Pro Tools Artist has five real-time automation modes. The active mode determines how the track's fader, pan, and other automatable controls will behave during playback. For this course, we focus on three of the five modes: **OFF** mode, **READ** mode, and **WRITE** mode.

Changing Automation Modes

You can choose automation modes on a track-by-track basis. To change the automation mode for a track, use the **AUTOMATION MODE SELECTOR** at the head of the track.

To select an automation mode:

1. In the Mix or Edit window, click on the **AUTOMATION MODE SELECTOR** for the target track. By default, this selector is set to **READ** mode on all tracks (displayed as **AUTO READ** in the Mix window).

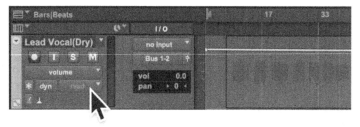

Figure 15.4 The Automation Mode selector for a track in the Edit window

2. Select the desired mode from the menu that appears. Available choices will include:

   • **OFF**: Automation will neither be written nor played back. This mode will suspend automation on a track that has been automated.

   • **READ**: Automation will not be written, but existing automation will play back. This mode will play back an automated track without running the risk of overwriting the automation.

   • **TOUCH**: Existing automation will play back until a parameter is touched or clicked; then automation will begin writing for that parameter until it is released.

   • **LATCH**: Existing automation will play back until a parameter is touched or clicked; then automation will begin writing for that parameter and will continue until playback is stopped.

   • **WRITE**: Automation will be written on all enabled parameters whenever the transport is rolling. The mode will replace existing automation on the track during playback.

Read Mode (Automation Playback)

By default, **READ** mode is active on all new tracks. In this mode, any automation that has been written or created on the track will be read (played) during playback. For example, if a volume automation graph goes downward over time, the fader will move accordingly.

When a new track is created, its automation playlist lines are flat and have only one automation breakpoint (at the very beginning of the track). In this state, the fader and other parameters do not follow the automation graphs, since no automation changes have been created. As a result, faders, pan controls, etc. will stay wherever you position them and not jump back to an automated position.

Read mode is a good general choice for tracks. In this mode, if you touch or move a parameter during playback, you will not write any new automation data. If no automaton exists for the track, the parameter will stay where you leave it. If automation does exist, the parameter will snap back to its automation graph and continue to play at the previously automated setting.

Write Mode (Automation "Record")

If you want to rewrite the automation on a track, you can use **WRITE** mode. In this mode, whenever the transport is rolling, new automation will be written to the track, overwriting any existing automation. This is a quick way to automate all of the parameters on a track so that the track will always play back the same way.

Write mode is very heavy-handed, though. This mode will ignore existing automation and write over the top of it. Anytime you roll the transport, you could potentially be destroying automation you've previously created that you intended to keep.

Off Mode (Automation Suspend)

When a track is set to **OFF** mode, no automation data will be read as your session plays, even if you have previously created or written automation on the track.

Changing the automation mode from **READ** to **OFF** will suspend automation on a track-by-track basis.

Global Suspend

If you want to suspend automation on all tracks, you have a couple options:

■ Hold **OPTION** (Mac) or **ALT** (Windows) while changing any track to **OFF** mode. All tracks in the session will change accordingly.

■ From the **WINDOW** menu, choose **AUTOMATION** to show the Automation window. At the top of the window, click the **SUSPEND** button. The button will turn red, and automation will be suspended throughout the entire session. To renable automation, click the Suspend button a second time.

Figure 15.5 Suspending automation on all tracks from the Automation window

TOPIC 15.3:
CREATING A MIXDOWN

When you play a multitrack Pro Tools session, you hear the component tracks combined by the Pro Tools mix engine. This is a great way to work while producing. When you want to hear your song *outside* of Pro Tools, you'll have to render the mix to a format that can play independently. This is a process known as creating a mixdown, or bounce, of your session.

A mixdown can be created in many different ways: by recording to an external device, by recording to a track within Pro Tools, and by bouncing your mix to disk. This course focuses on bouncing to disk.

Discussion: Bouncing a Mix to Disk

Bouncing to disk is the most popular way of mixing down a session. It has some powerful advantages. First, you will not need to create any new tracks or do any special routing. Second, you can preform a faster-than-realtime mixdown, mixing a long session in a short time. Last, you to easily change the sample rate and file format for the bounce, creating a final file in a format that any audio player can play back.

Considerations for Bouncing Your Mix

Bouncing your mix to a file on your storage drive is a simple process. However, you do need to pay attention to the details. The most important factors to consider before creating your mixdown are (1) what tracks are audible and (2) what portion of the timeline will be included in the bounce.

Audible Tracks

When you bounce a mix in Pro Tools, your mixdown will represent exactly what you would hear during playback. This means that any silenced tracks will not be included in the bounce. Tracks may be accidentally left out of your mix by being explicitly muted or by having other tracks soloed at the time of the bounce.

To ensure that all tracks are included in your bounce, make sure nothing is soloed or muted before using the Bounce Mix command.

Excluding Tracks

At times you may have tracks in a session that *should not* be included in a bounce. In this case, the best practice is to make these tracks inactive prior to creating the bounce, rather than muting them. You may also choose to hide the tracks so they don't appear in your Mix and Edit windows.

To make a track inactive, Right-click on the track name and select MAKE INACTIVE or HIDE AND MAKE INACTIVE from the pop-up menu.

In music sessions, it is common to have a click track. This track should NOT be included in your bounce. Be sure to disable the click using the Metronome button in the Transport window prior to using the Bounce Mix command.

Timeline Range

As mentioned above, your bounce will represent exactly what you hear during playback of the session. This applies to the bounce duration as well. If you have a 5-second selection in the middle of the second verse, you will get a 5-second bounce, containing just that portion of the mix. Said another way, Pro Tools bounces the selected range only.

To ensure that your entire session is included in the bounce, make a selection from the start of the program material to the point where playback should end. Be sure to include time at the end for any reverb or delay effects to decay to silence. After creating an appropriate selection, proceed with the Bounce Mix operation.

 The Timeline selection is the key here, not the Edit selection. It does not matter which tracks are included in the selection, only what range of time is included. (Track solos and mutes will determine which tracks are represented.)

You can bounce your entire session if you do not have a timeline selection. In this case, Pro Tools will bounce from the session start to the end of the last thing on the longest displayed track. This can produce unpredictable results, as you may have hidden information on a track, long after the actual program material has ended.

To control the start and end points of a bounce, it is best to create a selection of the desired program length first.

Creating Your Mixdown

Once you've verified that the session is configured for the desired content, you are ready to complete the mixdown process.

To create a mixdown:

1.   Select **FILE > BOUNCE MIX**. The Bounce Mix dialog box will display.

 To open the Bounce Mix dialog box from the keyboard, press COMMAND+OPTION+B (Mac) or CTRL+ALT+B (Windows).

2.   In the top section of the Bounce Mix dialog box, choose the **FILE NAME** and **FILE TYPE** for your bounce. (See Figure 15.6.) You will typically choose WAV (BWF) as the file type.

3.   In the **MIX SOURCE** field, verify that your main output path is selected. (It is typically selected by default.) This will ensure that the bounce matches what you hear through your monitor speakers.

Figure 15.6 File Name, File Type, and Mix Source in the top portion of the Bounce Mix dialog box

4.   In the **AUDIO** section, choose the parameters for the audio file that will be created.

   - **File Format:** This menu offers a choice of Mono (Summed), Multiple Mono, or Interleaved formats. You will generally want to select Interleaved so that your bounce results in a stereo file, containing both the left and right channels.

   - **Bit Depth:** This menu lets you select the bit depth for your bounce. Choices include 16 Bit, 24 Bit, and 32 Bit Float. You can generally set this to match your session bit depth, unless you need to do a bit-depth reduction for a particular delivery format or use case.

   - **Sample Rate:** This menu lets you select the sample rate for your bounce. Again, you can set this to match your session or select a lower sample rate for a required dellivery format or use case.

Figure 15.7 Options available in the Audio portion of the Bounce Mix dialog box

Selecting Bit Depth and Sample Rate for a Bounce

The choice of bit depth and sample rate for your mixdown file will depend entirely on what you plan to use the file for. A common convention is to follow the Red Book audio standard that was introduced for audio CDs. This standard requires audio for CD to be formatted as 16-bit, 44.1 kHz interleaved files. Many music deliverable formats still follow the Red Book standard; however, streaming services have also started to accept files at higher sample rates and bit-depths, often up to 96 kHz, 24-bit.

5.   In the **LOCATION** section at the bottom of the dialog box, select where your file will be saved, and optionally choose to have the bounce imported back into the session:

   - **Import after Bounce:** This option will import the bounced file into the session, on a new Audio track. This is available only when the mixdown file is the same sample rate as the session.

- **File Destination:** This section lets you choose where your bounced file(s) will be created. The simplest option is to use the default, saving your mixdown file inside the **BOUNCED FILES** folder within your session folder.

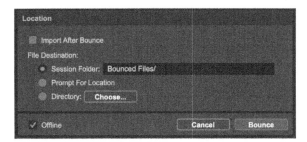

Figure 15.8 Options available in the Location portion of the Bounce Mix dialog box

6. At the bottom left of the dialog box, optionally enable the **OFFLLINE** checkbox to create your final bounce faster than realtime. (The speed of your computer's CPU and the complexity of the session will determine how fast your bounce will render.)

7. Click the **BOUNCE** button in the bottom right-hand corner to begin your mixdown.

   If the Offline box is *unchecked*, your session will play in real time during the bounce and a countdown window will display, indicating your mixdown's remaining time.

   If the Offline box is *checked*, you'll see a progress indicator for your bounce, along with a number in parentheses indicating how quickly the mix is rendering compared to a real-time bounce.

When your bounce completes, you will find your resulting audio file in the Bounced Files folder within your session folder (or another location you've specified in the Bounce Mix dialog box).

TOPIC 15.4:
BACKING UP AND ARCHIVING YOUR SESSION

After putting in so much hard work on your session, the last thing you want is to *lose* it. You'll want to safeguard your work, not only to recover from system problems, but also to retrieve your work years later. Your completed sessions can, over time, build a valuable archive of work and source material.

Discussion: Safegaurding Your Work

Computers, being complex machines, *will* fail. System crashes can arise from a variety of causes and result in loss of work. Our goal is to minimize that loss of work.

Session Backups

Pro Tools helps prevent data loss while you work with its *Auto Backup* preferences.

To change the Auto Backup settings:

1. From the **SETUP** menu, choose **PREFERENCES**. The *Preferences* dialog box will appear.

2. Navigate to the **OPERATION** tab. Midway down, you'll find the **AUTO BACKUP** section.

Figure 15.9 The Auto Backup section of the Preferences dialog box

This section has three settings:

*   **Enable Session File Auto Backup**—Verify that this option is enabled to turn Auto Backups on.

*   **Keep [#] most recent session backups**—Set the limit (up to 999) to specify how many backup files Pro Tools will keep before overwriting older backups. The higher the value, the more backup files you'll have available, allowing you to restore to points further back in your work.

*   **Backup every [#] minutes** — Choose how frequently backup files are created. Lower values will result in more frequent backups, minimizing the rework required in the event of a mishap.

3. After selecting settings, click **OK** to apply the settings and close the Preferences dialog box.

Session auto backups are saved inside your session folder, within the Session File Backups subfolder. They are designated with a .bak.[#].ptx file extension.

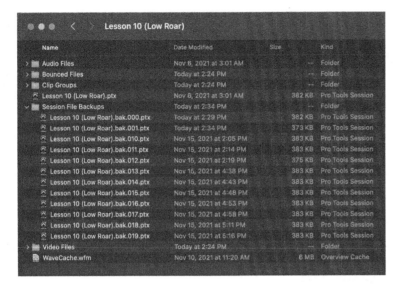

Figure 15.10 The Session File Backups folder

To restore from a backup, open one of the files in the **Session File Backups** folder as you would a normal session file. Once you've verified that the file represents the desired restore state, use the File > Save As command to give it a new name and save it at the top level of the session folder.

Creating an Archive

When you're done recording, editing, and mixing, you're ready to put your session on the virtual shelf and move on to the next project. This is what *archiving* is all about: Saving your work in such a way that it can be retrieved months and years down the line.

The goal of an archive is to not only protect your work from technical failure, but also from natural disasters like floods or fire. Many professional facilities have adopted the "3, 2, 1" rule:

- 3 different backups

- 2 different formats (for example, on disk and in cloud storage)

- 1 backup at an off-site location (to protect against natural disaster)

Though this might be unrealistic when you are first starting out, the important thing is to build good habits for archiving your work. This includes saving your sessions with all of the required media included. The Pro Tools **SAVE COPY IN** command can help achieve this.

Save Copy In

The **SAVE COPY IN** command is especially designed for archiving. This command lets you create a duplicate copy of your session and all of its media, collecting all files into one location. The result is a self-contained session folder that you can use in the future to revisit the session.

To create a self-contained archive for the current session:

1. Choose **FILE > SAVE COPY IN**. The Save Copy in dialog box will appear.

2. From the **FORMAT** pop-up menu, choose a format for the archive. You can use this menu to make the archive compatible with current softwarre or with an older version of Pro Tools.

3. Set the **SESSION PARAMETERS** section to match the settings of the current session.

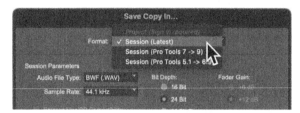

Figure 15.11 The top portion of the Save Copy In dialog box

4. Under **ITEMS TO COPY**, enable the **AUDIO FILES** checkbox. This will cause all of the audio files associated with the session to be copied into the Audio Files folder for the archive session, regardless of where the original files are located.

> (i) Using the Save Copy In command to copy audio files ensures that all of the files are collected into the Audio Files folder. This is especially useful for referenced files that you may have lost track of, so that they don't go missing in the future.

5. Click the **OK** button at the bottom of the Save Copy In dialog box.

   A file browser window will appear, enabling you to choose a location for your copy.

Figure 15.12 The bottom portion of the Save Copy In dialog box

6. Navigate to the desired locaation and click the **SAVE** button to start the copying process.

The copying process may take some time to complete, depending on the amount of media data that needs to be copied. A progress bar will display during the process.

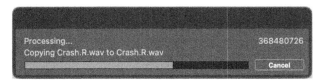

Figure 15.13 Progress bar showing the status of the Save Copy In operation

 After you complete the Save Copy In function, you will still be in the original session, not in the newly saved version. This is an important difference from the Save As command, which leaves you in the renamed version afterward.

Alternate Uses for Saved Copies

The **FILE > SAVE COPY IN** command is an essential tool for archiving. But its ability to change session parameters—sample rate, bit depth, and the Pro Tools format/version—makes it useful for other purposes as well. Here are a few other common uses for this powerful feature:

- Creating milestone "snapshots" or restore points of a work-in-progress without leaving your session

- Creating a version of a session at a different sample rate or bit depth

- Creating a version of a session that can be opened by older Pro Tools systems

- Converting a local session into a cloud-based project

- Converting a cloud-based project into a local session

LESSON 15 CONCLUSION

Lesson 15 wraps up a basic production process, tweaking your mix with automation and creating a mixdown of your session for final output.

Discussion: Summary of Key Concepts

In this Lesson, you learned:

- What mix automation is and how it is used in mixing

- How to view automation graphs in your Pro Tools session

- How to create and edit mix automation using the Grabber and Pencil tools

- How to select a real-time automation mode

- How to play back—and suspend the playing of—mix automation

- How to bounce your session using the Bounce Mix command

- How to back up and archive your mix, ensuring that your hard work is protected

Essential Keyboard Commands and Shortcuts

Below is a summary of modifier behaviors and shortcut operations that you should know from this Lesson.

- To delete an existing automation breakpoint, **OPTION-CLICK** (Mac) or **ALT-CLICK** (Windows) with the Grabber tool.

- To change the automation mode of all tracks, hold **OPTION** (Mac) or **ALT** (Windows) while changing any track's automation mode.

- To open the Bounce Mix dialog box, press **COMMAND+OPTION+B** (Mac) or **CTRL+ALT+B** (Windows).

Activity: Lesson 15 Knowledge Check

This quiz will check your knowledge on material covered in Lesson 15, Automation and Mixdown.

1. Refer to the image: Which control can you use to change the track to display Volume automation?

    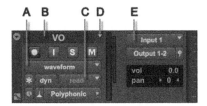

    a. The Track View selector

    b. The track nameplate

    c. The Automation Mode selector

    d. The Playlist selector

    e. The Audio Input Path selector

2. True or False? Automation lanes can be displayed underneath a track, letting you edit audio waveform on the track while you are editing the track automation?

3. Which modifier key can you use with the Grabber tool delete an existing automation breakpoint?

    a. Control (Mac) or Start (Windows)

    b. Option (Mac) or Alt (Windows)

    c. Command (Mac) or Ctrl (Windows)

    d. Shift (either Mac or Windows)

4. To create pan automation that sweeps back and forth from left to right, you can use the _____ mode of the Pencil tool.

5.   Which control can you use to put a track into Write mode for real-time automation?

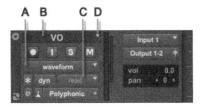

   a. The Track View selector

   b. The track nameplate

   c. The Automation Mode selector

   d. The Playlist selector

6.   Which of the following are ways to suspend automation for all tracks in a session?
       (Select all that apply.)

   a. Hold **OPTION** (Mac) or **ALT** (Windows) while clicking on the nameplate for any track.

   b. Hold **OPTION** (Mac) or **ALT** (Windows) while selecting **READ** mode for any track.

   c. Click the **SUSPEND** button in the Automation window.

   d. Click the **SUSPEND** button in the Mix window.

7.   The Automation window can be accessed from which menu?

8.   What are the two primary considerations when preparing to create a mixdown of a session?

9.   What function in the Bounce Mix dialog box allows for faster than real time mixdown?

   a. The File Format selector

   b. The Import After Bounce checkbox

   c. The Offline checkbox

   d. The Speed Bounce selector

10.   What menu command can you use to create a complete archived duplicate of your session, including
       all audio files?

Automating and Creating a Mixdown

In this exercise, you will finalize your session. You will start by copying the send assignment you created on the **Drums** track onto the **Hi Hat** track. Then you will automate the delay effect for the **VO** track using send mute automation. You will finish by bouncing the mix to a stereo file.

Exercise Details

■ **Required Media:** None

■ **Exercise Duration:** 10 Minutes

Downloading the Media Files

To complete the exercises in this book, you will use files included in the **PT Academy Media Files** folder that you previously downloaded from the course learning module on ElementsED.com.

To re-download the media files, click on the **Access Files** link in the sidebar after logging in to your account. Consult your instructor or visit **nxpt.us/make-music** for more details.

Getting Started

To get started, open the Pro Tools session you completed in Exercise 14. If that session is not available, you can use the provided **Exercise15-Starter** file in the **01. Starter Sessions** folder.

Open the session and save it as Exercise 15:

1. Open the session file that you created in Exercise 14: **Storage Drive/Folder > Exercises-XXX > Exercise14-XXX.ptx.**

    Alternatively, you can use the Exercise15 Starter file: **PT Academy Media Files > 01. Starter Sessions > Exercise15-Starter.ptx.**

2. Choose **FILE > SAVE AS** and name the session **Exercise15-XXX**, keeping the session inside the original folder. (Move the session into your **Exercises-XXX** folder if working from the starter file.)

Copy a Send Assignment

In the previous exercise, you created a send from the Drums and Guitar tracks to the Reverb return track. You might notice that this creates discontinuity for the drum kit, as the Hi Hat track does not have any reverb applied. The result is that the hi hat doesn't sound like it's in the same room as the rest of the drums.

To fix this, you can simply duplicate the send assignment from the Drums track onto the Hi Hat track.

Duplicate the send assignment:

1. Locate the send on the Drums track (Send A to Bus 3-4). **Do Not** click on the send button.

Figure 15.14 Existing Send on the Drums track (send window from the VO track in the foreground)

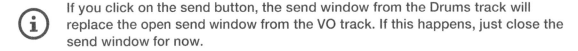 If you click on the send button, the send window from the Drums track will replace the open send window from the VO track. If this happens, just close the send window for now.

2. Hold **OPTION** (Mac) or **ALT** (Windows) and drag the send button from the Drums track to the Hi Hat track. The send assignment will be duplicated on the Hi Hat track.

Record Automation

In this part of the exercise, you will enable send mute automation for the session and place the VO track into Write automation mode. Next you will record automation during playback, toggling the mute state on and off for the send from the VO track.

Prepare the session for automation:

1. Verify that the Send window for the **VO** track is still displayed. If not, click on the send button on the **VO** track to open the appropriate Send window.

2. Press **COMMAND+=** (Mac) or **CTRL+=** (Windows) to activate the Edit window.

3. Choose **WINDOW > AUTOMATION** to open the Automation window.

4. **OPTION-CLICK** (Mac) or **ALT-CLICK** (Windows) on any enabled (red) automation button in the Automation window to disable all parameters.

5. Next, click on the **SEND MUTE** button (**S Mute**) to enable only send mute automation for the session. The button will be lit red when enabled.

Figure 15.15 Send mute automation enabled in the Automation window

6. Close the Automation window when finished.

7. Click the **MUTE** button (**M**) in the open send window to mute it at the session start.

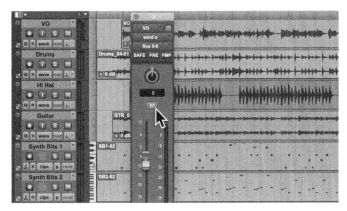

Figure 15.16 Mute button enabled in the Send window

8. Using the **VO** track's **AUTOMATION MODE SELECTOR**, put the track into **WRITE** automation mode. (If needed, resize the track to make the selector easier to view. See Figure 15.17.)

Figure 15.17 Automation Mode selector on the VO track set to Write mode

9. Press **RETURN** (Mac) or **ENTER** (Windows) to return to the session start.

In the next series of steps, you will be muting/unmuting the send on the fly during playback. This will add the delay effect on key words and phrases in the voiceover. You may need to practice the timing a few times to get the desired results.

 To practice the timing without writing automation, you can keep the track in Read mode while playing through the session and toggling the mute control on/off. Switch back to Write mode when you're ready to record automation.

Record send mute automation:

1. Begin playback, keeping the send muted for approximately 10 seconds.

2. Unmute the send just before the words "baked by the sun." Re-enable the send mute after the word "sun."

3. Continue playback for another approximately 10 seconds with the send muted.

4. Unmute the send again just before the words "sand-free technology." Re-enable the send mute after the word "technology."

5. Continue playback for another 8 seconds or so with the send muted.

6. Unmute the send at the end of the phrase, "stop by Spiccoli's surf shop" as the voiceover reaches the word, "today" so that this final word echoes repeatedly to conclude the ad.

7. Allow playback to continue through the end of the session; then press the **SPACEBAR** to stop playback.

   If you are not satisfied with the results, you can place the track back into Write mode and try the automation pass again.

8. When finished, close the send window and set the **AUTOMATION MODE** selector for the VO track back to Read mode.

Create a Mixdown

In this part of the exercise, you will maximize the output levels for the mix using a maximizer plug-in on the Master Fader track. Then you will use the Bounce Mix function to create a stereo file from your session mix.

Maximize the mix output:

1. Press **COMMAND+=** (Mac) or **CTRL+=** (Windows) to return to the Mix window.

2. Click on **INSERT SELECTOR A** for the **Master 1** track (under the **Inserts A-E** label) and choose **MULTICHANNEL PLUG-IN > DYNAMICS > MAXIM (STEREO)**. The plug-in window will open.

3. Press the **SPACEBAR** to begin playback.

4. In the Maxim plug-in window, set the **CEILING** slider around -0.5 dB. This sets the maximum allowable level for the plug-in, limiting the output levels to prevent clipping.

5. While listening to the mix, adjust the **THRESHOLD** slider to achieve a healthy output level without distortion. A setting of around -4.0 to -6.5 dB will likely be adequate for this session.

Figure 15.18 The Maxim plug-in showing Threshold and Ceiling settings

(i) Watch the histogram on the left side of the plug-in. Do not lower the Threshold significantly beyond the top of the histogram. (The level bars will turn red when the Threshold is set below them; too much red can result in distortion.)

6. Close the Maxim plug-in window when done.

7. Play through the session again and adjust the faders on various tracks as needed. The voiceover should be the most prominent element. Feel free to adjust the mix to taste.

(i) Reminder: You can use the Music Sub track to adjust the level of the music relative to other tracks in the session.

Bounce the session to a stereo file:

1. Press **COMMAND+=** (Mac) or **CTRL+=** (Windows) to switch back to the Edit window.

2. Click on the head of the **MIN:SECS** ruler so the ruler becomes highlighted, making it the main timebase.

3. Using the **SELECTOR** tool, make a selection on the **VO** track beginning at 1 second and extending to 31 seconds (0:01.000 to 0:31.000). Verify the selection using the **START** and **END** fields in the Counter display area.

4. Choose **FILE > BOUNCE MIX** to open the Bounce Mix dialog box.

5. Select the following options for your bounce:

   - File Name: YouInitials-SurfShop

   - File Type: WAV

   - Format: Interleaved

   - Bit Depth: 16 Bit

   - Sample Rate: 44.1 kHz

   - Offline checkbox: Enabled

6. Leave the other options set to their defaults (or as directed by your instructor).

Figure 15.19 The Bounce Mix dialog box configured for the mixdown

7. Click the **BOUNCE** button. Your bounce file will be created in the **Bounced Files** folder within your session folder.

Finishing Up

Congratulations! Over the course of these exercises, you have created a session from scratch, imported and edited audio, recorded audio and MIDI, added effects, recorded automation, and bounced the result to a stereo file.

1.   When your bounce completes, save your session and quit Pro Tools.

2.   Locate your mixdown file and play it back from your computer to verify the bounce.

Turn in your work as directed by your instructor. That concludes this exercise.

WRAP UP

Congratulations, you've made it! You've covered quite a lot of ground, but your journey is just beginning. Over time, you'll learn more about audio production and Pro Tools, and develop your own working style.

Here are a few things to focus on as you gain experience:

- Keep the fundamentals in mind—how digital audio works and the components of your system in particular. This will serve you well and help you make smart decisions.

- Take time to set up your sessions properly. Time spent up front will pay big dividends later in the production process.

- Allow time to experiment. As you advance, try new techniques and see how they fit in your workflow. Spend the time exploring and practicing when you can, so that when deadlines start to bear down, you'll have a solid foundation.

- Don't forget the *art*. Think of Pro Tools as a powerful musical instrument—it demands practice and discipline. As you refine your artistic skills (along with your technical skills), you'll achieve better and better results.

Your course instructor can provide additional project work, for those students interested in getting more hands-on experience. Certified Instructors can also provide students an opportunity to complete the Avid Certified Associate exam and earn an industry-recognized credential. Consult your instructor for more details.

If you want to learn more, you can explore Avid's advanced courses in Pro Tools. Avid's comprehensive curriculum (and courses offered through Avid Learning Partners) will move you confidently into the larger world of professional audio production.

To learn more about Avid's offerings, go to https://www.avid.com/learn-and-support.

At Avid, "Powering Greater Creators" is more than a slogan—it's a passion. On behalf of the whole Avid Learning team, we hope that this course has inspired you, and we wish you all the success.

Made in the USA
Coppell, TX
25 January 2025

44934988R00243